Elizabeth Bowen
The Enforced Return

Elizabeth Bowen: The Enforced Return

Elizabeth Bowen is a writer who is still too little appreciated. Neil Corcoran presents here a critical study of her novels, short stories, family history, and essays, and shows that her work both inherits from the Modernist movement and transforms its experimental traditions.

Elizabeth Bowen: The Enforced Return explores how she adapts Irish Protestant Gothic as a means of interpreting Irish experience during the Troubles of the 1920s and the Second World War, and also as a way of defining the defencelessness of those enduring the Blitz in wartime London. She employs versions of the Jamesian child as a way of offering a critique of the treatment of children in the European novel of adultery, and indeed, implicitly, of the Jamesian child itself. Corcoran relates the various kinds of return and reflex in her work-notably the presence of the supernatural, but also the sense of being haunted by reading-to both the Freudian concept of the 'return of the repressed' and to T. S. Eliot's conception of the auditory imagination as a 'return to the origin'.

Making greater interpretative use of extra-fictional materials than previous Bowen critics (notably her wartime reports from neutral Ireland to Churchill's government and the diaries of her wartime lover, the Canadian diplomat Charles Ritchie), Corcoran reveals how her fiction merges personal story with public history. Employing a wealth of original research, his radical new readings propose that Bowen is as important as Samuel Beckett to twentieth-century literary studies-a writer who returns us anew to the histories of both her time and ours.

Elizabeth Bowen

The Enforced Return

NEIL CORCORAN

OXFORD
UNIVERSITY PRESS

OXFORD
UNIVERSITY PRESS

Great Clarendon Street, Oxford ox2 6dp

Oxford University Press is a department of the University of Oxford.
It furthers the University's objective of excellence in research, scholarship,
and education by publishing worldwide in

Oxford New York

Auckland Bangkok Buenos Aires Cape Town Chennai
Dar es Salaam Delhi Hong Kong Istanbul Karachi Kolkata
Kuala Lumpur Madrid Melbourne Mexico City Mumbai Nairobi
São Paulo Shanghai Taipei Tokyo Toronto

Oxford is a registered trade mark of Oxford University Press
in the UK and in certain other countries

Published in the United States
by Oxford University Press Inc., New York

First published 2004
First published in paperback 2008

British Library Cataloguing in Publication Data
Data available

Library of Congress Cataloging in Publication Data
Data available
ISBN 978-0-19-818690-8 (Hbk.)
ISBN 978-0-19-953213-1 (Pbk.)

1 3 5 7 9 10 8 6 4 2

Typeset by Hope Services (Abingdon) Ltd.
Printed in Great Britain
on acid-free paper by
Biddles Ltd,
King's Lynn, Norfolk

Acknowledgements

I am very grateful for help, advice, and encouragement of various kinds to Roy Foster, John Kerrigan, Tony McBride, and, above all, Adam Piette, who generously read what I fondly thought was a final draft of my manuscript and made many valuable suggestions. I am also grateful to the Arts and Humanities Research Board for the research leave award which enabled me to complete this book, and to the Carnegie Trust for a very welcome research grant.

Some of this material, in substantially different form, has previously appeared in *Bullán: A Journal of Irish Studies*, *English: The Journal of the English Association*, and the *Irish University Review*.

Contents

Introduction Writing: The Enforced Return   I

I Ireland   17

    1. The Ghost in the House: *Bowen's Court* (1942) and
'The Back Drawing-Room' (1926)   19
    2. Discovery of a Lack: *The Last September* (1928)   39
    3. A Ghost of Style: *A World of Love* (1955)   61

II Children   79

    4. Mother and Child: *The House in Paris* (1935)   81
    5. Motherless Child: *The Death of the Heart* (1938)   102
    6. Childless Mother: The Disfigurations of *Eva Trout or
Changing Scenes* (1968)   126

III War   145

    7. Words in the Dark: *The Demon Lover and
Other Stories* (1945)   147
    8. War's Stories: *The Heat of the Day* (1946) and its Contexts   168

Works Cited   202
Index   207

Introduction
Writing: The Enforced Return

Laurence said—beating the bushes vaguely—'Imagine, sir, a small resurrection day, an intimate thing-y one, when the woods should give up their tennis balls and the bundles of hay their needles: the beaches all their engagement rings and the rivers their cigarette cases and some watches. . . . Last term I dropped a cigarette case into the Cher, from the bridge at Parson's Pleasure. It was a gold one, flat and thin and curved, for a not excessive smoker, left over from an uncle. It was from the days when they wore opera cloaks and mashed, and killed ladies. It was very period, very virginal; I called it Henry James; I loved it. I want to see it rush up out of the Cher, very pale, with eyeballs, like in the Tate Gallery. It wants a woman to be interested in a day like that, to organize; perhaps the Virgin Mary? Don't you think, sir?'

Mr Montmorency, startled at this address, replied: 'I have never been to the Tate Gallery.'

The Last September (42)

'You're not doing anything—I mean, only reading?'

Veronica to Sydney, in *The Hotel* (97)

I

Letters figure everywhere in Elizabeth Bowen, sometimes directly influencing action and plot, always re-directing readerly attention, re-focusing narrative, undermining or ironizing singularity of perspective. Some instances. In *A World of Love* Jane falls in love with the past or, more specifically, 'in love with a love letter' from Guy, a soldier killed in the First World War, and this love enables her transition to a different kind of future. In *The House in Paris* Leopold reads a letter from his foster-mother whose vulgar combination of prudishness and prurience disgusts him; and he then fantasizes a letter from his long unseen mother, pressing her empty envelope to his head as if in telepathic communication. In *Eva Trout* an entire chapter—called 'Interim'—represents an undelivered letter from a character whose sole appearance in the novel this is: a very dead letter indeed, in many ways, impeding the progress of plot but, in my view, including an essential, if easily missed, observation. In the story 'The Happy Autumn Fields' a dreaming woman in a bombed-out flat in wartime London, enters, by means of a collection of letters and other documents, into some strange form of sympathetic communion with a young woman in what is clearly Victorian Ireland. In 'The Demon Lover', more chillingly, an unstamped letter suddenly appearing in a shut-up house announces, apparently, the return of a vengeful ghost from the First World War to keep a long since organized tryst with a lover.

Then there are letters conveying information which the plots of the novels subsequently render void; letters with, therefore, the kind of incongruity or ironic discrepancy which makes for what Bowen once brilliantly called, in relation to J. G. Farrell's novel *Troubles*, 'unavailingness'.[1] There is the one which Lois posts, and then regrets posting, in *The Last September* announcing that she's fallen in love with a married man; the one written by James Milton to his family to announce his engagement, subsequently broken off, in *The Hotel*; the one which Mrs. Studdart writes from Venice in *Friends and Relations*, in which the half-sentence which she violently scratches out would have shown how much she understands of her daughter's true feelings—feelings which are, eventually, to constitute the novel's partially obscured plot of unrealized adultery; and her understanding is ultimately vented in appalled self-recrimination.

Such letters—and there are many others in the novels and short stories too—are so prominent in Bowen as to suggest almost a deliberate homage to one of the origins of the novel in eighteenth-century epistolary form; and in her brief wartime history of the English novel she says of Richardson's *Clarissa* that it has 'a saturation in its own moral atmosphere to which few novels have so completely attained'.[2] Such 'saturation' may well be one effect of letters in her own novels too, a suffusion of written representation to accompany the writing which represents speech; or, as the difference is recorded when Markie writes seductively to Emmeline across the table on a noisy flight to Paris in *To The North*, in 'letters' which eventually lead to a tragic denouement,

---

[1] Elizabeth Bowen, 'Ireland Agonistes', *Europa*, 1 (1971), 58–9, 59.
[2] Elizabeth Bowen, *English Novelists* (London: William Collins, 1942), 17.

'The indiscretions of letter-writing, the intimacies of speech were at once his'.

In addition to letters, other forms of writing are prominent in the novels too: the telephone message which Karen's mother leaves for her, and then erases after realizing that Karen has lied to her, but which remains (disastrously) legible, in *The House in Paris*; Portia's diary in *The Death of the Heart*, whose illicit reading is, arguably, both the register and the prompting of the various deaths of the heart which constitute the novel's plot; the newspapers which Louie reads fetishist-ically in *The Heat of the Day*, and, in her abjection, allows to construct a crudely propagandized identity for her; and, in the same novel, the crumpled message which Roderick finds in Robert's dressing-gown, which his mother will not permit him to read and which, after she glances at it herself, she says is 'nothing at all', although it may in fact be proof of his wartime treachery. In the writer Elizabeth Bowen acts of writing and reading are themselves constantly offered to readerly inspection and interpretation, and they are slippery with secrets, duplicities, treacheries, betrayals, the second selves which the traces of script inscribe on the page, the selves we may wish to eradicate but which remain ineradicably behind us, in evidence.

The self-consciousness about reading and writing in Bowen is one manifestation of what she says in the preface to a collection of her crit-ical prose: that 'For the writer, writing is eventful; one might say it is in itself eventfulness. . . . Reading is eventful also.'[3] Stylistically, her own writing is controversially eventful: it has been accused, even by some of her admirers, of mannerism, and it is certainly often deeply unconven-tional in its syntactical and grammatical structures; in some forms of negative construction, repetition, inversion, and ellipsis; in a reflexive turning back in upon itself rather than a committed motion forward; in its unyielding refusal of the obvious in spirited but sometimes very demanding favour of what she calls 'the affray of words, the vibrating force of their unforeseenness', which sounds as though she regards writing, or at least certain types of writing, as almost a kind of jazz improvization.[4] There is a nervousness in this, an anxiety that the mere writer herself may not remain in control of the riot; and one may certainly be unnerved, as a reader, by some of her styles and forms. 'When we write we endeavour to be exact,' she says, 'but also we must

---

[3] Elizabeth Bowen, *Afterthought: Pieces about Writing* (London: Longmans, 1962), 9.
[4] Ibid., 214.

be sensitive, imaginative as to words themselves—for they are there not merely to serve *our* purpose: they are charged with destinies of their own, haunted by diverse associations.'[5] This sounds much more like a lyric poet's than a prose writer's intense sensitivity to the semantic, acoustic, and etymological interconnections between words, to the autonomy of their dealings with one another, and to the way one might feel possessed or acted upon by them, passive before their suasions and invitations. W. J. McCormack, in fact, closely analysing a passage from 'The Demon Lover', says that 'Bowen's prose is post-Yeatsian poetry'; and I could imagine a meticulous and revealing linguistic study being performed on her prose of the kind which Adam Piette performs on the work of, among others, Joyce and Beckett, in his book *Remembering and the Sound of Words*.[6] I offer no such thing here but am, I hope, attentive to the way Elizabeth Bowen uses words throughout. Although hers is not a prose offering the confirmation of usual expectations, the critic who admires it must try to show that this is something other than 'mannerism'. The 'vibrating force' of her language is the force which precedes everything else in her; and it is, before everything else, why she is worth our attention.

In her formal structures also—from the relatively static *The Hotel* (1927), which is derivative of Forster and Woolf, certainly, as critics have said, but which maintains a tense edginess all of its own too, to the wildly and uncategorizably adaptive and fluid *Eva Trout* (1968)—she is variously inventive, experimental, unfixed: one intrinsic signature of her work is its sense of the corrosive and constricting boredom which would attend any act of formal repetition. The eventfulness of writing, and of reading, is the constant, testing novelty of further discovery and self-discovery; and Iseult Arble attempting to write a novel (but failing) in *Eva Trout* offers an emblem for the isolatedly alert receptivity of the venture: 'She angled the lamp lower over the typewriter, to see more clearly what it was about to tell her' (9). In these forms of stylistic and structural experiment Elizabeth Bowen is a writer deeply impressed by the ambitions of High Modernism, even if, until the final two novels, she never entirely loses touch with classic realism and its customary methods, including that of the omnisciently moralizing narrator. As

[5] *Afterthought*, 212.
[6] W. J. McCormack, *From Burke to Beckett: Ascendancy, Tradition and Betrayal in Irish Literary History* (1985; rev. and enlarged edn. Cork: Cork University Press, 1994), 403; and Adam Piette, *Remembering and the Sound of Words: Mallarmé, Proust, Joyce, Beckett* (Oxford: Clarendon Press, 1996).

such an inheritor she has suffered, in her critical reception, from her belatedness; and in this she has shared the fate of that other second-generation cisatlantic modernist writer, Henry Green, who is still also usually neglected or under-appreciated. Bowen was, in fact, almost surprisingly open to, if also sceptical about, even the most extreme experiments of Modernism—Joyce's, for instance, at a time when few others were. Of *Finnegans Wake* she said, in 1941, in an obituary appreciation, that 'He pounded language to jelly in his attempts to make it tell us what he was laughing at. One may say that he ended by laughing so much that he could not speak.'[7] She was also deeply admiring of what she called 'the untouched ice' in Virginia Woolf, 'the savage intractability of the spirit which must experiment.'[8] And she was exceptionally immersed in, and knowledgeable about, the post-Flaubertian tradition of French writing, and—as casual references throughout her work and an excellent late essay, 'The Art of Bergotte', attest—she was, throughout her life, a devoted reader of Proust.[9]

Just as she returns to modernist experimentation for her own sense of the possibilities of a modern writing, she returns to other traditions of writing too, and in ways which may suggest either an instinctive or a deliberate attempt at generic revision. In her treatment of Ireland, especially, but elsewhere too, she is, in part, adapting to her own purposes a gothic tradition, and notably one that has been characterized as 'Irish Protestant' gothic. In her treatment of childhood she is, I believe, returning to, and revising, Henry James and in her final novel, *Eva Trout*, Charles Dickens; in *The House in Paris*, she is sceptically engaging with the nineteenth-century European novel of adultery; in *The Demon Lover and Other Stories* she is, under the pressure of wartime's disruption of traditions of all kinds, very self-consciously returning to a variety of literary sources—Tennyson, Rider Haggard, anonymous balladry—which she then adapts and differently inflects. In addition there is, throughout her work, and in ways which sometimes raise interpretative difficulties, a constant return to the cultural resource and huge influential anxiety that is Shakespeare, who is as present to Bowen as he is to Joyce, even if in more muted and intermittent ways.

[7] 'In praise of Shem the Penman', *Irish Times*, 12 January 1991, 9, repr. from *The Bell*, March 1941.
[8] Elizabeth Bowen, *The Mulberry Tree: Writings of Elizabeth Bowen*, selected and introduced by Hermione Lee (London: Virago Press, 1986), 179.
[9] 'The Art of Bergotte' is reprinted in Elizabeth Bowen, *Pictures and Conversations* (London: Allen Lane, 1974), 77–109.

The return enforced in Elizabeth Bowen is always, then, a return to the already written, but it is one measure of her strength as a writer that this re-reading is also an invitation to us as readers to read the traditions themselves differently. The return may be enforced, since these traditions are what she has, but it may also be critical, sceptical, suspicious. Compulsion in Bowen is, paradoxically, a new kind of freedom. What the writer recognizes in return is constraint; what her readers might recognize is revision. So it is radically insufficient, for instance, for critics of Bowen to notice an indebtedness to, say, Henry James, without noticing also how we may read James differently in Bowen's later light. If James returns in Bowen, he returns, not exactly like the cigarette case which the dandyish Laurence names after him in my epigraph from *The Last September*, in a resurrection which accoutres him with the trappings of a later modernity, those incongruous and, no doubt, shockingly surrealist eyeballs in the wildly up-to-date artworks in the Tate; but newly and differently accoutred nevertheless. And 'it wants a woman to be interested in a day like that, to organize' (42): if Portia in *The Death of the Heart* is a revision of the Jamesian child heroine, as I claim she is, she is revised with a woman's knowledge and eye, with a differently gendered interiority; and the consequence for Bowen's fiction may even find a fault in James.[10]

So, part of what I mean by my subtitle is that the literary return may be enforced, but it is, in its turn, both an enablement and a resource. In Bowen's writing, the inevitability of belatedness is, I believe, accepted as the first premiss of transformation. In an essay entitled 'Disloyalties' she says of the writer's ethical responsibilities that 'His ideal is, to be at once disabused and susceptible, and for ever mobile'; and the essay counts the cost of this for any writer whose inevitable first pull is, on the contrary, in the direction of affection and attachment ('turning away from resting-places, from lighted doorways, to pursue his course into darker country').[11] 'Susceptible' is a much repeated word in Bowen's critical prose, and 'mobile' is a word everywhere in her work, both fictional and non-fictional. We may read this 'ideal' as an aesthetic as well as an ethical demand: her own stylistic, formal, and structural discoveries are the product of a restless, even nervous susceptibility to certain forms of writing, but also of a responsiveness intensely mobile

---

[10] Laurence's reference to the Virgin Mary in my epigraph is one of several such arrestingly peculiar references in this redoubtedly Protestant writer. I return to them.
[11] *The Mulberry Tree*, 61.

in its attentions and procedures. 'Plot', she says, 'is the knowing of destination': what the writer brings to the work 'is luggage left in the hall between two journeys, as opposed to the perpetual furniture of rooms. It is destined to be elsewhere.'[12] To be mobile is, of course, to be destined to be elsewhere, and her books are mobile in many senses: but in fact, characteristically open-ended, they give the impression rather of a certain bafflement before their own destinations than of any secure knowledge of where destination may lie; and they are very keenly pledged to the adventure of the journey itself.

The axiomatic belief in alternative, and further, destination is one explanation for the marked and, to some critics, unadmired and regretted, change in her entire style of writing after *A World of Love* (1955) in the final two novels, *The Little Girls* (1964) and *Eva Trout* (1968). A remark she makes about the style of Sheridan Le Fanu's *Uncle Silas*, that it has 'a voluptuousness not approached since', has often been cited; but much less stock has been taken of the parenthetical observation that follows it: '(It was of the voluptuousness in his own writing that Le Fanu may, really, have been afraid).'[13] In my judgement, Elizabethan Bowen herself has written some of the most voluptuous, as well as some of the most fearful, prose of the modern period, as sensuously gratifying as anything in Joyce or Nabokov, but, as in them, with a sensuousness permitted only by contexts which threaten to undermine it. The gaps, ellipses, and syntactical peculiarities in some of her earlier work may be read as a prophylaxis against too easy or unearned an elegance or ornamentation, too lax an indulgence in the modulations of the exquisite. With the completion of *A World of Love*, which contains some of the most voluptuous writing even in Bowen, there was also a recognition, I think, that the voluptuous itself had now to be forsworn unless the Bowen stylistic signature was actually to become repetitive. The final books therefore originate in a discipline of continence, or abstinence; even if 'continence' may not be the first word to occur to anyone wanting to describe *Eva Trout*.

I have to confess that I myself find *The Little Girls*—apart from its elegiac second section, whose picnic and parting on the eve of the First World War is one of the most haunting scenes in all Bowen, in which three words spoken by a mother to her daughter ('Oh Dicey—*Dicey!*') are inflected with a whole world of grief—a deeply flawed book, in

---

[12] Ibid., 35.   [13] Ibid., 103.

which the restless flurry of plotting, both busy and banal, seems almost
haplessly out of key with the haunting desolation of its theme; and I
therefore find myself with nothing of interest to say about it. Which is
doubly galling, since this theme—women in maturity literally returning to the scenes of their childhoods—would seem deeply germane to a
study of children, and return, in Bowen. But there it is. However, one
of the pleasures of writing this book has been for me the discovery of
how to appreciate *Eva Trout*, and to believe (self-deludingly, it may be)
that I know what this in some ways, at least initially, ferociously rebar-
bative novel is about and is up to. Whether I'm believed or not, I do
now think I understand how it was an inevitable product of a process
of intense writerly scruple on Bowen's part—as intense, I would claim,
as the disciplines of abstinence which characterize the later prose of
Samuel Beckett. Allying Bowen with this heroic strain of modernist
experimentation has not been common in criticism of her work, but it
gives body to what she said in her 1949 preface to the second edition
of her first collection of short stories, *Encounters*, published nearly
thirty years earlier. This clearly seemed an appropriate moment for
making the kind of programmatic statement she hardly ever permitted
herself: 'The sense of total commitment, of desperate and overweening
enterprise, of one's whole self being forced to a conclusive ordeal,
remains a constant.'[14] It is what I believe about her as a writer, and it
is exemplary.

II

The phrase 'the enforced return' is drawn from Bowen's essay 'Out of
a Book', an essay on childhood reading.[15] It is one of the several places

---

[14] *The Mulberry Tree*, 118. On the other hand, she can also be brusquely common-
sensical about writing, and you can admire this too. I particularly like an observation in
an exchange of public letters with Graham Greene and V. S. Pritchett: 'I don't see . . . that
we as writers differ in the practical sense—or can expect rightly to be differentiated—
from any other freelance makers and putters on the market of luxury or "special" goods.
Had I not been a writer I should probably have struck out in designing and making belts,
jewellery, handbags, lampshades or something of that sort—my aim being that these
should catch people's fancy, create a little fashion of their own, and accordingly be
saleable by me at a rising price.' (*The Mulberry Tree*, 226) 'Struck out' is good, and the
financial consideration is characteristic: she seems to be turning herself into her own
Mopsie Pye, the chain of 'novelty shops' owned by Clare Burkin-Jones in *The Little
Girls*.

[15] First published in 1946, it is reprinted in *The Mulberry Tree*, 48–53.

in her non-fictional prose where she conveys an acute sense of how, for her, reading is inseparable from remembering. Discussing what she calls 'the overlapping and haunting of life by fiction', she says that 'Reduced to the minimum, to the what did happen, my life would be unrecognizable by me. Those layers of fictitious memory densify as they go deeper down. And this must surely be the case with everyone who reads deeply, ravenously, unthinkingly, sensuously, as a child.'[16] We are given here another reason why acts of reading and writing figure so prominently in Bowen's work: in Elizabeth Bowen life itself is deeply, indeed inextricably, penetrated by text, what she calls 'living-ness' by writtenness. Given the presence of ghosts and hauntings of various kinds in her work, for Bowen to say that life is 'haunt[ed] by fiction' is to say a great deal: fiction is the second self, the other, the familiar stranger, the *doppelgänger*. It is what we see through, what we see with, and it is even what constitutes us: 'one stripped bare the books of one's childhood to make oneself'.[17] This sense of identity as itself constructed by fiction is one reason for the view of the tenuousness of identity apparent in a great deal of Elizabeth Bowen's work; and this is a matter to which I shall return often in what follows, since it is the matter to which her work often returns too. But that work is also liter-ally haunted, by ghostly returnees, or revenants, and by various forms of the *doppelgänger* figure; returns not unrelated, of course, to the ten-uousness of identity. Some of these have already been extensively explored by critics; others (and in the novels, notably in *The Last September*) have been barely noticed; so in what follows I make fre-quent return to these returnees too.

Bowen's writing may, then, in the terms of T. S. Eliot's notable for-mulation of what he calls the 'auditory imagination', engage in a rhythm of 'returning to the origin and bringing something back', of fus-ing 'the most ancient and the most civilised mentality'.[18] But it also manifests the entrapment of obsessive return, the inability to shake off a distressing, or distressed, past in a way which virtually demands to be read under the rubric of a Freudian return of the repressed, despite Bowen's occasional levity about Freud (when someone in *To the North* says she dreams about flying, for instance, the convert to psycho-analysis, Lady Waters, who is satirized throughout, says with knowing portentousness, 'That may have nothing to do with flying'). Fiction,

---

[16] *The Mulberry Tree*, 48–9.   [17] Ibid., 50.
[18] T. S. Eliot, *The Use of Poetry and the Use of Criticism* (1933; London: Faber & Faber, 1975), 119.

then, is ambivalently poised between pleasure and something more painful, even desolating; and when she writes about how fiction affects consciousness of place in 'Out of a Book', Bowen maintains, but only just, the affect of pleasure:

For the child, any real-life scene that has once been sucked into the ambience of the story is affected, or infected, forever. The road, cross-roads, corner of a wood, cliff, flight of steps, town square, quayside or door in a wall keeps a transmuted existence: it has not only given body to fiction, it has partaken of fiction's body. Such a thing, place or scene cannot again be walked past indifferently; it exerts a pull and sets up a tremor; and it is to indent the memory for life. It is at these points, indeed, that . . . synthetic experience has its sources. Into that experience come relationships, involving valid emotion, between the child reader and book characters; a residuum of the book will be in all other emotions that are to follow.[19]

There is, I think, a submerged eucharistic metaphor in the partaking of 'fiction's body' here, and there is certainly a quasi-religious dimension in Bowen's thinking about imaginative fictions and their effect on the malleable psyche of the reader. In her writing about writing and reading, at its most interesting, the attachments seem virtually occult, charged with high tension, scenes of dramatic encounter, self-recognition, and self-transformation, and often ambivalently poised between infection and affection, poison and salve. Writing and reading involve movements of danger as well as desire, compulsion, as well as attraction:

The imagination, which may appear to bear such individual fruit, is rooted in a compost of forgotten books. The apparent choices of art are nothing but addictions, pre-dispositions: where did these come from, how were they formed? The aesthetic is nothing but a return to images that will allow nothing to take their place; the aesthetic is nothing but an attempt to disguise and glorify the enforced return.[20]

It is more than fortuitously appropriate that Elizabeth Bowen should say this in an essay on childhood reading since one of the images that will allow nothing to take their place in her own work is what Peter Coveney, in the title of a famous book on children in literature, calls 'the image of childhood'. And reading in childhood is, for Bowen, crossed with a sense of how the writer is always in some sense writing in childhood too: as she puts it in her essay 'The Roving Eye', writers

---

[19] *The Mulberry Tree*, 52.   [20] Ibid., 63.

'are of a childishness which could seem incredible, and which is more than half incredible to their thinking selves. The childishness is necessary, fundamental—it involves a perpetual, errant state of desire, wonder and unexpected reflex.'[21] It is remarkable here how the writer's 'thinking self' is divorced from—indeed, makes a judgement on—the 'errancy' of the writing self; writing is a wondering which is also a wandering. The 'unexpected reflex'—what another essay calls 'The Bend Back'—is the constant return in Elizabeth Bowen: the reflex as the thing you do without thinking, which you cannot prevent yourself from doing, but also as the reflection and self-reflection which is the writing self bent back, again and again, on images which will allow nothing to take their place, images which are therefore close to being obsessions. The most substantial of these in Bowen are, I believe, images of Ireland, childhood, and war; and I have organized this book around those images, images which a contemporary criticism would probably rather perceive as themes.

III

For a long time Elizabeth Bowen, apart from a handful of exceptional critical studies—including William Heath's book in 1961, Hermione Lee's in 1981, and a smattering of outstanding essays—remained in a kind of critical limbo, not figuring much on university syllabuses, and even sometimes regarded, astonishingly, as a more or less middlebrow writer (not, perhaps, that she herself would have much minded that). In recent times, however, she has been placed very much at the centre of some highly sophisticated and resourceful literary and cultural criticism: deconstructive; feminist; psychoanalytical (with much use made of the work of Nicolas Abraham and Maria Torok on transgenerational haunting); Irish Studies-postcolonial; women's writing, and writing generally, of the Second World War. I have myself greatly profited from much of this work, and I record my debts to it in what follows. The more psychoanalytical-deconstructive elements of it, however, while valuably emphasizing and illuminating her sheer strangeness, do seem to me to present us with a Bowen endlessly death-inflected, dissolved, haunted, cryptic, modulated towards silence and negativity, in ways which I find too monotonous to account for a writer

[21] Ibid., 63.

in my view tonally very varied indeed. They also tend to underestimate the structural inventiveness and stylistic experimentation in her: difference from what has gone previously is sometimes—paradoxically, it may be—obscured when everything is a play, or a nightmare, of *différance*, and different texts may actually be made to sound rather similar. In some of this critical work too it can almost seem as though the whole writerly career is being read backwards through the lens of *Eva Trout*; and for me *Eva Trout* is, as I shall argue, a distorting mirror.

So, where do I come in? Not, certainly, with the certainty with which Harrison comes in to *The Heat of the Day*, seizing his wartime opportunity—'This is where I come in'—since greatly to admire any imaginative writing, particularly writing as elusive as this, is to know that it will resist as well as reward the critical intelligence. 'The poem', said Wallace Stevens—and Bowen is, we remember, a post-Yeatsian poet in prose—'must resist the intelligence almost successfully'.[22] Nevertheless, I do come in with a long-standing interest in Bowen, and a high sense of her worth. I first read her—*The House in Paris*, and then *The Last September*—when I was quite young, in my mid-teens, and I read her then alongside other modern literature which I was also encountering for the first time: Eliot, Joyce, Woolf. She seemed to me of their company in several ways: I knew I liked and was excited by what I found; I knew I didn't understand it very well, but thought that I might if I tried harder and found out more; I was haunted by certain moments and images in it—and still am—in exactly the way she says fiction may 'haunt' a life, outstandingly for me the encounter between Leopold and Henrietta after he is told that his mother is not coming in *The House in Paris*, and the episode in the ruined mill in *The Last September*, in which Lois and Marda encounter the IRA gunman.

Although my own background was closer to Joyce's as it may be intuited from *A Portrait of the Artist as a Young Man* than to what I could intuit of Bowen's from *The Last September*, in one respect I recognized a biographical affinity. The return sea trip from England to Ireland, and specifically to Cork, which Karen Michaelis makes in *The House in Paris*, was one with which I was myself extremely familiar, and the sense which Bowen's work gives of having its being between the two countries, of being most at home in the middle of the Irish Sea, was one I strongly felt too. When Bowen talks about this in her

---

[22] Wallace Stevens, *Opus Posthumous*, ed. by Samuel French Morse (1957; New York: Alfred A. Knopf, 1977), 171.

non-fictional prose she insists that there was no sentimentalism in her attachment to Ireland. In my own case there certainly was; but it nevertheless allowed me to appreciate, I think, something deeply intrinsic to Bowen: the gift or pain or dislocation of living between Ireland and England, of being bilocated. Perhaps because I came to her young, the social class of her characters never bothered me: it was as little a consideration as it was in, say, T. S. Eliot's 'Portrait of a Lady', although I suppose *The House in Paris* is the text of hers in which this is least an issue, since its register of damage is so palpable, accurate, and insinuating as to render all other considerations nugatory. I sometimes suspect, however, that there has been an element of inverted snobbery in her reception within the academy; and although my own snobberies are as likely as anyone else's to run in the inverted direction, I'm glad to have been spared such blinkers in relation to Bowen. There are things important in her work beyond all that fiddle; although that fiddle is, of course, also important within it, and I have things to say about this.

Whatever about all that, this early reading and partly shared experience allowed me access to the work of a writer I thought then, and think now, a great modern writer. I was taken aback as an undergraduate in the late 1960s to discover that my contemporaries had not heard of her and that the syllabus offered no lectures on her; and this is, I think, still more or less generally the case in UK universities, although perhaps not (so much) in Irish ones. My own Elizabeth Bowen is a deeply haunted writer too, and therefore, of course, one profoundly death-inflected, and I pay a great deal of attention in what follows to her gaps, ellipses, absences, hauntings, silences, and aporias; but I think too that to read her exclusively like this is to miss a great deal, and I'm reminded that, wandering the Protestant graveyard in Rome in her travel book *A Time in Rome*, she discovers there, extraordinarily, 'overflows of livingness'.[23] I think, that is to say, that there is an apprehensible and sometimes peculiar or disconcerting ethics in her work, and that it is to our advantage to discover it, and that, although she is drawn to fracture and disintegration, this is more inflected with affirmation—since she is often primarily a comic writer—than some recent criticism has made it seem. I think that she has arrestingly strange, but intelligible, things to say about Ireland and Anglo-Irishness, childhood, and war, and that these have not been exhaustively described or interpreted. And I think that it is worth attempting

[23] Elizabeth Bowen, *A Time in Rome* (1960; New York: Alfred A. Knopf, 1965), 224.

to historicize her work in contexts of written history itself and, as I have already said, of literary history. I see her as a writer deeply engaged with some of the most urgent matters of both personal and public history in her time, and as a writer whose books, bending back, say much more complicated things about these histories than the rather orthodox conservatism of some of her public political pronouncements would suggest. The writing self is not, indeed, the thinking self.

When she contributed to an exchange of public letters with Graham Greene and V. S. Pritchett in 1948 Bowen said that she was 'prepared to think' of her writing as 'a substitute for something I have been born without—a so-called normal relation to society'. But, she insists, with italics, 'My books *are* my relation to society.'[24] Precisely so. She is also, to me, emphatically an Irish writer, and nowhere more than in aspects of her work which have led some to refuse her the title which she very specifically, and repeatedly, chose for herself (an 'Irish' writer, not an 'Anglo-Irish' writer): in her ambivalences, exacerbations, antagonisms, and exhaustions with the country of her birth; in the way her writing is constantly abraded by the place, as well as in her deep—although not, perhaps, abiding—affections for it.

IV

In 'The Roving Eye' Elizabeth Bowen makes life hard for her critic:

Intellectually, the writer ought to desire and must expect to confront in his critic one who is his intellectual match; it may be, his intellectual senior.[25] Mind meets mind: style must stand up to hard analysis; structure at once reveals and defies its faults; method is there to sustain query; imagery is to be sifted through. All the same, there comes a point in the judgement process when intellect brings itself to a natural stop: the final value is rated by intuition. The vital test is the sense of truth in the vision—its clearness, its spontaneity, its authority. . . . Something has been beheld for the first time.[26]

Not much chance of measuring up; but I shall take the concessiveness of the third sentence there as permission to lapse from the judgement process into affirmation. This is a writer in whose work something is

---

[24] *The Mulberry Tree*, 223.
[25] Bowen was of the generation which took the masculine pronoun and possessive as universally applicable. This is sometimes disconcerting to the contemporary eye, but this is the only time I shall mention it in this book.
[26] *The Mulberry Tree*, 65.

indeed beheld for the first time and beheld uniquely. If Elizabeth Bowen's true achievement and value are only now coming to be adequately and generally recognized, this may well be because she was in advance of her time, a writer whose real operations went in disguise, a writer with whom we must catch up. She returns us anew to the history of her time, and of ours. She makes a difference.

I

Ireland

The Ghost in the House:
Bowen's Court (1942) and
'The Back Drawing-Room' (1926)

I

'There was Rome, and she would like to stay in a hotel by herself' (99) is one way in which *The Last September* (1928) formulates its heroine Lois's desire to escape from the constraining circumstances of a big house in 1920s Anglo-Ireland. Over thirty years after Elizabeth Bowen published the novel, we find her in *A Time in Rome* (1959), her only travel book, doing exactly that: staying in a hotel by herself in Rome and liking the experience of disorientation: 'Anywhere, at any time, with anyone', she says, in a remark we may read across the whole of her work, 'one may be seized by the suspicion of being alien—ease is therefore to be found in a place which nominally is foreign: this shifts the weight.' This may be read as Bowen's ratification of Sean O'Faolain's view of her as a 'resident alien' in both Ireland and England, an observation made in his critical study *The Vanishing Hero*, published three years earlier; and, at one point in *A Time in Rome*, in a kind of mirror image of Lois in the novel, Bowen thinks about Ireland.[1] It is the moment, strangely withheld until almost the book's conclusion, when she visits Keats's grave in the Protestant Cemetery near the Porta San Paolo—'Rome's permanent foreign colony', she mordantly calls it. After an elegiac meditation on Keats and his friend Joseph Severn, buried next to him, she notices a neighbouring grave and makes this remarkable observation:

[1] Sean O'Faolain, *The Vanishing Hero: Studies in Novelists of the Twenties* (London: Eyre and Spottiswoode, 1956), 116.

The pair of Englishmen have few neighbours in this fresh, desultory grassy stretch; it is natural to wander to see who the few are. Among them, two let us imagine beautiful Irish sisters, Miss Moores, from and of Moorehill, County Waterford—Helen, dying in Rome at eighteen, was three months later followed by Isabella, aged twenty-nine. The elder nursed the younger, then caught it, too? 1805, Moorehill lost its daughters; sixteen years later, Earth lost Keats. No, lost he could not be! Death does nothing to poetry. The loss, for us, is that of the 'more': otherwise, does it matter whether a poet, being what he is, is alive or dead? It could be said that the Miss Moores, being nothing but themselves, were the greater loss.[2]

Literally stepping to one side of Keats's grave, Bowen is also stepping to one side of his Englishness to find Irishness; of his masculine gender to find women; and of his posthumous fame to find its opposite in these usually unvisited tombs. His poetic immortality is, in a quite orthodox way, figured as compensation for his physical mortality; but that orthodox figure is given a radical revision by Bowen's observation— which occasions a kind of pastiche, but still rather arch, Romantic apostrophe, of a kind to which she is never normally prone—of what we might consider its complement: the lack of any such consolation for the ordinary dead, those who, lacking posthumous reputation, are 'nothing but themselves' and therefore more 'lost', more irretrievably vanished from the world, than the poet.

An entirely characteristic tough-mindedness permeates Bowen's thoughts at Keats's grave. Discontent with the customary forms and cadences of elegy, this adjunct to elegy is, we might say, emotionally disjunctive. There is also a characteristic distortion about the perception, which depends on the punning of 'Moore' and 'more' and on an almost seventeenth-century charnel conceit. Being nothing is to be, even if only in one precise sense, something greater than a great poet: a greater loss. Stepping aside from the orthodoxy of elegy, Bowen is here stepping into a tentativeness or experimentalism of feeling and thought, and the passage has a consequently arresting vibrancy and piquancy. In this it may be thought one instance of what, paradoxically for its elegiac occasion, Bowen has, earlier in this section of *A Time in Rome*, said Roman graveyards also are—'overflows of livingness'; and this engagement with the thought of death is spiritedly unflinching. The passage is itself another such manifestation, since it is also an instance of the creative capacity of imagination. 'Let us imagine,' the

---

[2] Elizabeth Bowen, *A Time in Rome* (1960; New York: Alfred A. Knopf, 1965) 228–9.

writer says, having found the Irish sisters; and she imagines them as beautiful and begins to create their story. It would be, were it written, a story of the goodness of unhistoric acts, such as those George Eliot celebrates in *Middlemarch* as 'incalculably diffusive' in their effects when, at the end of the novel, she reminds us of the 'unvisited tombs' occupied by women like her heroine Dorothea Brooke. Indeed, although Bowen appears almost to make a point of not saying so, it is also a story congruent with Keats's own, who nursed his brother Tom while he was dying from tuberculosis, before he 'caught it too'. (Severn, who nursed Keats, was luckier and died many years later.) Death may do nothing to poetry, but poetry, or fiction, may do much to death. Here, the act of Bowen's empathetic imagination gives a brief memorial fame to the otherwise unknown Miss Moores. Death obliterates; writing remakes.

Elizabeth Bowen's fiction frequently also makes the kind of detour to Ireland it does here, and in doing so undermines some conventional or accepted meaning with an alternative or even subversive one. Such detours are significantly determining, as we shall see, in both *The House in Paris* and *The Heat of the Day*, and a detour at the level of metaphor, or quasi-Homeric simile, supplies an extraordinary passage in *To the North*. Those novels of Bowen's set only in Ireland (*The Last September* and *A World of Love*) offer complex subversions of their own. For all of these works, the necessary contextualizing book is Elizabeth Bowen's own family history, *Bowen's Court* (1942), written mainly in London in the early years of the Second World War. It represents, we might say, the author stepping to one side of her own fiction to discover further family tombs: not the Moores of Moorehill, County Waterford, but the Bowens of the eponymous house in County Cork.

II

In a once celebrated, or notorious, critical essay, F. R. Leavis found George Eliot's *Daniel Deronda* such a self-divided work that he felt obliged to refer to two separate texts in his discussion of it: one with the title the author gave it; and the other with the title which Leavis, in an act of extraordinary presumption, invented for it, *Gwendolen Harleth*—'(as I shall call the good part of *Daniel Deronda*)'.[3] The

[3] F. R. Leavis, *The Great Tradition* (London: Chatto & Windus, 1948) 100.

reader of *Bowen's Court* may not feel driven to such an extreme, but the book does contain two narratives in a way that may well be disconcerting. In the main narrative Bowen is writing a history of her own Anglo-Irish family, beginning with their emigration from the Gower peninsula in South Wales and their consequent Cromwellian settlement in Ireland. This narrative includes the building of their Georgian house in Farahy, North Cork, in the eighteenth century, which Elizabeth Bowen had inherited at the time of writing this account; the rebellion of 1798, when the house was attacked; and the Famine of the mid-nineteenth century. It concludes with the period of Bowen's immediate predecessors, which included the war of independence and the civil war of the 1920s, when houses in the immediate vicinity of Bowen's Court, but not the house itself, were torched by Republican incendiaries: so even if Bowen's Court was the model for Danielstown in *The Last September*, in this crucial respect the actual house did not suffer the fate of the fictional one. Thus, *Bowen's Court* is Elizabeth Bowen's personal, insider inflection of a commonly written Anglo-Irish tale: a story of settlement, ascendancy, contraction, siege, and aftermath.

The ancestral piety of the book and the sense that it is a dynastic narrative are powerfully reinforced by Bowen's use of numerals, like the system of naming monarchs, to distinguish between her forebears (Henry I, Robert III, and so on), partly—but only partly, I think—because the same forenames, including the name 'Elizabeth', recur from generation to generation. The history is ostensibly constructed from Bowen's interpretation of family documents which have come into her possession as mistress of the house: wills, letters, marriage settlements, journals, the minute books of a Protestant association, the diary of the Cork chaplain to the Williamite army at the Battle of the Boyne, and so on. Sometimes, in fact, notably with regard to an extensive set of quotations from a Victorian children's journal, we may feel that the material has rather more significance for Elizabeth Bowen herself than it can ever have for us, and that it is given more than its reasonable due, making the book at times seem a kind of mosaic or tessellation, a sort of cento, in a way tending to disrupt narrative progress.[4]

---

[4] In the case of the children's diaries, however, the reader of one of Bowen's greatest short stories, 'The Happy Autumn Fields', may feel rewarded with a possible source for its quasi-supernatural crossing of the worlds of wartime London and Victorian Ireland by means of a cache of Victorian letters. I discuss the story in my chapter on *The Demon Lover and Other Stories*, below.

Nevertheless, the sense of a writer engaged in an act of imaginative family elegy and empathy is immediate and strong in *Bowen's Court* and gives it much of its distinctive tone.

Yet sympathy is frequently tempered by judgement, sometimes of a sharp-minded and unrelenting kind. Through the ages the family's vanity, fantasy, opportunism, and general abuse of power are exposed and derided, notably as they attach, in what seems almost a caricature of Anglo-Irishry, to a self-destructively obsessive land claim which persists litigiously, and in a financially crippling way, through the generations. Amidst all this plethora of citation Bowen prominently alludes to, but never actually quotes from, a treatise called *Statutory Land Purchase in Ireland*, which her own father, a lawyer, spent sixteen years writing. By the time it was published, it had already become, as a result of post-Treaty changes to the Irish constitution, 'a work of historic interest only' (444), as Henry Bowen himself called it—with what degree of ironic acceptance, or otherwise, his daughter does not say. In a book prominently parading its documentary sources for the history of Anglo-Ireland, this document, as long as Joyce's *Finnegans Wake* in the gestation, and redundant on delivery, has an almost emblematic force. Like some latter-day *Tristram Shandy*, its title takes on, in the latter part of *Bowen's Court*, an aura of near-terminal deferral and defeat; R. F. Foster calls the book a 'perfect metaphor for declining Ascendancy', although Bowen herself never, in fact, makes the metaphor explicit.[5]

Barbed expressions of the author's consciousness that she is uniquely a female inheritor of the house complement her father's book in undermining family pride. Bowen frequently notices the scant attention paid to the family's daughters and sisters compared to its sons and brothers in her documentary sources: of one pair of sisters, for instance, she notes that their 'sex did not even allow them capital letters in their father's will' (77). She caustically observes that 'the past does certainly seem to belong to men' (77), and she also tells us, although studiously avoiding reproach, that her parents had assumed that she would be a boy and had chosen the family name Robert for her. In these ways the book has a subliminally corrective and revisionist feminist impulse. This is not paraded and rarely even made explicit, but nevertheless it works from beneath through a subtle alteration of interpretative

[5] R. F. Foster, 'Prints on the Scene: Elizabeth Bowen and the Landscape of Childhood', in *The Irish Story: Telling Tales and Making it up in Ireland* (London: Allen Lane: The Penguin Press, 2001), 156.

perspective, and it focuses every so often on the ameliorative benefits brought to the Bowens by the women who married into the family. The nineteenth-century Eliza Wade is the outstanding case: she runs a soup kitchen from Bowen's Court at the time of the Famine when numerous locals, reaching the house too late, die on their way up the avenue. 'She would, I think, gladly have made soup of herself' (308–9), Bowen says, unforgettably.[6]

The specific family narrative is combined with a general history of the Anglo-Irish. Bowen's account is singularly lacking in class justification; at least, as we shall see, until the addition of an 'afterword' in 1963. She imputes blame consistently, notably for the refusal of subsequent generations to rescind the grossly unjust colonial land seizures of the Cromwellian settlement; for the Protestant Ascendancy's acceptance of bribes at the time of the Act of Union; for its prosecution and implementation of the Penal Laws in the eighteenth century; for its class 'hysteria' at the time of the Doneraile conspiracy in the early nineteenth century; and for a general willingness to plunder a country economically without accepting any adequate social responsibility. Her judgement is, on occasion, without illusion and absolute: 'The structure of the great Anglo-Irish society was raised over a country in martyrdom. To enjoy prosperity one had to exclude feeling' (248). In such judgements the book is probably influenced by Bowen's one-time lover, Sean O'Faolain, a former Republican soldier, who, in his own historically ruminative book, *The Irish*, published five years after *Bowen's Court*, meditates on the ways in which an Anglo-Irish culture flourished alongside political 'barbarism'.[7] Much of the time Bowen's critique is closer to the tone of O'Faolain's version of Irish history than it is to that of revisionist Irish historians like J. C. Beckett, F. S. L. Lyons, and R. F. Foster, who have been more wary about apportioning blame. Bowen is also writing during the Second World War, and in the atmosphere of rapprochement fostered by O'Faolain's journal, *The Bell*, to which she contributed; and her own contemporary, although short-lived, support for Irish neutrality was no doubt also a factor. The book is throughout, however, hostile to what she

---

[6] The churchyard in Farahy—once part of the Bowen's Court demesne, and standing at what was the bottom of the house's lower drive—contains a famine burial plot.

[7] Sean O'Faolain, *The Irish* (Harmondsworth: Penguin, 1947). R. F. Foster surmises that 'In its historical analysis the influence of O'Faolain is implicit and pervasive' in *Bowen's Court*. See R. F. Foster, *Paddy and Mr Punch: Connections in Irish and English History* (1993; London: Penguin, 1995), 117.

derides at one point as Anglo-Irish 'repining': it is oriented prominently towards the future, attempting to close a door on the past and unashamedly explicit about its 'hope' for 'an undivided Ireland', a view which led to Jonathan Cape's personal refusal to publish it with his firm on the grounds that it was 'subversive'.[8] These are all, as we shall see, matters which put great pressure too on Bowen's wartime fiction, the short stories of *The Demon Lover and Other Stories* and her novel *The Heat of the Day*.

Despite the 'subversive' element of the book, however, Bowen does also maintain a belief in the 'greatness' of Anglo-Irish society; and *Bowen's Court* celebrates the fact that the Bowens were in general more benevolent than most landowners and did cement local attachments. As a consequence, they built up a valuable style of living in the place of originally violent uprooting; although, very strangely, virtually no instances of Anglo-Irish cultural, as opposed to purely social, achievement, are ever adduced.[9] This history of achievement also frequently involves the quotation of documents, including Arthur Young's *A Tour in Ireland* (1780), the novels of Maria Edgeworth, a long account of the Doneraile conspiracy by the Cork journalist Thomas Sheahan, a wonderful and appalling passage from John Mitchel's journals on the Famine, and excerpts from the work of more recent Irish writers such as Aubrey de Vere and Stephen Gwynn. Both as national and as domestic historian, therefore, Bowen parades her sources: the book's method is juxtaposition, alignment, comparison, and, of course, interpretation. The historian herself defines the method of this dual history as an 'interleaving', and many critics have been impressed by the resourcefulness with which she manages her juxtapositions and alignments, as the local family history of North Cork

[8] See Heather Bryant Jordan, *How Will the Heart Endure?: Elizabeth Bowen and the Landscape of War* (Ann Arbor: University of Michigan Press, 1992), citing a letter from John Hayward to Frank Morley, 114.

[9] On the relative benevolence of the Bowens, it is, of course, significant that Bowen's Court was not burned in the 1920s. *Bowen's Court* is extremely reticent about this: 'I cannot go into this. At any rate Bowen's Court stood, and the kind inherited tie between us and our country was not broken' (440). I am able to add an element of oral history here. When I made a programme about Elizabeth Bowen for BBC Radio 3 in 1998, I interviewed people in Farahy and Kildorrery and was told that, while Elizabeth was in London, the local branch of the IRA—some of whose members worked, or had worked, in the house—took a vote *in the house itself* about whether to burn it. The vote was, of course, not to do so. I also had pointed out to me a 'mass path', which had run alongside the lower avenue of Bowen's Court in full view of the house—this being a path by which Catholics could gain access to open-air mass in Penal days; the implication being that the family had been an exceptionally tolerant one.

offers a perspective on the establishment, failure, and erasure of the Anglo-Irish, while also providing an exceptional insider's view of, and judgement on, the historical catastrophe which the colonial enterprise in Ireland represented.

I agree with this assessment of the book, but I still find something of Leavis's attitude towards *Daniel Deronda* stirring in me when I read it. It seems to me that alongside or underneath this interwoven narrative is a well-shaped subversive narrative which is at least as much obscured as it is delivered by the book's structure of 'interleaving'. It is not 'the good part' of *Bowen's Court*, or not the only good part, but it is, as it were, a parallel part; and this narrative, a ghost story, has relevance both to Bowen's actual view of Ireland and history, and also to some central elements of her fiction. So, what would the *Gwendolen Harleth* of *Bowen's Court*—we might call it *The Apparition*—read like?

III

The Apparition would be a circular narrative beginning and ending with both a haunting and a dispossession. 'There is no ghost in this house,' we are told a few pages into *Bowen's Court*, and in the 'Afterword' written in 1963, we are told so again:

The dead do not need to visit Bowen's Court rooms—as I said, we had no ghosts in that house—because they already permeated them. Their extinct senses were present in lights and forms. The land outside Bowen's Court windows left prints on my ancestors' eyes that looked out: perhaps their eyes left, also, prints on the scene? If so, those prints were part of the scene to me. (451)

One defining measure of the culture of the house is said to be its 'negation of mystical Ireland' (31), which culminates in the Bowens' early ignorance of, and their subsequent disdain for, the Gaelic Revival of the late nineteenth century. Even so, 'after dark, herons utter cries like lost souls' (30): and there have certainly been ghosts on this ground, even if there is no ghost now in the house, and they have been there from the beginning.

At the very start of *Bowen's Court* Bowen tells the story of 'the affair of the Apparition' which concerns Henry I, the first Bowen in Ireland, who accompanied Cromwell there from his home on the Gower peninsula in South Wales. Elizabeth Bowen takes the macabre tale from a treatise of 1691 which she calls *Baxter's World of Spirits* (its actual title is *The Certainty of the World of Spirits*). It relates how this first ancestor settled on the Farahy lands in County Cork and, while actually resident there, nevertheless appeared to his second wife, who had remained on the Gower, in the form of a putrefied carcass. The story of this apparition, a kind of grotesque *doppelgänger*, became well known to Henry's contemporaries in Ireland, and the odium attaching to him as a consequence led to his mental instability. The rationale which the seventeenth-century Puritan source gives for its story of possession is Henry Bowen's renowned atheism.

Although Elizabeth Bowen tells the story, she offers no interpretation of her own. We might feel more inclined to do so, particularly at the end of *Bowen's Court* when it is explicitly referred to again. There we are told that Elizabeth Bowen's father suffered from recurrent mental instability, known to the psychiatric medicine of the time as 'anaemia of the brain'. During these periods he would recall the story of the Apparition: 'the terrible vision of his illness contracted the Bowen history into the Bowen doom. . . . Through the empty rooms and on the land round them may have echoed ghostly tormented steps' (421). Of course, it is Bowen herself who is writing 'the Bowen history', and by linking beginning and end in this way it is she who is contracting a history into a doom, or at least extending the invitation to her readers to do so. The reason explicitly given for her father's illness is a lifelong feeling of guilt associated with his mother's death. His father, too, Elizabeth's grandfather, suffered a form of insanity, and a very Anglo-Irish one apparently connected with his outrage that his son had insisted on becoming a Dublin barrister instead of a traditional landlord: 'I think', says Bowen, 'of the Giotto figure of *Anger*, the figure tearing, clawing its own breast' (376). The equanimity of Bowen's treatment of these difficult, perturbing and—after all to her, recent—family circumstances suggests how capable an autobiographer she might have been in the work she projected towards the end of her life.[10] We may also think, however, that she was steeling herself into equanimity, since, as the scion of this dynasty, she must have feared a similar fate; and in *Seven Winters* she tells us that she was prevented from reading until she was 7 in case this should tax her brain in a way that might make her more readily prey to hereditary mental instability.

---

[10] What she wrote of it is reprinted in *The Mulberry Tree: Writings of Elizabeth Bowen*, selected and introduced by Hermione Lee (London: Virago Press, 1986), 251–98.

Victoria Glendinning says that Bowen 'was more afraid than most people of mental illness', and that during the period in which Bowen's Court was sold 'she drew as near to it herself as she was ever to get'; and she reminds us that in her penultimate novel, *The Little Girls* (1964), the character Dinah, 'facing the past head on, has a kind of breakdown'.[11]

When both insanity and *doppelgänger* possession figure in the narrative of *Bowen's Court*, so too do acts of dispossession and dislocation. The first Henry Bowen was a Cromwellian planter whose reward for service was the Farahy lands previously owned by a family called the Cushins, who were subsequently, in the usual way of these things, expelled from North Cork. Believing that she has found evidence that the daughter of the Cushin family remained on the land and had an affair with Henry's son, Elizabeth Bowen asks, 'Did she walk like a living ghost the lands her father had owned?' (77) In this trope, then, a member of the dispossessed family is figured as a ghost in her own home while she is still in fact alive, just as Henry the dispossessor appeared as a ghost on the Gower peninsula while living on the Farahy lands. A further intensification of, or irony in this, which Bowen makes explicit, is that Henry comes from a Welsh family, originally called the ap Owens, who were themselves victims of English dispossession when the Gower peninsula in South Wales was settled by the English after the Norman Conquest. Their Welsh origin leads Bowen at one point to remark of her family that they were 'not even pure Anglo-Irish' (277). This is said partly in order to distinguish them, to some extent, from the class against which her book makes, as we have seen, strong criticisms, but it also knowingly questions, or even mocks, the whole idea of 'purity' in relation to origin and development. To be 'pure Anglo-Irish' one would, presumably, have to be a 'pure' hybrid; but, how can a hybrid be pure?[12] And yet a further irony, or strange meeting, in this whole episode is that the Cushin daughter's first name was Elizabeth, which eventually became, of course, although only coincidentally, the Bowen forename inherited by the author of this book. Where dispossession is concerned in the writings of Elizabeth Bowen, that greatly over-cited phrase of Jacques Derrida's for the impossibility of ever

---

[11] Victoria Glendinning, *Elizabeth Bowen: Portrait of a Writer* (1977; London: Phoenix, 1993) 220.

[12] In this context it is of more than casual interest that *OED* gives as the word's first use in relation to human beings the following from Ben Jonson's *New Inn* (1630): 'She is a wild Irish born, sir, and an hybride'.

establishing origin, 'always already', seems to vibrate with an entirely new precision and aptness.

At the end of *Bowen's Court* the author describes the way she was sent from Ireland to England at the age of 7 as a result of her father's condition: the treatment recommended for him involved separation from his family. This Bowen version of the great Irish exile theme is of course relatively comfortable dislocation rather than dispossession, but nevertheless the result is to dispossess Elizabeth temporarily, but very woundingly, of a father and a house. In England she was also to be permanently dispossessed of her mother, who died of cancer when Elizabeth was only 13. The tough-mindedness and lack of self-pity of the mature woman writing *Bowen's Court*, admirable as they are, seem too intended and altogether too tight-lipped to ring true as an account of the child's responses. During the course of the book other Bowens in addition to Elizabeth's father and grandfather are subject if not to mental illness of her father's extreme kind then certainly to attacks of deep melancholia, and in evoking these Bowen's usually, in this book, rather brisk prose slows into something more strikingly figurative and unguarded. Of Henry III, for instance, she says that 'His infant—in fact, infantile—nervousness stayed, I feel certain, at the core of his being: under the superstructure of looks and manner moved moments of self-distrust and a sort of dread of the dark' (127). And of the incompetent Henry IV, who gives the house to his brother and retires to Bath, she says, 'Inside himself he was in an empty room' (237). The word 'infantile' is prominent in Bowen's considerations of the Anglo-Irish, notably in her preface to an edition of Sheridan Le Fanu's *Uncle Silas*, published in 1946, which is probably her finest critical essay; and moments of self-distrust and a sort of dread of the dark are precisely the material of her Irish short stories.[13]

Running underneath the family history of the Bowens and of the Anglo-Irish as a caste in *Bowen's Court*, then, is a closed circuit of narrative which I believe we should read as emblematic of colonial consequences, a kind of political unconscious of the text, joining together its beginning and its end. This may be considered a strain of that Protestant gothic which Terry Eagleton capably and extensively analyses in the Anglo-Irish novel generally in his book *Heathcliff and the Great Hunger*.[14] In Bowen's partly occluded gothic in *Bowen's Court*

---

[13] Elizabeth Bowen, '*Uncle Silas* by Sheridan Le Fanu', in *The Mulberry Tree*, 100–13.

[14] Terry Eagleton, 'Form and Ideology in the Anglo-Irish Novel', in *Heathcliff and the Great Hunger: Studies in Irish Culture* (London: Verso, 1995), 145–225.

the dispossessed become living ghosts of themselves when the possessions which largely construct their identities are suddenly and violently
removed. But the dispossessing colonizer is also a ghost of himself. In
the place he has come from he walks again as a putrefied carcass. Such
carcasses were, of course, the form to which the Cromwellian army
reduced huge numbers of the native Irish during its 'campaign'; and
Bowen is sceptically attentive to the motivation of that enterprise.
Cromwell's campaign, she says in one of those sudden epigrammatic
flourishes which characterize the book, was 'a speculation as well as a
holy war'(61), and she is satirical at Cromwell's expense when she
annotates some of the ways in which, in her view, the mixed motive
provoked hypocrisy and opportunistic duplicity.

When Bowen speaks of the isolation of the Irish big house as being
'innate . . . an affair of origin', emphasizing the more than usual isolation of Bowen's Court itself, she is making the necessary socio-political
point: that the topographical space dividing the Anglo-Irish from their
Irish neighbours is also the register of a huge religious, cultural, and
political space. Both *The Last September* and *A World of Love* elaborate metaphors of precisely such division and discontinuity. *Bowen's
Court*, however, makes the affair of the Apparition an affair of origin
too: it is present at (or even prior to) the beginning of this history and
persistent to the end, so much so that Bowen lets us know that it is read
by her own father as a 'doom', virtually a genetic fate. The act of colonization makes people ghosts of themselves while still alive: deraci-
nated, bilocated, manifestly powerful but also extremely vulnerable,
isolated by various kinds of space from those to whom they are also
attracted, always conscious of an elsewhere and an other to which they
may owe greater allegiance than they do to the present place and the
unstable, self-creating ego. To build a style upon a violent ruin is to
inherit the most profound consciousness of the potential for further
ruin, and such a consciousness becomes the single most enduring feature of both motive and self-perception. In Elizabeth Bowen the form
this takes is that of a Burkean conservatism of attachment permanently
shadowed by the fear of familial insanity, whose end may be catastrophic detachment, and a Burkean belief in the civilizing virtues of
property in fact permanently undermined by litigation, which may lead
to bankruptcy. The presence of ghosts of various kinds in Bowen's
writing, both literal and figurative, has, I believe, its own origin here;
but there is only one story, 'The Back Drawing-Room', which opened
Ann Lee's and Other Stories in 1926, in which the concept of a living

ghost figures as it does in the story of the Apparition: and the ghost appears in Ireland although the still living person is possibly in England.[15] It is worth observing that the ghost of a living person is very unusual in the genre of the ghost story (although it is a vicious and vengeful property in Dante, when he consigns some of the still alive to their already appointed circles of the Inferno, while their living bodies are possessed by demons). In fact, the only thing resembling it that I know of in modern literature is the ghost/*doppelgänger* of Spencer Brydon in Henry James's 'The Jolly Corner', and I shall propose a correspondence between the Jamesian and the Bowenesque ghost in what follows.

IV

Victoria Glendinning does not include 'The Back Drawing-Room' in a selection of Elizabeth Bowen's Irish stories, presumably because it is set in England; but, because in part a story within a story, it is most definitely an Irish story too.[16] It begins with several 1920s English intellectuals—pretentious, competitive, brittle—discussing spiritualism and survival after death. Although the First World War is not directly referred to, the war itself and in particular the grief it caused to bereaved mothers was a strong rationale for the popularity of spiritualism and its prominently gendered inflection in the 1920s. Thomas Hardy's and Walter de la Mare's poems, many of which include ghosts, are mentioned, and the discussion takes place in the kind of hushed, reverential atmosphere one associates with Madame Blavatsky or T. S. Eliot's Madame Sosostris in *The Waste Land*. Although at odds in various ways, the group is complicit in its snide condescension to one of its number who is repeatedly referred to as a 'little man', presumably with class condescension at least as much as with slighting reference to his stature; he is 'propped up and a little dejected, like an umbrella that an absent-minded caller has brought into the drawing-room'(200), and when he speaks it is 'as though the umbrella had spoken'(202): so he is a littler man even than Charlie Chaplin, he is a Chaplinesque umbrella.

---

[15] 'The Back Drawing-Room' can also be found in *The Collected Stories of Elizabeth Bowen*, with an introduction by Angus Wilson (London: Penguin, 1983), 199–210. My references are to this edition.

[16] See *Elizabeth Bowen's Irish Stories*, with an introduction by Victoria Glendinning (Swords: Poolbeg Press, 1978).

Never actually given a name, he is unknown to the rest of the group and appears to have joined it by some kind of accident or error. Nevertheless, he eventually offers to contribute to the discussion what he says will be a story of his encounter with a ghost. He is a hesitant and long-winded narrator, and the banality and literal-mindedness of his glumly sardonic self-composure fail completely to measure up to his audience's expectations of suspense and thrill, so he is frequently interrupted and his story is protracted. A framing device of some kind is characteristic of sophisticated ghost stories, but usually it is one in which the narrator has to convince a sceptical audience. In this story Bowen complicates the device, or even turns it on its head. The narrator's audience is more than willing to believe him; it is the narrator himself who can hardly believe the tale he is telling. These ironies supply a large part of the fascination and power of 'The Back Drawing-Room', as the sheer extraordinariness of the story which the little man tells eventually silences his immediate audience, who in the end have indeed been given the pleasurable terror they desired.

The little man has recently visited an Irish cousin just after what he calls 'these civic disturbances' have quietened down. His first mention of Ireland provokes a rhapsody of Celtic Revival-type melancholy from the woman who appears to be hosting the party, Mrs Henneker, and indeed English stereotypes of the Irish are much to the fore throughout Bowen's story, both in the little man's story itself and in the interruptions to it. The little man tells how, stranded in the rain a long way from his cousin's house with a punctured bicycle tire, he comes upon a big house at which, somewhere in the distance, a tennis party appears to be in session. Failing to attract attention, he wanders into the hall and then follows a woman into the back drawing-room ('really quite an intimate room, where I believe only favoured visitors are usually admitted', he says, in eager self-flattery). The woman lies on the sofa and sobs uncontrollably in a way eliciting sympathy from him; but this quickly turns into terror when he sees, in the room's deep gloom, her face looking as though it is 'drowning'. He dashes from the house in panic, 'simply not caring if they did think I was a burglar or a Republican, and fired at me from the bushes' (209), and pushes his bicycle all the way back to his cousin's house in the rain. There, over dinner, he learns that the only house he could have been in on the route he took, a house called Kilbarran, had in fact been burned down by Republican forces two years earlier, and the people who had lived there, the Barrans, had long since left the area. On hearing this, the little man surprises his hosts with a reaction of 'anger'. He then listens to his cousin's wife reflect on the fate of the Barrans:

She spoke as though they were dead; I rather assumed it, but asked. She said, 'Oh no; they're in Dublin, I think, or England.' I couldn't help saying she seemed to have rather lost interest in her old friends, and she looked at me (quite strangely, for such a practical woman) and said, 'Well, how can one feel they're alive? How can they be, any more than plants one's pulled up? They've nothing to grow in, or hold on to.' I said, 'Yes, like plants,' and she nodded. (210)

With this quoted speech about deracination the little man ends his story and leaves the party, even as he appears to wish to say more to Mrs Henneker, who ignores him. 'The Back Drawing-Room' concludes with Mrs Henneker's uncharacteristic, prominent, and enigmatic silence. This may be consistent with what she has earlier revealed of an unexpected fineness of understanding of the little man's meaning as the story unfolds, and notably when the woman of the house is said to have looked as if she was drowning. The little man says that if he were drowning he would not look at his life passing before him, but 'should be too much afraid, looking forward to all that was going to happen to me'. Mrs Henneker's response modifies what he says with an expansion of it which has a kind of Shakespearean largeness:

'No, to the world,' amended Mrs Henneker, 'to the whole of a world, your world. Because it is the quenching of a world in horror and destruction that happens with a violent death; just as one knows a whole world is darkened when one sees a child crying its heart out.' (208)

Clearly, she has intimate knowledge of such a 'quenching': it could be, of course, that her son had been killed in the war. 'The Back Drawing-Room', however, is inexplicit about her apparent sympathy for the narrated circumstances of the little man's story, and a significant implication in Bowen's story—as opposed to the little man's—seems to lie parallel to, but in an opposite direction from, that of the Apparition in *Bowen's Court*. In 'The Back Drawing-Room' the Anglo-Irish dispossessors are themselves dispossessed by the violent (Republican) forces which their original acts of colonization have ultimately unleashed at the point in their history, in the 1920s, when original settlement has become final siege. They become living ghosts not in the act of dispossessing others, as Henry I had done in the story of the Apparition, but in the act of being dispossessed themselves; and their ghosthood is similarly a matter of being in two places at the same time: which is the equivalent, as the cousin's wife glosses it, of being in fact nowhere at all, a death in life less grotesque than, but equivalent to, that represented by the putrefied carcass in the Apparition story. Uprooted from the only territory in which the Anglo-Irish possess an identity, they are in fact no longer 'alive' in any sense meaningful to others of their kind. They move into a sort of limbo of non-relation in which they are incapable of being at one with themselves, and the condition produces the most profound despair and grief: ' "She made me feel," the little man says of the weeping woman, "the end of the world was coming" ' (208–9). In James's 'The Jolly Corner' Spencer Brydon returns from a lengthy period in Europe to a New York whose modernity he finds it impossible to cope with, and he discovers in the house he has left the ghost of the self he would have become had he stayed. As in 'The Back Drawing-Room', the living ghost appears as an emblematic duality in a narrative of panic-stricken displacement, and of the end of a certain world.

By articulating such a meaning through the delicately achieved structure of her story, Elizabeth Bowen finds an emblem for the end of her class which has a kind of decorously baleful momentum. The careful framing of the Anglo-Irish ghost story within the English intellectual discussion, however, means that this momentum persists beyond the moment of the little man's story itself. However we understand his virtually enforced silence at the end of his story, and Mrs. Henneker's own pointed silence at the end of the story called 'The Back Drawing-Room'—and these are prominently foregrounded aporias in the story's construction—they may certainly be read as a moving of the Anglo-Irish plight into the English consciousness. The little man's story has, therefore, resulted in some modification of the Irish stereotypes raised during the narration: Ireland as a land of misty Celtic twilight, open-hearted hospitality, and reckless unconventionality. The banality of the little man's narration, where excitement and suspense had been anticipated, has impelled Mrs. Henneker's corrective and definitive restatement of his theme. Perhaps as the result of her own grief at the end of a world in the First World War, she is brought to an appreciation of the fact that this other, Irish, world has ended too. The two ghosts of the still living in *Bowen's Court* and 'The Back Drawing-Room' return to bring us the news that a colonial history includes its end in its beginning, becomes a ghost of itself in the act of first inscribing itself; and we might read the anger felt by the little man as the impotent emotion appropriate to the aftermath of a catastrophic history. Read like this, both narratives may also be thought to inherit, and to give a final malign shape to, some of the traits which R. F. Foster identifies in his definition of 'Irish Protestant supernatural fiction' as a genre in which 'occult preoccupations . . . mirror a sense of displacement, a loss of social and psychological integration'.[17]

V

The fact that violent acts of dispossession are at the origin and end of the stories Bowen tells of the Anglo-Irish—historiographically in *Bowen's Court* and fictionally in 'The Back Drawing-Room'—leads her to identify a paradoxical sharing of feeling between the Anglo-Irish and native Irish. In *Bowen's Court* we are told that in the eighteenth century 'the Gaelic culture ran underground, with its ceaseless poetry of lament', and this is glossed with the observation that 'It has taken the decline of the Anglo-Irish to open to them the poetry of regret: only dispossessed people know their land in the dark' (132). Declan Kiberd relates such belated identity of feeling to his striking conception of the figure of the 'dandy' in *The Last September* and intensifies Bowen's implication here, claiming that in her 'very disavowal of a native background and identity, she becomes a voice for all those uprooted, dispossessed Irish, for the Gaelic earls who fled in 1607, through the rapparees and exiled Fenians of later centuries, down to the Joyce and Beckett who had to put themselves at a distance from Ireland in order to convince themselves that the place had ever existed'. Bowen becomes, indeed, 'the Aoghan O Rathaille of her time and class'.[18] That this is a little strained, or even sentimental, is perhaps attested by the very odd claim indeed that Joyce and Beckett needed Elizabeth Bowen to 'become [their] voice', when they could speak so extremely well for themselves; and perhaps it says more about Kiberd's of course laudable desire to reconcile diverse traditions and move them towards a viable contemporary politics than it does about the actual spirit in which Bowen makes these observations. R. F. Foster much more sceptically suggests that what we have in such moments is 'an improbable echo of Daniel Corkery, possibly imbibed through O'Faolain but

[17] *Paddy and Mr. Punch*, 220.
[18] Declan Kiberd, *Inventing Ireland: The Literature of the Modern Nation* (London: Jonathan Cape, 1995), 378.

finished with a Bowen twist'; and Terry Eagleton, in *Heathcliff and the
Great Hunger*, may specify the actual politics involved in such alignments:

> There is a spurious kind of fellowship between oppressors and oppressed: if the
> exploiter is an outcast, then so are those on whom he battens; if they have no
> identity, then neither has he. What this conventionally overlooks is that if the
> ruler bears the mark of Cain it is because of his own actions, which is why the
> oppressed are outcast too; but in Ireland this symmetry can pass as plausible,
> since the governing class really does have good reason to feel paranoid. Their
> sense of persecution, in part at least, is a dread of the vengeance of those they
> have persecuted. Estranged from the populace by culture and religion, the élite
> can easily mistake itself for the marginal, and so misperceive itself as a mirror
> image of the people themselves.[19]

Nevertheless, Kiberd is right to identify an Anglo-Irish sense of 'dispossession' as the source of various kinds of imaginative sympathy in
Bowen. In particular it is striking, in a writer who so prominently
includes isolated and put-upon children in her work, that in *Bowen's
Court* she defines the lives of the Anglo-Irish, famously, as like those of
'only children . . . singular, independent and secretive' (20). In fact,
however, far from identifying Anglo-Irish and native Irish dispossession in most of *Bowen's Court*, she is usually saved from what Eagleton
calls this 'misperception' by the severity of her judgements on her own
class, however much she is tempted to it in a reflective moment or two.
There are stretches of the book in which, in relation to Bowen's perception of the Anglo-Irish, it is not Aoghan O Rathaille and the ceaseless poetry of lament which come first to mind but W. B. Yeats and the
combination of aggression and vulnerability which quivers and bristles
through such poems as 'Ancestral Houses' and 'Meditations in Time of
Civil War', where an understanding of Anglo-Irish motivation and
achievement involves '[taking] our greatness with our violence'.

However, there is, despite her better, perhaps O'Faolain-trained self,
a principle of animation in *Bowen's Court* which, deep down, cohabits
with the ancestral spirit. The tension between the book's historical witness, with its wartime desire for reconciliation, and this principle
obtrudes occasionally. There is the case, for instance, of the book's
major trope for the architecture, topography, and landscaping of
the house itself. This is purely and scandalously, although beautifully,
literary:

[19] *The Irish Story*, 151; *Heathcliff and the Great Hunger*, 191.

Inside and about the house and in the demesne woods you feel transfixed by the surrounding emptiness; it gives depth to the silence, quality to the light. The land round Bowen's Court, even under its windows, has an unhumanized air the house does nothing to change. Here are, even, no natural features, view or valley, to which the house may be felt to relate itself. It has set, simply, its pattern of trees and avenues on the virgin, anonymous countryside. Like Flaubert's ideal book about nothing, it sustains itself on itself by the inner force of its style. (21)

The effect of this is not merely to emphasize non-relation but to occlude a real politics of the place since, as *Bowen's Court* has itself, of course, made plain to us, this countryside was anything but virgin or anonymous when the house was 'set' there in 1775. The passage is suddenly as forgetful of actual originary circumstance as Robert Frost is, in the opening line of 'The Gift Outright'—'The land was ours before we were the land's'—of Native American precedence. It also aestheticizes the house into almost pure abstraction. A book of the proto-symbolist, proto-modernist kind Flaubert has in mind may indeed aspire to, although it could hardly be expected ever to reach, a purely non-relational sustenance; but a big house cannot so aspire, because the inner force of its style must, at the very least, be regulated and sustained by servants.[20] This myopia on Elizabeth Bowen's part is the crucial measure of her division from native Irish feeling, not least because it would, of course, have been—and was—the native Irish who were the servants.

This simile is matched by a revealing moment in her contemporaneous essay, 'The Big House', published in the first issue of O'Faolain's acerbically heterodox journal, *The Bell*, in 1942.[21] Tacitly salving the tragically bruised adverb of the final sentence of *The Last September*, when its big house is razed by the IRA ('Above the steps the door stood open hospitably upon a furnace'), she proposes a new socio-cultural role for the remaining big houses—congruent, as we shall see, with the way the big house is figured in *The Heat of the Day*—as places where members of both traditions may come harmoniously together. However, she ruefully acknowledges that the native Irish have shown no readiness to enter them. She appears genuinely perplexed at their reluctance, and undoubtedly wishes that they should do so, but

[20] Flaubert makes the observation in a letter to Louise Colet of January 1852. See Gustave Flaubert, *Selected Letters*, trans. and with an introduction by Geoffrey Wall (London: Penguin, 1997), 170. I am grateful to Geoffrey Wall for this reference.

[21] The essay is reprinted in *The Mulberry Tree*, 25–30.

Bowen's Court itself supplies one reason for their unwillingness when it tells us that a large portrait of Cromwell stood at the head of the main staircase of the house; and Bowen's Court was not, presumably, entirely exceptional in this regard. Bowen is not, I think, being disingenuous, but she is indicating a certain high-minded—or prejudiced—inattentiveness to cultural reality and a radical failure to appreciate the power of image and symbol in Irish history and politics. In *The Heat of the Day* Stella, in Ireland, shows a sensitive understanding of the effect of such symbolism and knows that if the houses are to continue at all the symbolism itself must be renovated or destroyed. But by the time Elizabeth Bowen wrote the afterword to the edition of *Bowen's Court* published in 1963, the idealizing tendency and the deeply ineradicable myopias have corrupted into nostalgia. In that later Anglo-Irish aftermath, in which Bowen had experienced the sale and subsequent destruction of Bowen's Court, she celebrates a tradition of stylish, even heroically stylish, *sprezzatura* against almost all the logic of her own earlier analyses:

> To live as though living gave them no trouble has been the first imperative of their make-up: to do this has taken a virtuosity into which courage enters more than has been allowed. In the last issue, they have lived at their own expense. (456)

R. F. Foster, citing the final remark here at the end of a chapter on the 'Ascendancy mind' in his history of modern Ireland, says that it is of 'equal inaccuracy' with Yeats's reinvention of Georgian Ireland as 'that one Irish century that escaped from darkness and confusion'; but he also says that 'in a very Anglo-Irish mode, this judgement reverses economic fact to express something not far from the psychological truth.'[22] This may be so; but psychology is dependent on economic fact too: and it is *Bowen's Court* itself, chastizingly to its now older author, that tells us so.

---

[22] R. F. Foster, *Modern Ireland 1600–1972* (London: Allen Lane: The Penguin Press, 1988), 194.

2

Discovery of a Lack:
The Last September (1928)

> Lois recalled with surprise that she had cried for a whole afternoon
> before the War because she was not someone in a historical novel.
> *The Last September*, 75

I

The Last September is a novel full of holes. Ellipses and lacunae characterize its dialogue, its detail, and its plotting, and several times it
opens into irresolvable aporia. As far as its dialogue goes, this is very
much one of the characteristic Bowen signatures, and not exceptional
in this novel. Nevertheless, it supplies one of the major sources of tonal
ambivalence in the book, as a wan, etiolated conversational style constantly punctuates or carries what is frequently a bright and brilliant, if
brittle, comedy of manners in the life of an Irish Big House immediately
prior to its destruction in the war of independence in 1920. In what was
only Bowen's second novel, the style is already secure and matured,
and also capable of defining itself: 'There was nothing to say, they did
not have to say anything: they exclaimed their thoughts casually, not
answering one another's, on the retreat towards silence' (53), where the
expressive oddness of exclaiming a thought, the near-oxymoron of a
casual exclamation, and the hint of telepathy, rather than conversation, in the phrasing serve to secure the strangeness or skewedness of
the perception being made, this intimation of a non-relation which is
melancholy but also companionable.[1] And in a novel in which the

---

[1] R. F. Foster observes that, although this manner has sometimes been linked by critics to that of Henry Green and Ivy Compton-Burnett, in fact it may be traced back in an
Anglo-Irish line to Maria Edgeworth. See *Paddy and Mr. Punch: Connections in Irish
and English History* (1993; London: Penguin, 1995), 107.

literal often shades into the figurative, as it frequently does in Elizabeth Bowen, and in which allegory is sometimes liable either to underwrite or to undermine realism, the retreat towards silence is that of the Anglo-Irish class or caste as a whole in the autumnal decline of their 'last September', and not just that of their engagingly disengaged representatives in this dialogue, Francie and Laurence.

What I want to call ellipses of plot, however, are exceptional, or at least exceptionally patterned and stressed, in *The Last September*, where they are both thematically functional and historically resonant. They are therefore at the heart of the book's effort and meaning; they are the way Bowen writes what she calls in her preface to the second American edition of the novel in 1952, 'fiction with the texture of history', emphasizing that the year of the novel's setting is eight years prior to its date of composition.[2] They are the mode in which she establishes herself as very much her own kind of historical novelist. The idea of the elliptical is signalled initially by the titles of the novel's three parts, in which an arrival, a visit, and a departure are announced. This is clearly to be a plot of transitions and instabilities, particularly since the 'visit' is in fact curtailed, and the 'departure' arguably refers to both an assassination and the burning of a house. Arrival, visit, and departure are all ironically positioned in relation to the putatively exceptionally stable setting of an ancient family home and Irish big house, Danielstown. And in fact, in so far as *The Last September* is a country house novel, some of the anticipated generic conventions of plotting are opened only to be abruptly foreclosed. Where typically in such novels characters are brought together so that they may interrelate in plots of social and erotic intrigue, in Bowen the relations never get very far. Lois Farquar, the niece of the house, an *ingénue* just out of school, is uncertain about her feelings for the English army subaltern Gerald Lesworth, and he is indeed worth less to her both than she wants to feel and than he desires; and their relationship is in any case terminated by the interference of her aunt, the mistress and *grande dame* of Danielstown, Myra Naylor—doing the right thing for all the wrong reasons, and in the most cynically manipulative way—before it is terminated for ever when he is assassinated by the IRA. Lois is altogether uncertain in her sexuality too, but her tentative relationship with Marda Norton, a visitor to the house, is itself terminated when Marda

---

[2] Elizabeth Bowen, *The Mulberry Tree: Writings of Elizabeth Bowen*, selected and introduced by Hermione Lee (London: Virago Press, 1986), 125.

leaves early because the married Hugo Montmorency, visiting Danielstown with his invalid wife, Francie, has fallen in love with her. The fact that nothing ever quite gets started or, if started, properly under way, makes the plot of *The Last September* one not so much of event as of interim, a long-drawn-out waiting—restless, anxious, hesitant, unresolved, and brought to conclusion only when most of the main characters have left the scene, and the house itself is razed from the landscape by the arson of the IRA during its guerrilla campaign.

There are respects too in which the novel ensures that its already elliptical plot is placed under further potential dissolution.[3] One such is the way that what fails to get started in Bowen's text sometimes gets further advanced in Lois's letters to her friend Viola in England. In letters which embarrass her as soon as she has posted them, she declares her love for a married man (Hugo, who has once been her mother's lover) and announces her decision to marry Gerald. These epistolary intimations of plots foreclosed vibrate in the novel with the melancholy of the road not taken, with an atmosphere of what, as we have seen, Bowen very tellingly calls 'unavailingness' in relation to J. G. Farrell's *Troubles*, a novel which pays a debt to *The Last September*.[4] Further, in the opening of the quite unanticipated Chapter 13, a chapter with an unlucky number, which I think of as Bowen's miniature Ulyssean 'Circe'—not a 'nighttown', but a 'nightcountry'—various of the novel's characters are sleepless or falling asleep and, doing so, they enter a world of dream and desire.[5] We know, for instance, that Laurence wants to be a novelist; and in effect he practises in this chapter when, falling asleep, he re-writes the plot of the novel in which he is a character. In an imagery of cobwebs and spiders' webs, he remorselessly unpicks what the novel has held tenuously together. In his dissolving oneiric version, 'in a kind of unborn freedom' (106)—which we might read as an arresting phrase for the novelistic imagination—

[3] 'Dissolution' is very much the word one wants here. It is a word that Bowen herself uses a lot; and John Hildebidle employs it in his essay on her work in *Five Irish Writers: The Errand of Keeping Alive* (Harvard: Harvard University Press, 1989). Andrew Bennett and Nicholas Royle register its significance in the title of their *Elizabeth Bowen and the Dissolution of the Novel: Still Lives* (London: Macmillan, 1995).

[4] Elizabeth Bowen, 'Ireland Agonistes', *Europa*, 1 (1971), 58–9, 58.

[5] The chapter is interestingly glossed by Bowen's observation in *A Time in Rome* (1959; New York: Knopf, 1965), 93, that 'People are most themselves when suddenly woken, or when they pull darkness over their heads, or when, in the middle of the night, they commit themselves to some momentous decision.' Maud Ellmann links the 'constant interruptions' of Bowen's first novel, *The Hotel*, to 'Circe' in *Elizabeth Bowen: The Shadow across the Page* (Edinburgh: Edinburgh University Press, 2003), 77.

Laura, Lois's mother, would have married Hugo; Richard Naylor, master of Danielstown, would have married Francie; Myra would have remained unmarried; and Laurence himself, the dandy, would have blown his brains out 'at—say—Avila, in a fit of temporary discouragement without having heard of Danielstown' (107). Lois 'naturally, was not born at all' (107)—since, of course, her parents would not have married.

This treats the untaken road with whimsical humour rather than anxiety or panic; and *The Last September* maintains throughout the parity, if not the primacy, of its comic tone. Inventing the marriage of Hugo and Laura, for instance, the fastidious Laurence also, with a shudder, envisages a time when they and four sons 'all hurried out to coarsen in Canada'; on the wedding morning, he thinks, 'the four young sons jiggled in excitement among the cherubim' (106). This is indeed a comic version of what I define below as an anxiety or terror attendant on the thought of one's own conception, which is intimately part of the characterization of Lois. But Laurence's rewriting of the actual plot of *The Last September* also reminds us of the accidental and contingent nature of all plotting, in novels and in marriages, and certainly in the marriages within novels. This stays only just on the right side of being deeply and deconstructively unsettling, particularly since Laura's actual marriage ends badly, and since this chapter opens with Hugo and Francie in bed together in an 'isolation of . . . proximity', childless, unsettled, and unhappy. Musing on the distressing circumstances of Laura's actual emotional life and marriage, however, Laurence—who has undoubtedly read Freud—eventually decides that 'there is a narrow and fixed compulsion . . . inside the widest ranges of our instability' (107). This determinism has its terrifying historical as well as psychological import, since Sir Richard, we are told at the end of this night-time section of the chapter, is busily dreaming of himself as a Black and Tan on a motorbike 'from which he could not detach himself'. In his dreams, therefore, he accepts the truth of the political situation which he will not admit to himself in daylight: that his very existence in this country—from which, truly, he cannot detach himself, but from which, nevertheless, he is about to be violently detached—is now dependent on the paramilitary terror of the state, with which, for all his traditional civility, he is inevitably collusive. Comedy in Elizabeth Bowen may cut very deep indeed, with a laughter on the other side of hysteria.

We may think of this chapter as the sudden lurch of *The Last September* into a kind of plot unconscious, one threatening sexual and familial disruption and chaos; and it is complemented elsewhere by what I have already called moments of aporia. There is one in Chapter 10 when a conversation between Marda and Hugo about the Irish war provokes this peculiar exchange. Hugo speaks:

'What's the matter with this country is the matter with the lot of us individually—our sense of personality is a sense of outrage and we'll never get outside of it.'
    But the hold of the country *was* that, she considered, it could be thought of in terms of oneself, so interpreted. Or seemed so—'Like Shakespeare,' she added more vaguely, 'or isn't it? . . .'   (82)

This begins as an acute piece of Anglo-Irish self-definition, and the usually irresolute Hugo is more than once in the book the articulator of unpalatable insight. It is one of Bowen's strengths as a novelist that we are invited to consider whether this is despite his weakness of character or, indeed, because of it: that is to say, whether his inertia—he is called 'a kind of echo'—is the only adequate reaction to his despair with what he has analysed as the sclerotic 'outrage' of his class, and therefore even a paradoxical strength of mind, a commitment to the only possible form of life consequent upon such knowledge. Also worthy of note here, however, is the Shakespearean reference which this provokes from Marda. What does it intend? It is, of course, impossible to say, since the novel keeps it in suspension with those marks of ellipsis, and we are uncertain what exactly Marda's comparison is attempting relation with, particularly since the phrase 'the hold of the country' is ambiguous: is this an objective or a subjective genitive, the country's hold over the Anglo-Irish, which might be virtually a sentimentalism; or their hold over the country, which would be much more charged with the realities of *realpolitik*?

    The Last September, however, is oddly intertextual with Shakespeare in at least one other respect too: it has, like *Twelfth Night*, characters called Viola and Olivia. Viola is, as we have seen, Lois's old schoolfriend in England; Olivia is her Irish friend. More usually called Livvy, her unabbreviated name is nevertheless pointedly given to us by Laurence when he objects to her diminutive: 'Why should they chop up the rather beautiful name of Olivia into something that sounds like cat's meat?' (55) Like Shakespeare, then, or isn't it? 'Outrage' is the word used for civil war by the Duchess of York in *Richard III* (II. iv. 63): so, is Marda saying that the relationship of the Anglo-Irish to the land they insecurely occupy, which is the cause of their sense of outrage, is like that of the baronial and monarchical classes to England in Shakespeare's history plays, and that therefore the outrage in fact reveals the vulnerability of those caught up in the fraught, disintegrative chaos of governmental transition and civil war which those plays witness? Or, is the text, as it were, saying that what should be comedy—the *Twelfth Night* element of its constitution (the changeable liaisons of the young and the ambivalences of sexual identity)—are inevitably, in this historical epoch, superseded by the exigencies of politics, as in the history plays? These seem to me reasonable interpretations of Marda's ellipsis here; and they are therefore an indication of the ways in which this novel may make so much dependent upon an ellipsis.[6]

In Chapter 7 there is a further aporetic moment, this one in relation to Lois. *The Last September* is acute about the consequences for privacy of living in an Irish big house on the Danielstown model; and at this point in the book Myra and Francie are discussing Lois's relationship with Gerald in the ante-room outside her bedroom. Lois, despite her best efforts, can hear them; and at the point when Francie says, 'Lois is so very—', she makes a noise in her room by kicking furniture to remind them forcefully of her presence. This conversational ellipsis or hiatus is registered as distress by Lois: 'Was she now to be clapped down under an adjective, to crawl round lifelong inside some quality like a fly in a tumbler?' (60), but it also persists as thwarted desire since, of course, part of her wants to know what was about to be said; and the chapter, like several in the novel, comes to a resonantly figurative conclusion:

She lifted her water jug and banged it down in the basin: she kicked the slop-pail and pushed the washstand about. . . . [ellipsis in text] It was victory. Later on, she noticed a crack in the basin, running between a sheaf and a cornucopia: a harvest richness to which she each day bent down her face. Every time, before the water clouded, she would see the crack: every time she would wonder: what Lois *was*—She would never know.   (60)

---

[6] Bennett and Royle in *Elizabeth Bowen and the Dissolution of the Novel*, 84, observe that 'references to Shakespeare's plays, whether in the form of narratorial allusions or in discussions between characters, are woven throughout Bowen's work: her novels are demonstrably and powerfully Shakespearean'. I agree, and shall refer to Shakespeare more than once again in this study; but I don't know that I follow them in their related view that Shakespeare's work is 'importantly Bowenesque'.

Lois's cracking of the basin is the price she must pay for security from embarrassing or distressing intrusion. It is also, figuratively, the fissure running through any assured sense of personal or even sexual identity, running between the sheaf and the cornucopia of potential gratification or satisfaction. This crack is, therefore, the aporia of her own lack of formation, her late adolescent unease, which is exacerbated by the fact that she is an orphan and was the child of an unhappy marriage, and—more peculiarly, but in a way entirely characteristic of Bowen's tangential perception—by her consciousness that she might not have existed, or might have been someone else, since her mother, Laura, might well have married Hugo Montmorency. Yet the crack or fissure also surely has its social and cultural dimension. For this scion of the Anglo-Irish at a time of violent revolutionary upheaval it is the crack which runs between what might once have been an identity—always defensive, probably, and frequently 'outraged', but nevertheless established—for the class from which she derives, and whatever it might become, or fail to become, in future. This Lois 'would never know' because, quite conceivably, there will never be anything to be known: this is an identity in transition only to abeyance. And it is that 'crack', the fissure opening between a politically and historically exhausted past and a potentially non-existent future, which opens again, running down the wall of the ruined mill in Chapter 15, and explicitly likened there, as we shall see, to the crack in the wall of Poe's House of Usher.

Constantly playing against the brightness of social comedy in *The Last September*, therefore—notably the comedy of edgy insinuation and misunderstanding that characterizes Anglo-Irish/English/Irish relations—is a pervasive effect of attenuation, bathos, desuetude. 'They were delayed, deflected,' it is said of Hugo's and Marda's lengthy failure to pay a return visit to Danielstown; but, in fact, this could be said more generally of the Anglo-Irish in the novel too. This mood is shadowed by the appropriateness of the book's Proustian epigraph: 'Ils ont les chagrins qu'ont les vierges et les paresseux . . .' which—that ellipsis again—in fact continues 'et que la fécondité ou le travail guerirait'. Bowen restrains herself from completing Proust's aptly and damningly judgemental sentence, in what is perhaps an effect of Anglo-Irish decorum, resisting the pull of her own most scathing critique, as well as the effect of a hermetically intertextual modernism: 'They suffer, but their sufferings, like the sufferings of virgins and lazy people, are of a kind that fecundity or work would cure.'[7] The sternness of this stricture is enforced, however, by at least one element of the novel itself: whatever suffering the characters endure is in part a function of their leisured, servanted culture of 'not noticing' the reality of their circumstances, a refusal to admit to the fact that an increasingly appalling guerrilla war is about to extirpate them for ever from the land they have lived on for generations. 'We never listen', says Sir Richard, as though it is a virtue; and indeed he fondly considers civil unrest a function of the season, one that will vanish when the days draw in.

It is in this primary sense that the novel's structural ellipses assume thematic significance. What is elided in brief reference, casual aside, throwaway remark, and willed silence is what Peter Hart, in his excellent *The I.R.A. and its Enemies: Violence and Community in Cork 1916–1923*, with an immense amount of detailed evidence, calls 'a kind of total war in miniature'.[8] It is to the point, in fact, that the name 'Cork' is itself elided in the novel, although this is hardly ever noticed. Presumably because the Bowen family home, Bowen's Court, was in Co. Cork, and Danielstown is too casually identified with its fictional representation, critics usually make the kind of assumption that Victoria Glendinning makes in her introduction to the Vintage Classics edition of the novel, where, in her first sentence, she refers to 'Danielstown, in Co. Cork'.[9] Bowen's elision of the county's name is, however, consistent with those others I have been identifying. It is the index of authorial scruple before the facts of a history whose most violent effects defy the capacity of her own fiction. To read Hart against Bowen is to take the full, hideous force of the reality behind words which float nebulously through the novel, signifiers deliberately unattached to the enormity of their signifieds: 'patrols', 'raids', 'Black and Tans', 'Cork Militia', 'reprisals', 'army of occupation', 'an offensive'. There is a real, if paradoxical, sense therefore in which history is most present in *The Last September* when it is most absent. As it is, prominently, when, after Gerald's assassination, Sir Richard allows himself a

---

[7] Marcel Proust, *Remembrance of Things Past*, Vol. III, trans. by C. K. Scott Moncrieff and Terence Kilmartin, and by Andreas Mayor (London: Chatto & Windus, 1981), 927; original in *New Pléiade* iv. 470. This forms part of Proust's great meditation on time and art in the final volume of the novel, a passage significant in many ways for Bowen. I am grateful to Professor Malcolm Bowie for supplying me with the source of this quotation.

[8] Peter Hart, *The I.R.A. and its Enemies: Violence and Community in Cork, 1916–1923* (Oxford: Clarendon Press, 1998), 39.

[9] Introduction to Elizabeth Bowen, *The Last September* (London: Vintage, 1996), 1.

brief, stunned recognition of the entirely likely truth—that Gerald has been the victim of a family, the Connors, or their friends, with whom his own has been on extremely good terms (and a visit to whose farm by Lois and Hugo supplies a superb early scene of tender *rapprochement*). This momentary, muffled, and almost missable recognition provides what is probably the most chastening and despairing ellipsis in the book, as Sir Richard veers away from the truth he approaches, trailing into the ineffectuality of his kind: 'it did not do to imagine . . .'.

II

The shared sense of historical lacuna produces an unlikely imaginative sympathy between Lois and Laurence, the two 'vierges' of the book. Young members of the next Anglo-Irish generation, they are both orphans—significantly, since the condition already cuts them off from their most immediate roots. Laurence is Myra's impecunious nephew, staying in Danielstown during the Oxford vacation. He is Bowen's wry portrait of the 1920s undergraduate—bookish, a bit camp, cynical, with all the 'wrong' politics: he sympathizes with the aims, and understands the reasons for the methods, of the IRA. A mordant if callow realist, he seems strangely transposed to Ireland from the world of Evelyn Waugh. He and Lois are antagonistic for most of the book's length, although, after Gerald's death, they explicitly come to the kind of mutual recognition which the reader senses as already inherent in their edgy friction from the start. But what they share throughout is a view of the 'situation' far removed from the myopia or deliberate blindness of the other Anglo-Irish characters. Both are exceptional among the inhabitants of Danielstown in that they actually encounter the 'other' of the IRA—Lois when she sees a gunman walking through demesne land and, in an episode I shall analyse in some detail in a moment, when, accompanied by Marda, she meets another gunman in a ruined mill; and Laurence when he has a near-farcical 'unusual night' as the victim of an IRA ambush. They are also exceptional in their attunement to the historical moment they are living through. This is particularly clear when both respond to a subaltern, Smith, when he tells them that he intends to leave the army for a colonial career in East Africa once the Irish question is 'settled':

But to Laurence and Lois this all had already a ring of the past. They both had a sense of detention, of a prologue being played out too lengthily, with unnecessary stress, a wasteful attention to detail. Apart, but not quite unaware of each other, queerly linked by antagonism, they both sat eating tea with dissatisfaction, resentful at giving so much of themselves to what was to be forgotten. The day was featureless, a stock pattern day of late summer, blandly insensitive to their imprints. The yellow sun—slanting in under the blinds on full-bosomed silver, hands balancing Worcester, dogs poking up wistfully from under the cloth—seemed old, used, filtering from the surplus of some happy fulfilment; while, unapproachably elsewhere, something went by without them. (118)

And after tea, outside the house—not Danielstown, but the neighbouring Mount Isabel, which also burns at the novel's end—Laurence looks up at the mountain:

A sense of exposure, of being offered without resistance to some ironic uncuriosity, made Laurence look up at the mountain over the roof of the house. In some gaze—of a man's up there hiding, watching among the clefts and ridges— they seemed held, included and to have their only being. The sense of a watcher, reserve of energy and intention, abashed Laurence, who turned from the mountain. But the unavoidable and containing stare impinged to the point of a transformation upon the social figures with their orderly, knitted shadows, the well-groomed grass and the beds, worked out in this pattern. (119)

The exquisite, Chekhovian ennui of Lois's and Laurence's responses here has, nevertheless, its historically corrective virtue. What they share, in their queerly antagonistic link, is the recognition of termination: both understand what the novel calls at another point 'the fear behind reason'. The 'pattern' about to be disrupted or transformed is figuratively cultural and political, as well as literally meteorological or horticultural, and these passages have behind them a neo-classical horticultural aesthetic and morality: the house is a kind of Appleton House, as in Marvell's poem, but one now about to suffer the indignity of its undoing. Lois and Laurence, unlike the majority of the inhabitants of these houses in the novel, well understand, and have internalized, their own supersession. In Laurence's abashment—his shame—before the gaze of the other or outsider there is an almost sexual violation; in his idle listlessness there is an almost naked 'exposure' to the focused energy and intention which will be his ruin. There is admiration as well as understanding in this, and if Laurence is subjected here, he is also a harbinger of the future. That future is 'unapproachable', indeed, by those whom it exhausts, but it is not unknowable; and these passages may be said to find their gloss in W. J. McCormack's observation that 'when the social world of the

Anglo-Irish was finally eclipsed it was as if the hyphen, which had always been a signally diminished equation mark, became a minus sign, a cancellation'.[10] Laurence, for all his whimsicality, is able to sense and define the moment of that cancellation; and my view of the political *nous* of whimsicality has a correlative in Declan Kiberd's perceptive reading of the novel, citing Walter Benjamin on Baudelaire, as 'one of the very few works of literature to consider the dandy as a fit subject for tragedy'.[11]

If Lois and Laurence are queerly linked by antagonism, they are queerly linked in another way too. Laurence's name is, as it were, the masculine version of 'Laura', the (Petrarchan) name of Lois's mother, which is frequently reiterated in the book, and figures in its initial form 'L. N.', scratched on whitewash in the boxroom in which Lois hides from Livvy in Chapter 16. Both names are congruent with the word 'laurel', and laurel—the shrub—also figures several times in the narrative. It does so, for instance, when Lois encounters the man in the trenchcoat:

A shrubbery path was solid with darkness, she pressed down it. Laurels breathed coldly and close: on her bare arms the tips of leaves were timid and dank, like tongues of dead animals. Her fear of the shrubberies tugged at its chain, fear behind reason, fear before her birth; fear like the earliest germ of her life that had stirred in Laura. (33)

This extraordinary passage is complemented by others: when, for instance, during the tennis party which forms one of the novel's most emblematic social scenes, 'The strong and dreadful smell of laurels made them all irritable' (43); and when, during Lois's interview with Gerald just before it becomes clear that she will not marry him, 'The laurels creaked as, in his arms, she bent back into them. His singleness bore, confusing, upon her panic of thoughts, her physical apprehension of him was confused by the slipping, cold leaves' (172), and Gerald is forced to say that he doesn't like 'the smell of the laurels' (172).

Andrew Bennett and Nicholas Royle have noticed the recurrence of laurels, and, citing the first of these passages, they read it, in the context of an argument about the presentation of 'the physicality of thought', as 'a fear of the name of the mother: the "laurel", plant of

[10] W. J. McCormack, *From Burke to Beckett: Ascendancy, Tradition and Betrayal in Irish Literary History* (Cork: Cork University Press, 1994), 52–3.

[11] Declan Kiberd, *Inventing Ireland: The Literature of the Modern Nation* (London: Jonathan Cape, 1995), 373.

poets, the signifier of linguistic profusion, is also the path down which Lois walks in the name of her mother Laura'; and they pursue this perception into an idea of the ways in which, in Bowen, 'people are figured, characterized, given identity, precisely by the thought of the dead'.[12] There is a lot in this, and Bennett and Royle's book is notable for relating Bowen's perception of the 'thought of the dead' to certain kinds of literary and psychoanalytic theory. Clearly, this passage anchors Lois's lack of secure identity in thoughts of her dead mother and associates her fundamental anxiety with her very genetic constitution, in her now dead mother's womb. I would want, however, to return the perception from theory to history and topography by emphasizing the reverberance of Laura's name in Laurence's too, as well as emphasizing Laura's figurative inscription in the pervasive laurels, that vegetation—smothering, overpowering, cold, slippery—of the house Danielstown, and a vegetation deeply associated with war and victory, and therefore prominently iconic in Anglo-Irish history and representation. Laura, I propose, becomes thereby a presence of virtually occult significance in the novel. Sister of the master of the big house, and southern wife of a failed northern marriage, she is the Anglo-Irish ghost *par excellence* in *The Last September*. In the entrapment and failure represented by her ghosthood, she is what Lois and Laurence understand about the entrapment and failure of the class they come from, and she is what they must overcome; which they can do eventually only by leaving the house, and which, the novel appears to insist at its close, can finally happen only when the house itself is razed from the Irish landscape. The figure of Laura may therefore be comprehended by Paul Muldoon's poignant formulation—made in relation to other texts of Bowen's—of 'the dispossessed Anglo-Irish gentry who are turning into possessing "gentles" [as in 'gentle people': that is, fairies], ghosts of themselves who are implicated in, but cut off from, their own lives'.[13] Something of the kind is surely what is being formulated when Lois returns to Danielstown from the dance towards the end of the novel, and is questioned by Laurence in the garden:

'It is extraordinary,' said Lois. 'I feel as if I had been away for a week. Yet you find us going on much the same?' He looked at her through the stems ironically but without intelligence. And she could not try to explain the magnetism they all exercised by their being static. Or how, after every return—or awakening,

---

12 *Elizabeth Bowen and the Dissolution of the Novel*, 17.
13 Paul Muldoon, *To Ireland, I* (Oxford: Clarendon Press, 2000), 24.

even, from sleep or preoccupation—she and those home surroundings still further penetrated each other mutually in the discovery of a lack.   (166)

This is virtually a final return for Lois, however, and we may regard the 'discovery' made by it as the impulsion to escape. Lois and Laurence, who have already vanished from *The Last September* before its final catastrophe, have pulled away from its magnetic stasis, in order to attempt to supply, in their own personal and cultural histories, an alternative to this lack.

III

In what is usually regarded as a crucial episode of the novel, the encounter between Lois, Marda, and the IRA gunman in the ruined mill in chapter 15, during which Marda's hand is grazed by a bullet, lack is clearly the issue too, and the idea of the ghostly figures prominently. Hugo, Marda, and Lois approach the mill in a state of sexual tension and awkwardness. Hugo has fallen in love with Marda but can express this only in frustrated irritability; this part of the country was once the scene of a highly charged moment in his disintegrating relationship with Laura, which he is now remembering; and Lois is attracted to Marda too in a way she can barely formulate to herself, so unexpected and perturbing is the emotion.[14] This erotic undercurrent flows throughout the episode, and is part of what lies behind the evocation of the scene inside the mill as 'strangely set for a Watteau interlude', a '*fête-champêtre*' of dalliance and diversion. In fact, the

---

[14] It is not to my purpose here to pursue the implications of Lois's sexual ambivalence any further, but it is a recurrent strand in the book's complex interweavings: she wants, for instance, to be 'a woman's woman' and she wishes of Gerald 'that he were a woman'. The erotic ambiguity of the relations between Olivia and Viola disguised as Cesario in *Twelfth Night* may suggest a reason for Bowen's use of both names in *The Last September*. Woman-to-woman relations in some of Bowen's novels, including *The Last September*, are exhaustively examined in Renée C. Hoogland, *Elizabeth Bowen: A Reputation in Writing* (New York: New York University Press, 1994); and Patricia Coughlan has very illuminating things to say in 'Women and Desire in the Work of Elizabeth Bowen', in Eibhear Walshe (ed.), *Sex, Nation and Dissent in Irish Writing* (Cork: Cork University Press, 1997), 103–31. She reads the relationship between Lois and Marda as 'a woman-to-woman attachment which takes place in the margins of the accepted social narrative and which has little or no place in the allotted scheme of things (and . . . in most of the published criticism of Bowen to date)' (124). The parenthetical observation has become much less true since Coughlan wrote this.

encounter itself goes on to pitch this in a different key when Marda and Lois are 'ashamed' to look at the sleeping gunman, presumably because of the intrusion or violation of a privacy; when they are 'embarrassed' by the suggestively phallic pistol, which neither have ever seen 'at this angle'; and when he looks at them 'with calculating intentness, like a monkey'—which also, of course, has a simianly sexual suggestiveness.

Marda is already prominently identified as, on many occasions, the source of accident or catastrophe. The chapter, therefore, has an air of the ominous even before the mill is sighted. When Marda first sees it, it appears to her as 'the ghost of a Palace Hotel', and the ensuing descriptions—'staring, light-eyed, ghoulishly, round a bend of the valley'—pursue the gothic associations. These climax in an allusion to Edgar Allan Poe when Lois enters the mill: 'Cracks ran down; she expected, now with detachment, to see them widen, to see the walls peel back from a cleft—like the House of Usher's' (124); and this sexually stirred context inevitably activates the sexual connotations of the words 'cracks' and 'cleft'. Lois, as we have seen, is already associated with a crack, the crack between a sheaf and a cornucopia through which her own identity might fall. Here, suggestively in several senses, that crack widens to include the history of Anglo-Ireland itself. In Poe's 'The Fall of the House of Usher' the cracks in the walls open and the house falls after a terrible secret has been revealed. This ruined mill is, as it were, the terrible secret of Anglo-Irish history still architecturally articulate on the land, even in its desolation; and Hugo begins to elaborate something like this before he is prevented by yet one more elision:

'Another,' Hugo declared, 'of our national grievances. English law strangled the—' But Lois insisted on hurrying: she and Marda were now well ahead. (123)

That ellipsis is the gap through which a long Anglo-Irish history falls: the issue is raised, as so often in Bowen, only to be turned from, but in a way that makes it in some ways all the more insistent, with the insistence of the hauntingly irretrievable.

What Hugo is alluding to here is the English economic stranglehold which, in the nineteenth century, ensured—by means of custom duties, tariffs, and so on—the virtual destruction of Irish industry. Peter Hart, for instance, tells us that 'Cork had once been the most populous county in Ireland, with extensive industries; nowhere had nineteenth-century changes been more costly'.[15] The mill as the ruined scene of

---

[15] *The I.R.A. and its Enemies*, 39.

this conflicted history then becomes the scene for the return of the historically repressed when the IRA man—it appears by accident—shoots and inflicts a minor injury on Marda. It is as though the Anglo-Ireland represented by Danielstown still contains or harbours the violence which will be its own disintegration. Julian Moynahan writes penetratingly about this episode and reads the shedding of blood as a vampiric touch, 'the nightmare vision of the "undead", the dead still putting on an act at living'.[16] This would harmonize with what I have already characterized as the sexual tension of the episode, since its opening erotic emotions are transposed to Lois's feelings about the mill too—'It was a fear she didn't want to get over, a kind of deliciousness'—and it is consistent with the feeling of the uncanny which many readers get from the scene and which, of course, the reference to Poe both confirms and enforces. Indeed, the whole episode may be read in the light of Terry Eagleton's analysis of Protestant gothic in *Heathcliff and the Great Hunger*, where he defines it as 'the political unconscious of Anglo-Irish society, the place where its fears and fantasies most definitively emerge':

It is as though every drearily predictable process of labour and exchange, every casual act of domination or collusion, is leaving its stealthy impress in some region altogether elsewhere, which will return in the shape of literary fantasy to confront us with the terrifying inner structure of all that we take for granted.[17]

The mill episode is not, of course, presented as fantasy but as reality; and yet its gothic colouration and allusions, and its sharing something of that atmosphere of dream or nightmare already registered in what I have called the 'little Circe' chapter, ask to be read under this rubric too. The mill becomes, then, the novel's ultimate ellipsis. The actual history—the story of England's colonial relations with Ireland—which has produced its present ruinous condition is interrupted before it can be properly articulated; but the violence which is the contemporary product of that history of 'grievances'—the shedding of Anglo-Irish blood—is all too actually represented in the scene. Even so, in a further continuation of the trope of ellipsis, it is itself not to be articulated further: Lois swears Marda to secrecy about the episode when she returns

---

[16] Julian Moynahan, *Anglo-Irish: The Literary Imagination in a Hyphenated Culture* (Princeton: Princeton University Press, 1995), 244.

[17] Terry Eagleton, *Heathcliff and the Great Hunger: Studies in Irish Culture* (London: Verso, 1995), 187–8.

to Danielstown. This is because she has promised as much to the IRA man, a promise which the narrative describes as 'priggish', but which may certainly be read as the signification that for Lois the ethics of the personal life always countermand the pragmatics of the political one. Yet it is also because, as this narrative has long since taught us, this kind of 'political unconscious' simply cannot be raised to the consciousness of the Anglo-Irish themselves. This secrecy, therefore, the removal into hermetic impenetrability of the actual, is a further intensification of Lois's feeling after her encounter with the man in the trenchcoat much earlier in the novel that 'it was impossible to speak of this'; and therefore, as a result, as now once more, she must be silent. The imaginative space opened by this politicized gothic is also the scene of judgement:

Banal enough in life to have closed this valley to the imagination, the dead mill now entered the democracy of ghostliness, equalled broken palaces in futility and sadness; was transfigured by some response of the spirit, showing not the decline of its meanness, simply decline; took on all of the past to which it had given nothing. (123)

This passage has been the occasion of some puzzled commentary, and it certainly compacts an understanding of the ways in which the aesthetic satisfactions of romantic ruin are, in fact, produced by a deeply unimpressive economic actuality. Julian Moynahan's comment on it moralizes the Bowen scene:

one may recoil from the spectacle of the ruins of the nongiving mill to a thought that if the dominant and empowered class in Ireland during the nineteenth century . . . had given more—had given *something*—to the country, then perhaps the Gothic strangler, English law, might not quite have been able to do its worst.[18]

This is an understandable reaction, but it seems to me at least conceivable that this is precisely Bowen's point. The mill—which would almost certainly have been owned and operated by a member of the Anglo-Irish class—is judged here for its failure to have given anything, economically, to the land it stands on: this was, precisely, its 'meanness'. Only in its more recent 'ghostliness' does it reveal to the responsive imagination its collusion in terminal 'decline'; and this ghostliness, like Laura's in the novel, is the entrapment which cannot be avoided, except by release into the alternative history which the gunman—who seems almost bodied forth by the mill itself, its incarnate form or

[18] *Anglo-Irish*, 244.

denizen—represents. If Anglo-Irish customs and traditions may be considered in some ways still 'feudal'—and the word is used, only half ironically, several times in *The Last September*—then this new 'democracy' will enforce its alternative, and will do so by nailing the old feudalists in the ruins of their despotism. It takes a democracy of the imagination, however, to perceive this, releasing the mill from its historical banality into corrective sublimity: it 'took on' all of the past in the sense, certainly, of manifesting it, but also in the sense of offering it challenge and confrontation. Which is why for Hugo, 'The mill behind affected him like a sense of the future; an unpleasant sensation of being tottered over' (125). What is behind is also to come; and what is to come will involve his destruction.

The narrative says of Lois, just before she enters the mill, that 'This was her nightmare: brittle, staring ruins' (123); and this is, of course, the novel's nightmare too, as it is that of a great deal of Anglo-Irish literature. It is also the nightmare which becomes, yet again, the Anglo-Irish reality in the novel's concluding paragraphs, in which Danielstown and two neighbouring houses, Castle Trent and Mount Isabel, are burned in the same night. Danielstown, we might say, bears a relation to the ruined mill similar to that borne by the sociable house, Knowl, to its satanic alternative, Bartram-Haugh, in Sheridan Le Fanu's *Uncle Silas*, which, as I suggested in my last chapter, is a seminal text for Bowen.[19] It is the other, the opposite, the suppressed, the repressed, the deviant, with which the socially acceptable norm is nevertheless darkly intimate and collusive. At the centre of *The Last September*, then, the mill is both prolepsis and metonym; which are functions which the gothic and the ghostly frequently serve in Elizabeth Bowen too when they become more transparent and explicit.

IV

I have written here of the several ways—Lois's letters, the fantasy or dream life of the 'little Circe' chapter—in which *The Last September* courts deconstructive alternatives to, or remakings of, its own in any case attenuated plot. I want to think now about something inherent in the plot itself, which is nevertheless also heavy—indeed ominous—with alternative, and, I think, very revealingly so. I mean Lois's

[19] See '*Uncle Silas* by Sheridan Le Fanu', in *The Mulberry Tree*, 100–13.

relationship with the English army senior subaltern Daventry, which is prominent in the episode of the barrack dance towards the end of the book, and which, like the episode of the ruined mill, also features, in my view, a mode of displaced or redistributed gothic. It is extra-ordinary that Daventry's role in the novel has received so little com-mentary.

The dance is brilliantly managed, in what is in effect an early version of the vertiginously quasi-expressionist style which Bowen uses most notably elsewhere in the grill-bar scene crucial to *The Heat of the Day*. Taking place in the army barracks, behind barbed wire and under armed guard, the dance is certainly nevertheless part-Jane Austen, pre-occupied as it largely is with the flirtations between the young women and the soldiers of a garrison town, under the chaperoning but inter-estedly encouraging eyes of the older army wives. However, it becomes increasingly a kind of whirling *Walpurgis* night of emotional confusion and desire played out, in a 'dementedly' windy night, to the sound of a gramophone which is eventually shattered in an accident. The dance, in fact, gradually assumes into itself the various elements of a trans-ferred siege mentality, its state of 'exalted helplessness' and its 'high impetuousness out of everybody's control'. It is to some extent remi-niscent once more of the 'Circe' episode of *Ulysses*, in which Stephen eventually, in a Wagnerian gesture, shatters a lamp with his ashplant. Bowen's shattered gramophone may remember this; and the dance in *The Last September* is instinct with kinds of disruption to the norma-tive patterns of social and psychic existence comparable to those which preoccupy Joyce in 'Circe', although we may also recall the crucial role played by the dance—that publicly licensed erotic act—in both *Madame Bovary* and *Anna Karenina*; and Daventry's role is crucial here.

Daventry is, like many of those in the British army in Ireland during the 1920s, a survivor of the First World War; and indeed a minor char-acter in this episode thinks of the atmosphere of the dance as 'post-war madness' (150). The First World War is explicitly recalled elsewhere in the novel too: in the many photographs of dead soldiers in Mrs Fogarty's drawing room, and in the information that Marda's first fiancé died at the Somme; and *The Last September* is comparable in this regard to Virginia Woolf's major novels, with their reflections of post-war trauma. Daventry, like Septimus Warren Smith in *Mrs Dalloway*, is a victim of shell-shock and is, as a result, disenchanted, cynical, even brutal, in a way that none of the other soldiers we encounter in the novel is. He swears in front of women; he is heavily dependent on whisky to alleviate his distresses; and he brings into the novel its sole evocation, in anything other than oblique report, of the grisly actualities enforced, and endured, by this soldiery:

> He kept shutting his eyes; whenever he stopped dancing he noticed that he had a headache. He had been out in the mountains all night and most of the morning, searching some houses for guns that were known to be there. He had received special orders to ransack the beds, and to search with particular strictness the houses where men were absent and women wept loudest and prayed. Nearly all beds had contained very old women or women with very new babies, but the N.C.O., who was used to the work, insisted that they must go through with it. Daventry still felt sickish, still stifled with thick air and womanhood, dazed from the din. Daventry had been shell shocked, he was now beginning to hate Ireland, lyrically, explicitly; down to the very feel of the air and smell of the water. (144)

The 'lyrical' hatred of Ireland is a tellingly ironic touch, when so much lyricism has been expended in Irish literature on love of the place; and it is accompanied by other breaches of norm and expectation too. (Indeed, the information that Daventry 'had been shell-shocked' here leaves it open whether he has been literally so, by the war, or metaphorically so, by these Irish activities.)[20] Daventry is, in particular, sexually forthright and leeringly flirtatious with Lois. She, however, is unexpectedly responsive to this: 'There was a desperation about Mr Daventry she could have loved' (146); and, dancing with him, 'she had no idea she could dance so beautifully' (149). Also unexpectedly, however, Daventry is friendly with the much more restrained, gentlemanly Gerald, who praises him extravagantly to Lois during a walk they take together in this chapter.

These realist elements of the narrative are, however, accompanied by another. Daventry is twice associated with the satanic: once in the narrative itself, when he is first introduced, and again in Lois's perception of him: 'she thought, "you laugh like Satan" ' (157); and this further gothic element is reinforced in several ways. Lois is described as Daventry's 'revenge' for another woman's dancing with Gerald; Gerald is said to ask a question of Lois 'like the ghost of Daventry' (151); during the walk 'Gerald and Daventry passed in the dark with, it

---

[20] Daventry's ransacking of Irish homes should also remind us that, while the IRA burned down big houses in the 1920s, the Black and Tans burned down many small ones and, in 1920, torched the entire centre of Cork city.

seemed, a queer silent interchange' (153); Lois, looking at Daventry, suddenly 'saw there was not a man here, hardly even a person' (157). In addition, Lois is grateful to be interrupted by others after the breaking of the gramophone, just as a drunkenly laughing Daventry has begun a prying inquiry about Gerald: 'About our young friend—Tell me this—' (157). This is, of course, one more ellipsis or aporia:

She was glad of them, for under the storm of his mirth that swept their island, disarranging the interlude, she had sat cold and desolate. A gramophone passing, a gramophone less in the world, it was not funny. But between bursts of laughter she had felt him look at her lips, at her arms, at her dress, like a ghost, with nostalgia and cold curiosity. About their young friend?—she wasn't to know. (157–8)

The tone of this is hard to judge, in a way not uncharacteristic of Bowen, since a gramophone passing, a gramophone less in the world, may not be funny but, even so, hardly deserves elegiac lament—and, in fact, may be felt to be funny enough. Whereas a person less in the world is certainly never funny, and Daventry here becomes, at least in simile, exactly that: a person less in the world, a ghost; and, furthermore, one with what appears to be a strong, if stealthy, sexual interest in Lois. There is, surely, a first distillation here of that figure which crystallizes out terrifyingly in Bowen's utterly unnerving story of a later war, 'The Demon Lover'.

What does all this signify? It signifies, I think, that beneath the surface realism of Lois's relationship with Gerald and Daventry in *The Last September* there is the shadow of a gothic plot, in which Daventry is Gerald's *doppelgänger*, a ghostly survivor of the First World War not only brutalized but rendered a satanic ghost by his experience of the actualities of military combat. Gerald's recognition of Daventry, his 'queer silent interchange', implies that he is what Gerald might become after such experience too, experience of the kind his premature death, of course, terminates. During the episode of the dance Lois's emotions sway between the two men. Frightened and wary of Daventry, she is nevertheless manifestly attracted to him, allowing herself indeed to be commandeered by him. Drawn to encourage Gerald in a proposal of marriage, she is nevertheless deeply self-doubting. She speaks the final words of the chapter 'with Mr Daventry's best irony' (158)—her voice, as it were, occupied by his, not by Gerald's. With Gerald, Lois 'felt she was home again; safe from deserted rooms, the penetration of silences, rain, homelessness. Nothing mattered: she could have gone to sleep'

(150). But to Daventry she confesses, precisely, her enduring homelessness: 'I don't live anywhere, really', she tells him, to his assured
response, 'I do: I live near Birmingham' (157). In fact, of course,
Daventry's name—in this novel in which at least some names maintain
an almost eighteenth-century emblematic quality—is also the name of
a place near Birmingham, so that his identification with place, an
English Midlands industrial place, is intense.

When Gerald is killed, it is Daventry who reports his death to Lois at
Danielstown, where she is expecting the visitor to be Gerald himself. If
during the episode of the dance Gerald appears 'like the ghost of
Daventry', here Daventry appears, as it were, like the ghost of Gerald;
and he comes confrontationally:

Mr Daventry arrived before the postman. He had not paid an unofficial visit
since he had been in Ireland; it seemed to him odd there should be nothing to
search for, nobody to interrogate. It was early, wet tarnished branches came
cheerfully through the mist. He had come to the gate with a convoy on its way
over to Ballyhinch; two lorries had ground into silence and waited for him at
the gate, alarming the cottagers. He walked up the avenue lightly and rapidly:
nothing, at the stage things had reached for him, mattered. And superciliously
he returned the stare of the house. (200)

The others in the house do not 'care for the look' of Daventry: 'They
felt instinctively that he had come here to search the house' (202). The
Anglo-Irish feel, that is, that he is about to put them in the position of
subjection which has been the lot of their 'Irish' neighbours. In this
intrusion and confrontation, then, we have the actuality of English military power in Ireland establishing its force and its threat to Anglo-Irish
as well as to Irish. Like the ghostly Laura, like the ghostly mill,
Daventry is another ghost returned from the dead: superciliously meeting the house's confrontation of him, in a revision of that trope of personification generically typical in big house literature, he is, with his
rootedly English name, the insistence to the inhabitants of Danielstown
that, if a house is sustained only by the means he represents, then it is
liable, like the House of Usher, not to stand very long. Daventry, we
might say, is the final discovery that *The Last September* makes about
Danielstown's lack; and there is surely an implied allegorical resonance
in his departure. It is middle England leaving Anglo-Ireland to its own
devices: 'He took leave with unfriendly courtesy and went off abruptly,
with an air that obliterated them, as though he had never been into
their house at all' (203). Which appears to remember—and with what

larded ironies—the nationalist metaphor used by the Irish for the colonial Anglo-Irish, the 'stranger in the house'.[21]

Given this discovery, it is hard not to read the burning of the house at the end of the novel as the register as much of authorial desire as of anxiety. Lois appears to want it earlier in the book, thinking of Marda: 'she hoped that instead of fading to dust in summers of empty sunshine, the carpet would burn with the house in a scarlet night to make one flaming call upon Marda's memory' (98). This has its consonance with Yeatsian ideas of the heroic consigning of ancestry to preservative commemoration, the kind of thing that led him to 'recognize', as Terence Brown says, 'that the destructive fires of revolutionary change were a heroic climax for what he believed was a noble caste, preferable to the indignities of taxation, poverty and gradual decay that were to be the lot of ancestral houses elsewhere in this egalitarian century which Yeats detested'.[22] This was a 'lot' which, as we have seen, Elizabeth Bowen, mistress of Bowen's Court, inherited and endured, writing the experience autobiographically into *Bowen's Court*, in whose afterword she does console herself with the fact that the ultimate destruction of the house by its new owner was at least 'a clean end', and fictionalizing its distresses and follies in *A World of Love* (1955). Laurence also wants it, however, out of a kind of whimsical and cavalier boredom which is itself only the surface of a much deeper malaise of superfluity: 'I should like something else to happen, some crude intrusion of the actual. I feel all gassy inside from yawning. I should like to be here when this house burns' (44); and he is absolutely certain that it will. Where its (putative) inheritors desire the house's demise, the IRA 'executioners' are, it might be thought, virtually acting as their agents in that very carefully phrased 'design of order and panic' which the novel's plangently memorable conclusion describes. And this is to collapse the hyphen between 'Anglo' and 'Irish' in a literally explosive way:

At Danielstown, half-way up the avenue under the beeches, the thin iron gate twanged (missed its latch, remained swinging aghast) as the last unlit car widened, gave itself to the open and empty country and was demolished. Then the first wave of a silence that was to be ultimate flowed back, confident, to the steps. Above the steps, the door stood open hospitably upon a furnace. (206)

---

[21] 'We want no more strangers in our house,' says the citizen at one point in the 'Cyclops' episode of *Ulysses*, for instance.

[22] Terence Brown, *Ireland: A Social and Cultural History 1922–1985* (London: Fontana Press, 1985), 133. For a careful, and accurate, differentiation of Bowen's own attitudes from Yeats's, however, see C. L. Innes, *Women and Nation in Irish Literature and Society 1880–1935* (Hemel Hempstead: Harvester Wheatsheaf, 1993), 165–77.

3

A Ghost of Style:
A World of Love (1955)

Had the facade not carried a ghost of style, Montefort would have looked, as it almost did, like nothing more than the annexe of its farm buildings—whose slipshod gable and leaning sheds, flaking whitewash and sagging rusty doors made a patchwork for some way out behind.

A World of Love, Chapter 1

Troubles, a novel, is on a scale of its own—a major work made deceptive as to its size by apparent involvement with what is minor. That was inevitable, since the setting is Ireland, where either everything matters or nothing does.

Elizabeth Bowen, on J. G. Farrell[1]

I

In *The Last September* the cook, Kathleen, makes only a one-paragraph appearance; but it is an exceptionally memorable appearance, in which she is etched with a casually authoritative particularity. Gerald has been invited to tea; but, as we have seen, Lady Naylor considers him an inappropriate suitor for her niece, Lois. Kathleen is discussing with Lady Naylor the preparations for tea:

Kathleen, the cook, who resembled her mistress in personality so closely that their relation was an affair of balance, who had more penetration than Lady Naylor and was equally dominant, inferred much of the situation from her mistress's manner. Herself, she had felt this was bound to occur. For an hour or so, they had countered each other amiably in the lime-washed gloom of the kitchen, over a basin of green-pea soup. Lady Naylor announced with unusual deprecation, there would be an officer coming over to tea. Kathleen, refolding

¹ 'Ireland Agonistes', *Europa*, 1 (1971), 58–9, 58.

her hands royally, asked, would she slap up a sally-lunn? On the whole, Lady Naylor thought drop-cakes. Kathleen immediately placed the officer. Strolling down the yard in the course of the afternoon to execute a couple of chickens, she watched dispassionately from under the chestnuts Gerald crouch on his motor-bicycle up the avenue. Lois, standing about with the dogs, went down to meet him. For tea, Kathleen sent up an unaccountable iced cake, ironically festive. (169)

The finely judged social comedy of this, the acme of the early Elizabeth Bowen manner, is revelatory of the social world of the well-regulated Anglo-Irish big house in the early years of the century, which is also 'an affair of balance', that between masters, or mistresses, and servants, whose mutual understanding may even involve a close resemblance, or sometimes a transfer, of roles. Here it is Kathleen, rather than Lady Naylor—who is usually formidable—who behaves regally and who, in the end, and in her absence, sets the tone of this teatime encounter with her presumptuous gesture of culinary irony. In the well-regulated rituals of this world, a sally-lunn, drop-cakes and, supremely, an iced cake may, to those in the know, speak volumes about social and cultural distinctions; and such gestures are also an index of the exclusion of those not in the know, like the hapless Gerald here. 'Dispassionately' carries the impersonal authority of the well-regulated system which is, in part, a system in which an Anglo-Irish *hauteur* is disdainful about the mere English; and the iced cake may be 'unaccountable' to some of the participants in this tea party, but it is most assuredly not unaccountable to Lady Naylor, to whom it is the continuation by other means of an always tacit conversation. (The passage has, proleptically, more than comedy in it too, since the word 'execute' applied to the killing of chickens may mock-heroically announce the violent duty Kathleen is about to do on behalf of this social system; but all too soon in *The Last September* Gerald himself will be executed by the IRA as the representative of an occupying colonial power, and, in the novel's final paragraph, this house itself will similarly undergo its 'execution'.)

In the generally less highly regarded and, in my view, under-appreciated *A World of Love*, published over twenty-five years after *The Last September*, the servant in the ironically named house Montefort—which is neither strong nor any longer much of a fortification against anything—is called not Kathleen but Kathie; and we may read in that diminutive the catastrophic diminution of Anglo-Irish existence between the 1920s and the 1950s which this book,

Elizabeth Bowen's sole novel after *The Last September* to be wholly set in Ireland, unillusionedly expresses.[2] Kathie is the only servant remaining in this big house, and she more or less shares the family's life. Indeed, they spend a great deal of time in her kitchen, which, it is emphasized in a striking prose-poem or hymn to this room in the novel's opening chapter, is the place in the house which has changed least: 'routine abode in its air like an old spell' (21). In every other respect Montefort defines Anglo-Ireland in its virtually posthumous life after the Second World War; and on one level, the realistic one, the novel presents a vivid portrait of what has been called the 'descendancy', the remnant of the Protestant Anglo-Irish ascendancy living, in various states of frustration and resignation, with an attenuated 'ghost of style' (21).

Montefort is vividly realized in its appurtenances, all of them bathed in an almost sultry residual aura in the novel's emphatically and exceptionally hot June in Co. Cork. The crack near the house's keystone; the felled trees and broken barometers; the torn curtains and the chipped Crown Derby crockery; the forsaken dovecote—all are redolent of an even more terminal kind of interim than that explored in *The Last September*, which is the interim in which the Anglo-Irish await their fate at the hands of the IRA during the war of independence. In *A World of Love*, 'The room seemed to be waiting, perhaps for ever, for its dismantlement to be complete' (31)—which is a kind of 'eternal interim', as Paul Muldoon has it, in a brilliantly unsettling oxymoron, in another Irish context.[3] And, as the narrative observes elsewhere, with a sudden fine flicker of Bowen's arrestingly skewed perceptiveness, 'A wait is something being done to you' (147). Making what is usually agency disquietingly passivity, Bowen approaches here, as she does elsewhere too, both the ontology and the cadence of Samuel Beckett (whose novel *Watt* (1953) is a big house novel, of a kind). *A World of Love*, like *Waiting for Godot*, is a remarkable representation of the desuetude, melancholy, exasperation, and resignation attendant on 'waiting' for what will almost certainly be nothing very much, and a representation also of how waiting has become a chronic condition, simply what you do with yourself in the absence of anything else to do.

---

[2] If generally under-rated, however, the book has been highly rated by Andrew Bennett and Nicholas Royle in *Elizabeth Bowen and the Dissolution of the Novel: Still Lives* (London: Macmillan, 1995). They say that it marks 'an eloquent and subtle shift in the unfolding of the Bowen œuvre' (104).

[3] Paul Muldoon, 'Lull', in *Why Brownlee Left* (London: Faber & Faber, 1980), 17.

The novel's portrayal of the intense isolation of a house which the postman rarely visits, and whose family's credit at the local grocer's has long since stopped, is accompanied by its recognition of the kinds of social change in Ireland which have permitted another house, or 'castle', nearby to have been newly taken over by the venal English Lady Latterly. Her emblematic name may indicate that she is lately come, or come at the end of something, and that she is *nouveau riche* ('but, as Antonia said, better late than never' (57)); and the central scene in the book occurs in her house. But if Anglo-Irish regret, melancholy, and envy are part of the emotional structure of *A World of Love*, so too is a strong sense of accusation. This is concentrated into the symbolic obelisk which casts its shadow on the house in the novel's opening pages and figures prominently throughout. Indeed, its assertive architecture plays a role in the book comparable to, if lesser than, that played by the eponymous lighthouse in Virginia Woolf's *To the Lighthouse*. It is redolent of the different passions and yearnings of the novel's characters, and it has a phallic insistence verging on the parodistic. We learn towards the novel's close, however, that it has been raised as an act of flagrantly self-deluded and almost defiantly absurd Anglo-Irish arrogance by an early owner of the house, in order to commemorate himself while still alive. This may be read as a further, now satirical, version of the living ghost *motif* which I have discussed in relation to *Bowen's Court*; and the fact that this man's name has, in fact, been virtually forgotten is a telling instance of one, not entirely untypical, Anglo-Irish case. The shadow of the obelisk falling across the now decayed house of Montefort is therefore also the shadow of a terminal judgement.

If the novel depicts a ghost of style, however, its plot concerns a rather stylish ghost; and *A World of Love* is the novel of Bowen's which comes closest—although in a guarded, hesitant, and ironized way—to the explicit supernaturalism of some of her short stories.[4] Its heroine, the beautiful, 20-year-old Jane, discovers in Montefort's attic a cache of love letters to an unnamed addressee. They turn out to have been written by Guy, the one-time master of the house, who was killed in the First World War; and Jane falls in love with him, or at least with the

---

[4] W. J. McCormack regards it as a self-conscious 'experiment with the possibility of a supernatural story written at novelistic length'. This may be so, but conceivably runs the risk of appearing to underestimate the degree to which the novel's form is impelled by its preoccupations. See *From Burke to Beckett: Ascendancy, Tradition and Betrayal in Irish Literary History* (1985; revised edn., Cork: Cork University Press, 1994), 409.

idea of him, when she reads them. This relationship between the dead and the living provokes a kind of spectral appearance of Guy to Jane at a dinner party at Lady Latterly's house, and two more of the novel's characters, Lilia and Antonia, also experience Guy's 'presence' at different points in the narrative. Lilia is Jane's English mother and had been Guy's fiancée; but, when he died intestate, Montefort went to his cousin Antonia. Partly out of a sense of duty to Lilia, however, Antonia encouraged her to live in Montefort and organized, or perhaps even ordered, her marriage to the promiscuous Fred Dancy, an illegitimate relation of hers and Guy's, who now farms what is left of the estate and by whom Lilia has had two children. These are Jane herself and the younger, very strange, isolated, and vengeful Maud, who is by far the most peculiar child in Bowen's extensive gallery of isolated children, and whose conversations with an imaginary companion, hobgoblin, or familiar called Gay David supply a kind of distorted obverse side to the quasi-supernatural material of the main plot. Antonia—who is now, in the present moment of the book, 50, as is Lilia—has taken charge of Jane and educated her in England, making her, in her mother's envious view, a 'changeling': this is one of several fairy-tale, romance, and mythical emblems which the novel associates with Jane. Antonia retains the right to visit Montefort when she wishes; which is what she is doing this June, accompanied by Jane. Fred and Lilia have, over the years, and after an initially passionate relationship, become deeply estranged.

During the course of the novel it becomes clear that Guy, although engaged to Lilia, had also loved and had an affair with Antonia: there are several flashbacks to his final wartime departure from Charing Cross station, when both Lilia and Antonia come to say their good-byes, not acknowledging each other, and when both appear to feel that yet a further 'last-moment comer' has also been present. In addition, we discover as we read that there is a prominent sexual element in the relationship between Fred and Antonia too, and, further, that Fred has feelings about Jane bordering on the incestuous. Finally, towards the end of the novel, Antonia's manifest emotional dependence on Jane itself appears erotic in its intensity. So the tensions of insecure or unclear relationships of property ownership and inheritance, along with those of strong, if sometimes suppressed or muffled, sexual feeling, are vibrant in the book's highly charged human atmospheres. In this respect, it is as though the kinds of plot which sustain the major work of Somerville and Ross (*The Real Charlotte*, *The Big House of*

Inver) are being given one intense final recapitulation-in-miniature, a brilliant coda, by this succeeding novelist of the Anglo-Irish. The opening sentence of *A World of Love* reads, 'The sun rose on a landscape still pale with the heat of the day before', and therefore, as several critics have noticed, self-consciously encodes an allusion to the title of Bowen's previous novel, *The Heat of the Day*, published almost ten years earlier; but the novel's retrospect is a larger one than this. Despite its relative brevity, the book is a kind of Anglo-Irish fictional summation, a fantasia on themes from the brilliant and fractured history of the Anglo-Irish novel, and, as we shall see, a moving away or forward from such themes.

Possession is therefore central to the book's preoccupations and explorations, and in three senses of the word: the ownership of a house; the security of another's sexual faithfulness; the sense of being taken over by the spirit of someone or something. When Antonia senses Guy's presence in chapter 6, the word itself is used: 'All round Montefort there was going forward an entering back again into possession' (77). This sentence may seem inflected with what those who dislike it consider Elizabeth Bowen's stylistic mannerism, but I would argue that it is, in fact, in its hesitant progression and doubling back upon itself, an exact syntactical representation of the novel's deepest intimation or insinuation: which is to do with the way an entering back again may be, or may become, a going forward. *A World of Love* is a novel about what can be done with the burden of a difficult or even impossible history. It is a book about how an inheritance may be renounced and a necessary dispossession, or even a kind of exorcism, voluntarily accepted.

II

Although Hermione Lee says, rightly, that '*A World of Love* is full of echoes of Bowen's earlier works', and Andrew Bennett and Nicholas Royle discuss the 'citational' in the novel, the specific relationship between *A World of Love* and *The Last September* has, I think, been underestimated: there is a real sense in which the later novel is an entering back again into possession of the earlier one.[5] The presence of a

[5] See *Elizabeth Bowen* (1981; revised edn., London: Vintage, 1999), 186 and *Elizabeth Bowen and the Dissolution of the Novel*, 104–20.

servant in Montefort who shares her name with the cook of the earlier novel and the fact that this is Bowen's only subsequent novelistic return to the big house setting, apart from episodes in *The House in Paris* and *The Heat of the Day*, suggest strongly that the books are interestingly and intricately related. Jane in *A World of Love* is in the same position as Lois in *The Last September*: uncertain, indecisive, waiting for a future to declare itself to her. She is also dressed in a manner closer to that of Lois in the 1920s than to that of a young girl in the 1950s, since she is wearing, when we are introduced to her, the Edwardian muslin dress in which Guy's letters had been wrapped. (In an erotically charged way this is consonant with what we shall discover as the novel's central plot, since it is possible to read this dress as a kind of shroud become wedding gown.) Jane's relationship with Antonia has elements in common with Lois's with Marda, although Antonia's loneliness and vaguely alcoholic desperation make her more vulnerable and threatened than the resolutely independent Marda. The books share a similar, and similarly not easily interpretable, Shakespearean motif. Jane is described in androgynous terms as being 'like a boy actor in woman's clothes', which recalls the way Lois's friends in *The Last September* are named Viola and Olivia, names out of *Twelfth Night*, in which, in Elizabethan England, the female characters were played by boy actors, and in which Viola when disguised as Cesario would therefore have been a boy actor playing a girl playing a boy. *A World of Love* also alludes to *A Midsummer Night's Dream*, *Antony and Cleopatra*, *Hamlet*, *Macbeth*, and, in its climactic concluding sentence, *As You Like It*. Where Marda in *The Last September*, as we saw, asks, apparently of the situation in Ireland in the 1920s, 'Like Shakespeare or isn't it?', *A World of Love* says of its general atmosphere at one point, 'Even Shakespeare had stalked in'. Despite these specific allusions, however, we may well feel that the Shakespeare who actually stalks in to this novel is the writer of the late romances, those dramas of re-enactment, transformation, and return.

The Co. Cork setting of both books is the same: *A World of Love*, unlike *The Last September*, actually names Cork, even though the local town, a representation of Mallow, retains its previous fictional name, 'Clonmore'. And there is, finally, a brief allusion in *A World of Love* to the fate of such houses as Danielstown and its neighbours at the end of *The Last September* when Jane experiences 'the absolute calmness, the sense of there being almost no threat at all, with which one could imagine fighting one's way down a burning staircase—there *was* a licking danger, but not to her; cool she moved down between flame walls' (65). This is, as it were, a heroine far too young to have had any direct experience of the Irish 1920s who has nevertheless internalized, made an intimate part of her present subjectivity, a miraculous survival of that political nightmare: indeed, the passage has the hallucinatory calm or 'cool' of an image from a much-repeated dream.

Given these correspondences between the two books, it is possible to read Guy, the dead soldier of the First World War, as both an echo and an epitome of the many dead soldiers whose photographs fill Mrs Fogarty's parlour in *The Last September*, and of Marda's fiancé who was killed on the Somme, all those lives violently and prematurely destroyed; and, as I suggested in my chapter on *The Last September*, the aftermath of the First World War is as acute in Bowen as it is in Virginia Woolf. A photograph of Guy, a 'studio portrait', is prominently on display in Montefort, and many of the characters are seen reacting to it. The place of photography in Elizabeth Bowen's work is a large topic, and I return to it again in my chapters on *Eva Trout* and *The Heat of the Day*. Bowen knows as keenly as Roland Barthes in *Camera Lucida* that photographs are spectres too, as keenly as Susan Sontag in *On Photography* that 'all photographs are *memento mori*'; and her writing is shaken by the perception.[6] Like Alexander Gardner's riveting photograph of the about-to-be-executed Lewis Payne for Barthes, the photograph of Guy also inevitably insists the lacerating knowledge that, as Barthes puts it, 'he is dead and he is going to die'; and this shadowing or traversing of times across one another, a kind of temporal derangement, is crucial to this novel's atmosphere and also to its meanings.[7] In this context it is, of course, highly significant that Antonia is a famous photographer, although one whose career now appears to have fallen into abeyance: so she too has been what Barthes calls the photographer, an unwitting 'agent of death', in this novel which so deeply intertwines the lives of the living with the presence—to memory and to imagination—of the dead.[8]

For Jane, however, it is Guy's letters more than his photographs which construct his identity; and in this too *A World of Love* maintains an edgily retrospective congruence with *The Last September*. At the

---

[6] Photography, says Barthes, is 'a figuration of the motionless and made-up face beneath which we see the dead'. See *Camera Lucida*, trans. by Richard Howard (London: Jonathan Cape, 1982), 186; and Susan Sontag, *On Photography* (1977; London: Penguin, 1987), 15.

[7] *Camera Lucida*, 95.   [8] Ibid., 92.

beginning of Chapter 15 of that novel, the crucial chapter set in the mill, which I analysed in my last chapter, Hugo is remembering a quarrel there with Laura, Lois's dead mother, at the point when their relationship was disintegrating. But he finds it impossible to recreate Laura's presence in the landscape:

And, having given proof of her impotence to be even here, Laura shrank and drew in her nimbus, leaving only—as in some rediscovered diary of a forgotten year—a few cryptic records, walks, some appointments kept, letters received and posted. (121)

'Letters received and posted', the written traces left by the dead, actually form the plot of A World of Love; and Guy's letters are cryptic in the sense that they are mysteriously or enigmatically unaddressed. Although the novel tantalizes its characters and its readers for a long time with the possibility that the addressee is either Lilia or Antonia, in fact in the end it turns out that it is neither, but another woman altogether—with whom Guy also clearly had a passionate relationship.[9] As we shall see, however, Guy's is a very different spectral presence from the one Laura's cryptic remains make in The Last September.

The scene in which Guy 'appears' to Jane is skilfully managed, given its potential for absurdity. She is attending a party at Lady Latterly's castle and is conscious of the mercenary nature of this new friendship: she 'was paying by being the lovely nobody, exhibited but not introduced'(61). Inexperienced with alcohol, she very quickly gets drunk: the quasi-expressionist style which Bowen uses elsewhere for comparable material—the dance in The Last September, the grill-bar in The Heat of the Day—also works well here, where elements of social comedy gradually become farcically but also menacingly skewed. When, therefore, Jane senses Guy's presence at the dinner table, which has one empty seat—a guest has either failed to arrive, or not been properly invited—both she and we as readers are unsure whether she is seeing things in a visionary sense or merely as the result of intoxicated hallucination. So the novel withholds the gothic supernatural in the same gesture with which it invites it in, inheriting, in the act of revising to its

---

[9] Maud Ellmann, thinking of the way 'Gay David' resonates with 'Guy', and noticing a misprint at one point in the novel which names a 'Guy David', proposes that Guy may have been gay, or bisexual, and that the letters may in fact be addressed to a man. Given the novel's potently polyvalent eroticism, and Bowen's interest in homosexuality, this is conceivable, if also (of course) unprovable. See Elizabeth Bowen: The Shadow across the Page (Edinburgh: Edinburgh University Press, 2003), 188–9.

own purpose, a tradition with strong Anglo-Irish antecedents. And the spectre at this feast is also a Barthesian spectre of the photograph:

Snapshots taken before Antonia was a photographer fused with the 'studio portrait' taken in uniform for Lilia, on the hall wall at Montefort (oakframed, overcast by the flank of the stopped clock, all but secretively to be disregarded) and with what was inadvertently still more photographic in shreds of talk. Over the combination of glance and feature, the suggestion of latitude in the smile, rested a sort of indolent sweet force. Now more than living, this face had acquired a brightened cast of its own from the semi-darkness, from which it looked out with an easy conviction of being recognized. Nothing was qualified or momentary about it, as in the pictures; this was the face of someone here to the full—visible, and visible all at once, were the variations and contradictions, the lights and shades of the arrested torrent of an existence. . . . Here he is, because this is where I am.   (68–9)

I quote here only part of a lengthy passage which appears to allude to T. S. Eliot's *Four Quartets*, that other work containing spectres and, written during the Second World War, commemorating the dead of history's wars: Guy's voice, which Jane cannot quite hear, is 'just not here or there, just not now or then but at the same time everywhere and always'. 'Burnt Norton', the first of the Quartets, includes the line 'Quick, now, here, now, always', and the final poem of the sequence, 'Little Gidding', moves towards its climax with an evocation of 'England and nowhere. Never and always.'[10] Bowen's novel at this point, we might say, is Anglo-Ireland and nowhere, everywhere and always. Jane's 'Here he is, because this is where I am' is the register of a communication or, indeed, communion with the dead which establishes identity and transformation. It is the place where 'the arrested torrent of an existence' fetches up; which may explain the very peculiar reference to 'what was inadvertently still more photographic in shreds of talk', as the living conversation itself comes, for Jane, to share in the spectral illusionism—if it is that—of Guy's photographic presence. The novel subsequently tells us that Jane's peculiar possession by the spirit of Guy releases in her the capacity to 'love'. In this way the tragedy of a brilliant young life terminated by war—its 'arrested torrent'—is turned towards a future and to something other than tragedy. There is Christianity in this as well as Shakespearean romance; and the title of *A World of Love* derives from *Centuries of Meditations* by the

---

[10] The guests at Lady Latterly's dinner party include a man called Peregrine, and it is tempting to think that he also derives from *Four Quartets*, with its 'spirit unappeased and peregrine'.

seventeenth-century poet and mystic Thomas Traherne, which is cited as the novel's epigraph: 'There is in us a world of Love to somewhat, though we know not what in the world that should be . . . Do you not feel yourself drawn by the expectation and desire of some Great Thing?'

Undoubtedly, continuous with this, part of Bowen's meaning here is equivalent to Eliot's summative statement of the relationship between living and dead in the fifth section of 'Little Gidding':

> We die with the dying:
> See, they depart, and we go with them.
> We are born with the dead:
> See, they return and bring us with them.

Traversing the orthodoxy of Christianity, however, there is something more occult and contingent in the sense of the interrelationship between dead and living in the novel; and R. F. Foster has defined, in relation to Yeats, a tradition of Anglo-Irish 'Protestant magic' which may well also structure Bowen's attitudes here. Foster includes her in 'the line of Irish Protestant supernatural fiction' running from Charles Maturin and Sheridan Le Fanu to Bram Stoker and W. B. Yeats, and he proposes a socio-economic reading of the tradition: 'Marginalised Irish Protestants all, often living in England but regretting Ireland, stemming from families with strong clerical and professional colorations, whose occult preoccupations surely mirror a sense of displacement, a loss of social and psychological integration, and an escapism motivated by the threat of a takeover by the Catholic middle classes.' He also suggests a strong Neo-Platonic and Swedenborgian pedigree for 'ideas about the dead partaking in the life of the living'.[11] Earlier in *A World of Love*, at the opening of Chapter 4, and associated with Antonia's reflections on Guy, a significant generalized statement is made on precisely this matter, defining the 'incompleteness' of the lives of those the dead leave behind, and specifically associating the impossibility of a 'sense of finality' with one generation's experience of two world wars:

Life works to dispossess the dead, to dislodge and oust them. Their places fill themselves up; later people come in; all the room is wanted. Feeling alters its course, is drawn elsewhere or seeks renewal from other sources. . . . But the

---

[11] R. F. Foster, 'Protestant Magic: W. B. Yeats and the Spell of Irish History', in *Paddy and Mr Punch: Connections in Irish and English History* (1993; London: Penguin, 1995), 220.

recognition of death may remain uncertain, and while that is so nothing is signed and sealed. Our sense of finality is less hard-and-fast: two wars have raised their query to it. Something has challenged the law of nature: it is hard, for instance, to see a young death in battle as in any way the fruition of a destiny, hard not to sense the continuation of the apparently cut-off life, hard not to ask, but was dissolution possible so abruptly, unmeaningly and soon? And if not dissolution, instead, what?   (44)

Guy's appearance to Jane is the novel's answer to that question. It means, at the very least, that the dead maintain so forceful a presence in the consciousness of the living as to become, at certain quasi-visionary moments, immediate in an overwhelming, possessing form. Elizabeth Bowen is a novelist very delicately attuned to the ways in which our conscious and unconscious lives are structured by thoughts and memories of the dead; and *A World of Love* is a novel in which she finds a sufficient and unsentimental fable for the acuteness of the resulting emotions. The novel is, at its deepest imaginative level, a work of profound personal and cultural mourning; and, in the Freudian sense, it performs the work of mourning too.[12] This passage reminds us that the 'query' raised by two world wars has itself frequently been the material of Bowen's own fiction: obliquely, sometimes even subliminally, in the case of the First World War, throughout her work; and, of course, directly in relation to the second in *The Heat of the Day* and her wartime short stories. *The Last September* is also taken up with yet another of the twentieth-century's wars, the Irish war of independence; and Gerald Lesworth, a central character, is another instance of 'the apparently cut-off life'. *A World of Love* returns to both Ireland and the history of Anglo-Irish fiction to find a form capable of coping with the grief while also working—against 'life'—to return possession to, and to repossess, the dead.

But *A World of Love* also asks the other question which Eliot raises in the *Four Quartets*: to what purpose ('But to what purpose | Disturbing the dust on a bowl of rose leaves . . .'). Guy, in fact, makes comparably ambivalent appearances to both Antonia and Lilia and, as in Jane's case, the visitations issue in motions of love. In the wake of Guy's appearance a new rapport develops between the

---

[12] I had written and, indeed, published a version of this before Maud Ellmann's book on Bowen appeared; but she also describes the novel in these terms, although she inflects them rather differently. See *The Shadow across the Page*, 186. In addition, she says— accurately and, in fact, movingly—that it is 'a work of mourning . . . for the kind of novel that Bowen will never write again' (189).

estranged Lilia and Fred, one initiated when Fred gains access to the letters on Lilia's behalf. Antonia's relationship with Lilia has been a long bond of tense antipathy, but Guy's appearance provokes from her an act of empathetic generosity: although she knows otherwise, she chooses to offer Lilia the consoling illusion that Guy's letters were, in fact, addressed to her. If both Antonia and Lilia are brought to new sympathies and generosities by the dead man, Jane is moved towards love of another kind, a kind Antonia senses when she reflects that Guy 'came back, through Jane, to be let go' (135). A World of Love ends when, in a radical structural move, its plot is simply abrupted in order to bring Jane to the start of a new, unwritten one. Lady Latterly's chauffeur drives her (and Maud) from Co. Cork to Shannon airport to meet a visitor from the United States, whom Jane assumes, wrongly, to be one of Lady Latterly's discarded lovers. As Richard Priam descends from the plane and raises his eyes to Jane, the book resoundingly utters its romance-like final sentence: 'They no sooner looked but they loved' (149). This has a Shakespearian echo or reverberation: Orlando says to the suddenly smitten Oliver in As You Like It (V. ii. 1–2), 'Is't possible that on so little acquaintance you should like her? That but seeing, you should love her?' In fact, 'echo' may be too strong a word for what Bowen's final sentence does here. Andrew Bennett and Nicholas Royle perhaps do better to call it a 'citational haunting'.[13] Bowen is, in my view, here concentrating the Shakespearian references made earlier in the novel, which I have already noted, by suddenly and (it must be said) very riskily introducing, as a conclusion, the Elizabethan plot motif of love at first sight; but the risk is justified by the breathtaking brazenness with which the effect is carried off, which has behind it the whole countervailing potential for negativity that is the burden of Anglo-Irish history in the twentieth century.

Jane, that is to say, has been released by Guy, but also enabled by her love for him to love another. The encounter, which is accompanied by the first rain to fall in this sultry novel, has a radiant and transfiguring intensity comparable to the meeting of Clarissa and Peter Walsh at the end of Virginia Woolf's Mrs Dalloway, and for a comparable reason: the plots of both novels, compelling and intricate as they are, seem, once we have reached these moments, in a sense only delaying or diversionary preparations for them, clearings of the necessary space for their inescapability. However, where the conclusion of Mrs Dalloway—'It is

---

[13] Elizabeth Bowen and the Dissolution of the Novel, 171.

Clarissa, he said. For there she was.'—is earthed in retrospect, and indeed foreshadowed in flashback, that of *A World of Love* is pitched towards prospect, and quite without prediction or predication. This is a novel which, originating in aftermath, culminates in projection, as it opens welcomingly to the future.

III

In this, its visionary or mystical elements imply a political meaning too; and, like *The Last September*, the book, for all the delicacy and transparency of its motifs of fairy tale and romance, has allegorical resonances. Jane searching the attic of Montefort in Chapter 2 is wandering among the losses and depredations of Anglo-Irish history: 'The flame of Jane's candle consumed age in the air; toppling, the wreckage left by the past oppressed her—so much had been stacked up and left to rot; everything was derelict, done for, done with (27).' Her own sense of history is that 'too much had been going on for too long', and her exhaustion is explicated like this:

... she had an instinctive aversion from the past; it seemed to her a sort of pompous imposture; as an idea it bored her; it might not be too much to say that she disapproved of it . . . . Oh, there lay the root of all evil!—this continuous tedious business of received grievances, not-to-be-settled old scores. Yes, so far as she was against anything she was against the past; and she felt entitled to raid, despoil, rifle, balk or cheat it in any possible way. (35)

Compared to *The Last September*, the portrayal of the contexts of these 'grievances'—the highly charged word also used in the ruined mill episode of that novel—is minimal and parenthetical in *A World of Love*, but they do nevertheless figure: when, for instance, Antonia bars the door of Montefort for the night:

Not since Montefort stood had there ceased to be vigilant measures against the nightcomer; all being part of the hostile watch kept by now eyeless towers and time-stunted castles along these rivers. For as land knows, everywhere is a frontier; and the outposted few (and few are the living) never must be off guard. (79)

Guy, the last master of Montefort before its decline, represents this specific Anglo-Irish past, with the grievances and old scores of a 'frontier' or colonial society, in which 'land' is so pressing a concern as to demand personification: what land 'knows' is that it holds people in servitude. Despite feeling as she does about history, Jane must come to terms with this past before she can move towards any kind of future. History cannot be merely ignored: it must be faced, absorbed, and transformed: 'He came back, through Jane, to be let go' (135). And, in being let go, he also undergoes a self-transformation, his living faithlessness or promiscuity being converted into the generous posthumous desire for the happiness of others. Guy is therefore the opposite kind of ghost from Laura in *The Last September*: not damaging, restricting, and inhibiting, as she is there, but enabling and releasing. He is also, I think, a benign version of the malign spectre of the dead First World War soldier, K, in Bowen's Second World War story, 'The Demon Lover': his return brings not terror, as K's does to Kathleen Drover, but love. Guy's possession of Jane is the opportunity for the second chance: he represents the potential for making it over, making it new, the possibility that history's defeats may have a translatable value; that they will not corrode as stultifying or sclerotic neurosis, but may act as the spur to a more satisfactory future.

When Jane, as it were, leaves the plot of *A World of Love* behind her on her lengthily described, exhilarating journey to Shannon airport, which may itself be regarded as a benign version of Emmeline's final suicidal and murderous drive at the end of *To The North*, she is discovering a future which will not include the 'continuous tedious business of grievances'; but it is one which arrives from outside Ireland itself. In driving to pick up the American Richard Priam from Shannon, Jane passes through country—the west of Ireland—which has itself been much mythologized in Irish literature, notably, of course, by W. B. Yeats. In *A World of Love*, however, Co. Clare ends in 'a mad void utter rocky declivity to the West', an unpunctuated zero space, almost a kind of Beckettian nowhere; and Elizabeth Bowen's West is the scene not of noble fishermen and peasants but of a new international airport whose causeway 'looked like the future'. This is a very brief moment in the novel, but it does appear to criticize the long tradition of Irish self-mythologizing, which might well be regarded as a preservation under other, cultural, forms, of 'received grievances'. Richard, coming from America, is from that new world which once attempted to create itself in reaction to this old one; and, in doing so, he might he said to fulfil the promise of the novel's opening paragraph which turns from the past—'the heat of the day before'—towards an unfamiliar light which 'brought into being a new world—painted, expectant, empty, intense'. Even if there is no prediction of, or predication for, Richard Priam, then, in the plot of *A World of Love*, the spectre of his future presence at the novel's close may, as the 'new world' which Jane is about to enter, be nevertheless verbally encoded in its beginning.

Richard's extraordinary surname, Priam, is the name of the father of Hector, who, towards the end of the *Iliad*, embraces his son's killer, Achilles, in forgiveness.[14] Consonant with that, Antonia presents Kathie, towards the end of the novel, with the ribbon which has tied Guy's letters together, and Kathie wears it in her hair. This occasions what might seem a disproportionate amount of business, unless we read it as a further generous-spirited and reconciliatory gesture: the letters which represent the Anglo-Irish landowning past, but which also effect a transformation of that past and an enablement of a different kind of future, are also the agency of an act of courtesy from the once dominant class to those whom it previously kept in servitude; and the Catholic servant now turns the ribbon which has been merely of use into something decorative and delightful, in this country where, as we discover in the announcement made at Shannon airport, Irish, not English, is now the official first language of the polity. This, in my view, must offer some qualification to R. F. Foster's judgement that *A World of Love* portrays 'the ice-age Ireland of the 1950s . . . [when] the reconciliatory ideas of the *Bell* [Sean O'Faolain's liberal journal, to which Bowen contributed] had receded beyond recognition'.[15] This is, of course, the actual Irish state in which the novel is set, and many would agree with Foster's characterization of it; but the plot of *A World of Love* itself, as I hope I have shown, intends apology, rebuke to Anglo-Irish arrogance, reparation, and reconciliation from the losing side in the revolutions of the 1920s. Arguably, there is a tincture of sentimentalism in all of this, an absence of the tough-mindedness which perceives, as Bowen does in a review of a book on seventeenth-century Ireland 'after Cromwell', that 'nothing in Ireland is ever over'.[16] If

---

[14] John Hildebidle says that Richard is 'improbably named' but doesn't speculate on what the probabilities might be: see *Five Irish Writers: The Errand of Keeping Alive* (Harvard: Harvard University Press, 1989), 97. William Heath, in *Elizabeth Bowen: An Introduction to Her Novels* (Madison: University of Wisconsin Press, 1961), 140, calls the name 'a literary joke'. Heath's early study still reads very well, and this observation may even derive from a conversation with Bowen, but I can't myself think that she would play a joke at this climactic moment of the novel, or that she would only play a joke.

[15] *Paddy and Mr Punch*, 121.

[16] Elizabeth Bowen, *Collected Impressions* (London: Longmans Green & Co., 1959), 173.

there is sentimentalism, however, it is the surplus of that desire manifest everywhere in the book's subtle intricacies of interrelationship. If nothing in Ireland is ever over, something in *A World of Love* almost is. Which is why, I think, Bowen is brave enough so suddenly to abrupt her plot: the unexpected and unpredictable exigency of loving at first sight is a doing away forever with the military metaphors of Jane's earlier engagement with history ('raid, despoil, rifle, balk or cheat').

<h2 style="text-align:center">IV</h2>

In leaving the novel's historical as well as literary plot, however, Jane is also leaving Antonia and, although she does so with a kiss which has a marked erotic quality, her thoughts are cruel: 'Somehow she's gone. She's old' (130). Since Antonia does behave well to Lilia at the end of the book, this is bound to seem heartless, and Jane is certainly not a study in tender-mindedness; but it is a realistic evocation too of generational supersession: Lilia understands exactly how Jane is 'ready, empty, apt—the inheritor; foreign in her beauty with the foreignness of this supplanting new time' (51). In order to live on her own terms, Jane must leave Antonia to the past. As a result, however, the final effect of the novel is to mingle with the 'love' recorded in its concluding sentence a poignancy associated with the isolated and increasingly desperate figure of Antonia. If Jane is not as cruel as Hal dismissing Falstaff in *Henry IV*, Antonia's fate is, nevertheless, like Antonio's in *The Merchant of Venice* and the other Antonio's in *Twelfth Night*, to remain resolutely outside new or renewed coupledoms: those of Fred and Lilia, of Jane and Richard Priam. So Antonia's name too may have its Shakespearian origin, a feminized version of his 'Antonio'. Antonia, the well-known photographer who can no longer find a theme or subject, whose early marriage has long since failed, who finds solace in alcohol, and whose life oscillates increasingly meaninglessly and whimsically between England and Ireland, London and Co. Cork, is, I suggest, a kind of black self-portrait of the artist in advancing age, a portrait of a personality Elizabeth Bowen feared she might herself eventually assume. If so, Jane, in taking leave of her, is both a later version of Lois in *The Last September* doing what would have been impossible for her—rejecting her overbearing aunt and mentor, Lady Naylor—and also, more complexly, the author's farewell to versions of herself which she has scripted into her work. The abruption of plot in

A World of Love is Elizabeth Bowen consigning her writing, and particularly her writing in its historically superseded Anglo-Irish dimension, to the past: abandoning it, as Guy's letters are abandoned in the Anglo-Irish attic. Since the novels which eventually followed, *The Little Girls* in 1963 and *Eva Trout* in 1968, are notoriously difficult to attach in any unproblematic way to the remaining canon of her work, we may feel that *A World of Love*, by ending Bowen's fictional engagement with Ireland once and for all, but also by ending, as it were, nowhere at all, pitches Bowen the novelist towards the most unsettling kinds of further writing.

II

Children

4

Mother and Child:
The House in Paris (1935)

'Perhaps a child smells history without knowing it.'

Seven Winters

I

'Your mother is not coming; she cannot come.' This is to me one of the most wrenching sentences in modern fiction. Wrenching the first time we read it, at the end of Part I of *The House in Paris*, and more wrenching still when we read it again at the opening of Part III, the most notable repetition in this novel much preoccupied with repetition and return. It is addressed by Naomi Fisher, who inhabits the house, to the 9-year-old Leopold, temporarily in Paris from Spezia in order to meet the mother he does not know, but about whom he has endlessly fantasized: Naomi is giving Leopold the news from a just-arrived telegram. Also present in the house's 'salon' to hear the statement, as she has been since early morning, is the 11-year-old Henrietta, out of England for the first time and spending the day in the house while in transit to her grandmother in Mentone. During the course of the day the children, who are both lonely, anxious, intensely nervous, and highly sensitive and intelligent, show themselves capable of intense cruelty, but have also entered into an edgily envious and self-protective collusion as they observe adult behaviour, and as they tell each other about the circumstances which have left them stranded together in this brief Parisian halt.

The first time we read the sentence Leopold is all febrile anticipation, fantasizing a mother who will remove him from his despised foster-parents and take him with her to England. When we next read it, as the novel repeats it across the gap of its second, lengthiest section, entitled 'The Past', we have been given an account of the circumstances of

Leopold's conception, and of the relationships which have entangled his origins with the lives of the mother and daughter (Naomi) of this Parisian house. As readers of *The House in Paris*, therefore, we read the sentence twice, where Leopold hears it only once: so that we are given the clearest possible indication of the weight with which it falls upon him. It becomes a sentence in the judicial as well as in the grammatical sense. In the passage succeeding it in Part III Henrietta is distressed by Leopold's apparently haughty disengagement from the news he has just been given. Threatening to leave the room, she challenges him to say why he has just refused to be shown around Paris by Naomi. 'Because my mother is not here', he says; and—stating the fact, using the word 'mother'—his pride immediately collapses:

His hands went behind his back and she saw his shoulders shake. He became like a boy who is the butt of a dancing class. 'Well, say something!' he said.

She only clutched the door-knob. When she could not speak, Leopold turned round facing the mantelpiece and suddenly ground his forehead against the marble. One shoulder up dragged his sailor collar crooked; his arms were crushed between his chest and the mantelpiece. After a minute, one leg writhed round the other like ivy killing a tree. The clock ticked away calmly above his head. If it were just crying . . . thought Henrietta. The first sound torn from him frightened her so much that she began to count the white lines round his collar. At first each sob was like some terrible accident, then they began to come faster. He wept like someone alone against his will, someone shut up alone for a punishment: you only weep like that when only a room hears. She thought: But none of us are punished like that now. His undeniable tears were more than his own, they seemed to be all the tears that ever had been denied, that dryness of body, age, ungreatness or anger ever had made impossible. . . . Disappointment tears the bearable film off life. Leopold's solitary despair made Henrietta no more than the walls or table. This was not contempt for her presence: no one was there. Being not there disembodied her, so she fearlessly crossed the parquet to stand beside him. She watched his head, the back of his thin neck, the square blue collar shaken between his shoulders, wondering without diffidence where to put her hand. Finally, she leant her body against his, pressing her ribs to his elbow so that his sobs began to go through her too. Leopold rolled his face further away from her, so that one cheek and temple now pressed the marble, but did not withdraw his body from her touch. After a minute like this, his elbow undoubled itself against her and his left arm went round her with unfeeling tightness, as though he were gripping the bole of a tree. Held close like this to the mantelpiece he leant on, Henrietta let her forehead rest on the marble too: her face bent forward, so that the tears she began shedding fell on the front of her dress. An angel stood up inside her with its hands to its lips, and Henrietta did not attempt to speak. Now that she cried, he could rest. His cheek no longer hurt itself on the marble. Reposing between two friends, the mantelpiece and her body, Leopold, she could feel, was look-ing out of the window, seeing the courtyard and the one bare tree swim into view again and patiently stand. His breathing steadied itself; each breath came sooner and was less painfully deep. Henrietta, meanwhile, felt tears, from her own eyes but not from a self she knew of, rain on to the serge dress, each side of the buttons that were pulled a little crooked by Leopold's hand. They stayed like this some time. (196–7)

Part of the tremendous force of this derives from its merging of two elements: intense physical specificity; and large moral generalization. The physicality is awkwardly, childishly unformed: the hands not knowing what to do; the shoulders shaking; the forehead rammed against marble; the shoulder dragging a collar crooked; the legs writhed around each other. Henrietta is being morally extended, coming to a new comprehension and consciousness of a 'self' previously unknown to her by learning, with an extraordinarily intense inwardness and empathy—which we are to presume derives from at least comparable sufferings of her own—that language, with its words of solace and com-fort, is exactly what is not needed here. What the inarticulacy of Leopold's suffering, which is as open as if it has no witness, demands is that she become a 'friend' to his pain in the way the inanimate marble is a 'friend': by learning to become 'disembodied' so that her very body itself will paradoxically allow her to feel out the only response he can tolerate. The passage itself articulates an empathy discovering what Wilfred Owen calls, in 'Insensibility', 'the eternal reciprocity of tears': 'pressing her ribs to his elbow so that his sobs began to go through her too'. It is a passage whose own tender inwardness with the pain of chil-dren is both the permission for, and the justification of, its sudden extension of the moralistic into a quasi-metaphysical figuration, when the knowledgeably instructive 'angel stood up in her', a protective guardian of desolate children. Henrietta has earlier noticed that Leopold has a scar on his neck and another on his knee; and this passage from *The House in Paris* is the novel's most concentrated expression of the psychological and emotional wounding that is parentlessness.[1]

---

[1] Andrew Bennett and Nicholas Royle, in *Elizabeth Bowen and the Dissolution of the Novel: Still Lives* (London: Macmillan, 1995), 43, read the novel as 'a traumaturgy, both a work and a theory of wounds'.

II

Part II of the novel is intricately related, through numerous images and motifs, to Parts I and III. Indeed, *The House in Paris* is a kind of formal oxymoron in its delicately managed combination of anguished emotional material and a sharp elegance of structure: the book is 'wieldy, shapely and unencumbered', indeed, the ideal which Bowen admires in an essay on writing fiction.[2] Part II is set ten years previously and tells the story of the affair which Leopold's mother, Karen Michaelis, has, while she is engaged to someone else, with Max Eberhart, a French Jew, who is himself at the time engaged to Naomi Fisher, a close friend of Karen's (and, of course the Naomi who, in Part III, brings Leopold— once again as it were—the news of his mother). In some way never made entirely explicit, but which certainly has its sexual connotations, Max has also been heavily involved with Naomi's own mother. She is only ever known in the novel as Mme Fisher, in a way which perhaps inevitably associates her with that earlier Mme in English fiction, Mme Merle in James's *The Portrait of a Lady*; and in the present moment of Parts I and III she is now secluded, close to death, in a bedroom in the house in Paris.

In the course of their affair Karen becomes pregnant with the child who becomes Leopold; but Max, before he knows this, commits suicide in the house—in fact slitting a wrist in front of the very mantelpiece against which Leopold slumps in his misery: the mantelpiece has become an enemy to Max as it becomes a friend to Leopold. Max, who is neurotically hypersensitive, kills himself after a conversation in which Mme Fisher reveals that she has been self-interestedly and cynically manipulative of both his and Naomi's emotions in relation to their engagement. Naomi, in an act of breathtaking selflessness or masochism—it is one of the novel's many strengths of ambivalent characterization that we are unable to decide which—arranges Leopold's adoption by an American family, the Grant Moodys, whose name he bears and with whom he lives, out of all contact with his mother and her family. Karen has assumed that her fiancé, Ray Forrestier, will abandon her, but the marriage, in fact, goes ahead, which necessitates Ray's giving up a promising diplomatic career. Now, ten years later, in

---

[2] Elizabeth Bowen, 'Exclusion', in *Afterthought: Pieces about Writing* (London: Longmans, 1962), 220.

Parts I and III, both entitled 'The Present', Leopold is in Paris because
Ray has persuaded a still reluctant Karen to meet him. In fact, at the
very last moment, Karen, who has suffered some kind of breakdown,
finds herself emotionally incapable of leaving her hotel in
Fontainebleau: hence the news which Naomi gives Leopold. Ray, in a
decision of his own, goes instead and, at the end of the novel, delivers
Henrietta to her next chaperone at the Gare de Lyon for the onward
journey to Mentone, keeping Leopold with the intention of returning
him to his mother.

In Bowen's portrayal of the Forrestier marriage the wound of parentlessness uncovered at its rawest in the passage between Leopold and
Henrietta is matched with a credibly unsentimental view of the wound
that is childlessness too. This is a childlessness haunted by an abandoned child; and it is unexpected but psychologically convincing that,
even though we learn that Ray and Karen have lost a child, and that
Karen can have no other children, it is Ray who pines, or at least pines
more, for the lost child:

When, travelling, they might have been most together objects would clash
meaningly upon those open senses one has abroad. That third chair left pushed
in at a table set for a couple. After-dark fountains playing in coloured light, for
no grown-up eye. The transcontinental engine, triumphant, with flanks steam-
ing, that men and boys stop to look at when they get out at the terminus, while
the woman hurries ahead thinking: Here I am. Cranes and fortifications.
Someone being arrested, a good street fight. The third bed in their room at the
simple inn. France being France at nights, with lights under trees, over tables,
a band, an outdoor cinema. (But, after all, he has Italy.) A tale of blood in a
guide-book. The quickening steamer-paddle churning the lake. The woman
sitting unmoving, smiling at cramp, with a child's head on her shoulder. The
man explaining how something works. Venice, New York, places seen too
often, crying out to be seen for the first time. Children's eyes excited and dark
from sitting up so late. (219–20)

Even if the register of boyhood masculinity may be found a little
over-insistent to contemporary ears, childlessness here is brilliantly
figured as a permanent part-rejection by the world, as the almost
malevolent clash of objects insisting a meaning which your subjectivity
would rather ignore or deny. The world becomes a place into which
you can never comfortably fit, a place in which, because you are permanently missing something, you are also missing yourself. The
inevitable absence is made vividly particular and present in that desolate parenthesis in which Leopold's own Italian circumstances briefly

intrude: '(But, after all, he has Italy)'; which is a futile concession, doubling vengefully back upon itself, since 'after all' is to place him after
all he has suffered, and that he 'has' anything at all is of no consolation
at all to him if he does not have what he wants, and neither do you. *The
House in Paris* evokes, and then defines, this sense of absence as an
unending and sometimes argumentative 'dialogue' between Karen and
Ray, which Ray calls 'the old fight that makes us three all the time'. A
lengthy section of Part III is a passage of this dialogue presented, like
the 'Circe' episode of Joyce's *Ulysses*, in dramatic form. Its distress-
ingly claustrophobic circularity is an epitome of enforced return—the
return, again and again, of what happens 'all the time' in this marriage.
The novel is itself a dialogue, across its three parts, between parentlessness and childlessness; and, in one of its most experimental narrative techniques, Part II is represented as a kind of dialogue between
Karen and a proto-Leopold at the moment of his conception.

In *The Last September*, as we have already seen, Lois meditates,
strangely and strikingly, on her own conception; and *The House in
Paris* is, more intensively, a novel about conceiving and being conceived, and about how knowing about your own conception may let
you begin to know who you are. The word 'know' and its cognates—
which inevitably take an edge in this context from the Biblical sense of
the word 'know'—echo again and again in the book, most notably
when, in an interview with the still deeply malevolent Mme Fisher in
Part III, Leopold invites her to confirm his own identification of his
plight: 'People who know me must not know I was born, and people
who know I was born must not know me?' In its childish abjection this
is painfully self-knowing and shrewd, since the narrative itself tells us
that 'No one knew about Leopold. The hush of silence round him was
complete.' (219) In his attempt to break this silence, Leopold becomes,
we might say, the epistemologist of his own conception, of the act of
carnal knowledge which generated him; and it is the peculiarity and
originality of Bowen's structure in *The House in Paris* to have discovered a narrative method in which his questions can be answered.

Part II oscillates between first-, second-, and third-person address,
between interior monologue, free indirect speech, and objective narrative in a way which makes narrative technique itself mobile. But it is the
strangeness of its second-person address which strikes most, when we
read, of the moment of conception itself, that 'the idea of you, Leopold,
began to be present with her'. Here the narrator, or the narrative,
weirdly interpellates Leopold, naming and addressing him before he

exists in an almost vertiginously unnerving way. The act of interpella-
tion effects a kind of cross-fertilization of the three parts of the novel,
permitting Karen to address Leopold with her story as though he were
her equal in emotion, intellect, and rationality. Part II becomes, therefore, the ideal conversation which a separated mother and child might
have were they, in fact, impossibly, contemporaries, the kind of conversation inconceivable—perhaps the *mot juste*—in life. It is the only
possible true response from the self-narrating mother to the deepest
craving of the hopelessly baffled child, and the novel figures it, self-
reflexively, as what the art of fiction itself might manage as a response
to the fall, or rise, from childhood into adulthood:

Actually, the meeting he had projected could take place only in Heaven—call
it Heaven; on the plane of potential not merely likely behaviour. Or call it art,
with truth and imagination informing every word. Only there—in heaven or
art, in that nowhere, on that plane—could Karen have told Leopold what had
really been. . . . The mystery about sex comes from confusion and terror: to a
mind on which these have not yet settled there is nothing you cannot tell.
Grown-up people form a secret society, they must have something to hold by;
they dare not say to a child: 'There is nothing you do not know here'. (67)

Part II of *The House in Paris* is the fictional 'nowhere', the artistic
'plane', where the adult may say exactly this to the child, a space where,
in the relation between mother and child, 'the mystery of sex' is not
derided or diverted or dissipated but made manifest, both self-
excoriatingly and self-justifyingly. The Gospel's 'Except ye . . . become
as little children, ye shall not enter into the kingdom of heaven'
(Matthew 18:3) may lie behind this astonishing narrative conceit and
its projection of the figure of 'Heaven'; and we remember that an
angel—whose location would also presumably be Heaven—stood up
in Henrietta to bring her too to a new plane of empathetic comprehension. Andrew Bennett and Nicholas Royle write excellently about what
they call 'this singular apostrophic formulation', describing it, wittily,
as 'an uncanny conception of Leopold in writing'.[3] Its depth psychology pushes towards a kind of literary experimentation entirely congruent with the fraught complexity of the novel's material, an
experiment which is, for me, as richly challenging and satisfying as anything comparable in Woolf or Joyce. Further, it is a narrative technique
which embeds in the deepest structure of the book a knowledge of the
inextricability of sexuality and childhood; it is a way of fully including

[3] *Elizabeth Bowen and the Dissolution of the Novel*, 57.

Leopold, the child, in the implications and operations of human sexuality, and thereby a way of saving him from the miseries of self-opacity. 'No one knew about Leopold', but Leopold must know; and, 'There is nothing you do not know here.'

Or, we might say, Part II of *The House in Paris* is the letter which Karen might actually write to Leopold who, in Part I, before he learns that his mother is not coming, finds an empty envelope addressed by her to Naomi: it is one of the novel's most reverberating moments, and perhaps the most striking use of letters in this many-lettered novelist (Maud Ellmann ingeniously says that the novel itself is 'structured like an envelope').[4] In Naomi's handbag he first finds a letter from Marian Grant Moody advising Naomi on how to treat him, and telling her that he has not yet 'received direct sex-instruction'. In its vulgarity, presumption and unscrupulous intrusiveness this letter causes 'revulsion' in Leopold, a revulsion impelling him to read yet another private letter: 'The revulsion threatening him became so frightening that he quickly picked up Mrs. Arbuthnot's letter and read it, as though to clap something on to the gash in his mind' (42). Finding the empty envelope from his mother, he then, as it were, attempts to apply it as a salve to his wounded mind:

he began to pace the salon, with his eyes shut, pressing her empty envelope to his forehead as he had once seen a thought-reader do. Then he began to read slowly aloud, as though the words one by one passed under his eyelids: 'Dear Miss Fisher,' he said.   (45)

'Dear Leopold,' Part II of *The House in Paris* implicitly says—yes, 'you, Leopold'—passing under his eyelids all he will ever need of 'direct sex-instruction', and giving it in exactly the terms in which it may be adequately received.

III

John Rodker famously called Ford Madox Ford's *The Good Soldier* 'the finest French novel in the English language',[5] but I think that *The*

---

[4] Maud Ellmann, *Elizabeth Bowen: The Shadow across the Page* (Edinburgh: Edinburgh University Press, 2003), 117.

[5] Quoted in Ford Madox Ford, dedicatory letter to Stella Ford, in *The Good Soldier: A Tale of Passion* (1915; London: Penguin, 1972), 8. Victoria Glendinning tells us that Victor Gollancz wrote to Bowen asking of *The House in Paris*, 'I wonder if you

House in Paris can lay claim to the title too, profoundly immersed as it is, in its sense of structural and psychological possibility, in the work of Flaubert and his successors. Indeed, its title may be, in part, an acknowledgement that this is a novel set up in the house of French fiction also, and Bowen may be offering us a little instruction in, or an ironic joke about, this when she calls the Parisian street in which her titular house stands the 'Rue Sylvestre Bonnard', after the eponymous hero of a novel by Anatole France, *Le Crime de Sylvestre Bonnard* (1890), an instruction reinforced when she eventually tells us in a late essay on Proust that France is the assumed original of Bergotte, the novelist in *A La Recherche du Temps Perdu*.[6] When Bowen devises a literary mode in which the adulterous, or quasi-adulterous, mother may speak to her son—unashamedly and with entire frankness—of the sexuality which has produced him, and does so in a world in which, as the novel makes amply plain, concepts of women's 'ruin' are still well within earshot, with their potentially devastating social consequences, she may also be offering a return with a difference to—that is to say, a revision and a critique of—the nineteenth-century French tradition of the female novel of adultery. As Naomi Segal has shown, in that tradition adulterous women are frequently 'punished' (by male authors) by having daughters rather than sons.[7]

Tony Tanner, in his study of the European novel of adultery more generally—which discusses, among other texts, *Madame Bovary* and *Anna Karenina*—notes the 'curious phenomenon' that, 'although there invariably are children, or at least a child, often there is curiously little interest in them or it, even on the part of the mother (or especially on the part of the mother)' and that children 'are seldom very notable presences; if anything, they seem to incorporate some sense of negativity, a weak hold on life, and a latent indifference to things that seem to have been transmitted to them from their parents (and more particularly

---

realize how *un-English* it is?'. See *Elizabeth Bowen: Portrait of a Writer* (1977; London: Phoenix, 1993), 97. She also says that in the early 1930s Bowen 'had read a lot of French, starting with Stendhal' and that in 1932 she began a translation of Flaubert's *L'Education Sentimentale*. Bowen herself, in an interview in 1942, says, 'if I've been influenced by anything it's been by the French novelists and short-story writers of the past fifty years'. See 'Meet Elizabeth Bowen', *The Bell*, 4: 6 (September 1942), 420–6, 425.

[6] 'The Art of Bergotte', in Elizabeth Bowen, *Pictures and Conversations* (London: Allen Lane, 1975), 77–109, 97.

[7] Naomi Segal, *The Adulteress's Child: Authorship and Desire in the Nineteenth-Century Novel* (Cambridge: Polity Press, 1992).

their mothers)'.[8] Structuring her novel by opening with the illegitimate male child himself, who longs for an account of his origin and very firmly refuses negativity, and then folding that child's longing into the mother's unashamedly explicit account of the act that produced him, Bowen is, I propose, taking on this tradition, this literary house in Paris. She adopts elements of its generic structure, but she also combats it, on behalf of the usually excluded child. Where the tradition shows 'curiously little interest' in the child—and the adverb there is a very mild one for the scandal of the phenomenon—*The House in Paris* displays enormous interest in the child and shows the mother displaying enormous interest too, although not, certainly, of the conventional kind; and Leopold is the embodiment of a refusal of exclusion who wants to know everything there is to be known about what has been transmitted to him from his parents, and more particularly from his mother. When, towards the very end of the book, Ray Forrestier has decided to return Leopold to Karen and waits with him outside the Gare de Lyon, he thinks, 'the child commanded tonight, I have acted on his scale'. *The House in Paris*, unlike numerous novels of female adultery in the European tradition, acts on the child's scale.

IV

Like smoke coming under a door the dead silence of Mme Fisher seemed to pervade everywhere.

The House in Paris, 229

The ideal trust required for Karen to impart to Leopold the ideal knowledge he demands is everywhere contrasted in the novel, however, with the violation of trust. *The House in Paris* includes a conversation made in Heaven, but its actual settings often evoke something more like a Hell. It is very much a chamber novel, a novel of enclosed, shut-off spaces: hotel-rooms; restaurant tables; garden-ends; drawing-rooms; salons; the study at Chester Terrace (the Michaelis home); taxis; railway carriages; the train corridor in which Karen and Max are accidentally thrown against each other and then fatefully compelled to gaze deeply into each other's eyes; and also the whole of the tiny house in Paris itself, where the stripes on the wallpaper seem like the bars of

---

[8] Tony Tanner, *Adultery in the Novel: Contract and Transgression* (Baltimore: Johns Hopkins University Press, 1979), 98.

a prison. Inside these confined, claustrophobic spaces people betray one another. Karen betrays Ray, her fiancé, and Naomi, her close friend, by sleeping with Max; Max betrays Naomi, his fiancée, by sleeping with Karen (so that Leopold, the product of the union, is, in a sense, the incarnation of the double treachery perpetrated upon Naomi); Karen lies to her mother, who lies, in a different sense, by refusing to acknowledge that she knows she has been lied to: her silence becomes the betrayal of any future trust between herself and her daughter. The novel choreographs these treacheries by never permitting secure response to motivation or morality: *The House in Paris* is, as I have already said, a novel with an entirely credible ambivalence of characterization. Karen, for instance, betrays friendship, but Naomi's relationship with her has always had a self-laceratingly masochistic element which may prompt such treachery; Karen does attempt to resist Max, but the novel is vibrantly insightful about the irresistibility of sexual passion. So that, even concerning the hurtfulness of betrayal to the betrayed, the flow of readerly sympathy in *The House in Paris* is never straightforward.

Mme Fisher, in the most enclosed space of all, the bedroom in which she is dying, betrays everyone, notably her own daughter—who, in an emblem for her mother's intrusiveness on her life, has no lock on her door. She also violates the trust of both Leopold and Henrietta by giving them her perverse version of the narratives in which she has figured in relation to them, narratives in which they would, if they believed her, feel, in Tony Tanner's term, 'negative' about themselves. Doing this to these children in the novel's present moment, Mme Fisher is doing yet again what she has already done to her daughter. So, in the book's most elegantly articulated symmetry, both Karen and Naomi are portrayed as unhappy daughters: they too figure in their functions as the children of unsatisfactory mothers.

This is, prominently in the modern novel in English, a Jamesian theme; but it is pursued in *The House in Paris* into Bowen's most formidable representation of a type persistent in her work. If Mme Fisher has James's Mme Merle somewhere in her origins, as I have suggested, she is also a compound—or a compost—of those earlier domineering elderly women in Elizabeth Bowen, beginning with Mrs Kerr in *The Hotel* and prominently including both Lady Naylor in *The Last September* and Lady Waters in *To The North*, who all presumptuously interfere in the lives of younger women and daughters, sometimes disastrously—in the case of Lady Waters to the point of the young woman

Emmeline's final act of murder and suicide. Leopold, in a superb phrase entirely consistent with his high intelligence and imagination, thinks of Mme Fisher as 'septic with what had happened', poisoned by a past for which she is herself largely responsible. Mme Fisher's interference with Naomi's emotional life, first urging Max on her and subsequently urging him, instead, towards Karen, culminates in Max's self-destruction. Since Mme Fisher, we learn, was, before her marriage, a governess in England, we may read her as a coda to the long line of socially and sexually thwarted governesses in nineteenth-century Romantic and gothic fiction. She collapses into herself, she is also septic with, those figures of intertwined powerlessness (in relation to adults) and power (in relation to children) who fetch up at the turn of the twentieth century in James's governesses in *What Maisie Knew* and *The Turn of the Screw*. Mme Fisher is Bowen's intertextual portrait of the deep damage done by the servility demanded of intelligent women by economic necessity.

There is a pseudo-gothic element in the title of *The House in Paris*— we might think in particular of Sheridan Le Fanu's *The House by the Churchyard*, since Bowen herself wrote on Le Fanu—and several critics have drawn attention to a certain fairy-tale aspect of the book: R. B. Kerschner Jr, in a fine essay, for instance, calls the plot 'a dream narrative masquerading as bourgeois realism'.[9] There *is* a kind of spilt gothic in the novel, nowhere more than when, in the final chapter of Part 2, Naomi imagines her mother as quasi-vampiric: 'I saw then that all her life her power had never properly used itself, and that now it had used itself she was like the dead, like someone killed in a victory.' Mme Fisher does indeed draw blood from Max, when he slits his wrist in the house in front of her, after a conversation in which, we learn, he is 'commended' by her—for, we are to presume, his seduction of Karen. It is Mme Fisher's presumption of a comparable cynicism in him—for Karen has money, Naomi does not—which devastates to the point of suicide a Max whose emotional instability is by then very well attested.

If Mme Fisher is the wicked witch of a modern *Hansel and Gretel* narrative, however—and Karen thinks of her as 'a woman who sells girls . . . a witch'—there is also something virtually satanic about her as she lies formidably static in her bedroom, with its 'tabernacle' of bed-curtains in a permanently shuttered darkness, and with what to Leopold is her 'frightening lightness of humour' about God. She is the

[9] R. B. Kershner Jr, 'Bowen's Oneiric House in Paris', *Texas Studies in Literature and Language* (Winter, 1986), 407–23, 411–12.

darkly perverse maternal matrix in which the novel's plot is bred, as all of the characters are drawn inevitably towards her, and then driven away: Max into suicide; Naomi into the wounded disconsolateness of the utterly unloved and perversely used child; and both Henrietta and Leopold, during their enforced interviews with her, into new and, we anticipate, desolatingly maturing, formulations of the perversities of adult behaviour. This has its quasi-incestuous element, since Karen believes that it is Mme Fisher's own sexual desire for Max which has made her jealously push him away from Naomi towards Karen herself; and it is therefore, of course, Mme Fisher who is 'responsible' for the conception of Leopold. This quasi-incestuous element in the book's relationships—the closed circle that is Mme Fisher–Max–Naomi–Karen–Max—is the emotional and psychological interior of its inward-turning chamber structures, its claustrophobic and sometimes dream-like atmospheres. This is a novel in which thwarted energies of repression and desire constitute the only available family romance.

Max's own family origins are not made clear, apart—and, of course, significantly—from the information that he is Jewish. We do learn that his father died when he was young, but we know nothing at all about his mother; and we are perhaps to infer that, like Leopold, he is illegitimate, and has been abandoned by a mother. In any case, he has clearly first encountered Mme Fisher as a maternal substitute. What Naomi eventually realizes is that her mother has corrupted the young, hypersensitive, and deeply impressionable Max, dispossessing him of a viable self and taking a kind of possession of him: 'He could do nothing that she had not expected; my mother was at the root of him' (182). The novel finds an altogether arresting figure for Mme Fisher as the incarnation of destructive maternity when Max thinks that she has performed 'the madonna trick' on him. Max, the French-Jewish outsider, is, in his over-dependence, deeply compelled, even overwhelmed, by the irresistible 'force' of a 'figure of stone pity' but one whose customary solace is perversely turned to destruction: the image of a pernicious Madonna.

In this, *The House in Paris* itself returns to the startlingly unexpected figurations of the ending of *Friends and Relations*. There, the upper-class and very English Anglican Mrs Studdart meditates on the marriages of her daughters, which have formed the novel's plot. She knows with horrified certainty that, partly through her own doing, one daughter has married the man whom her other daughter loves, and is loved by, and her knowledge produces her appalled internal outcry, '*I can't*

bear life for her!' Stepping outside the usually, although not exclusively, realist register of the novel, the 'never confidential' Mrs Studdart
constructs for herself 'a confidante, an intimate' to whom such things
might actually be said out loud: 'A lady. With her one would be certain
of being understood; there prevailed a perfect good taste in which,
while anything could be mentioned, too much had never been said'
(157). There is a sad comedy in this, since the confidante is figured as 'a
kind of sublime Mrs Studdart'; but there is more than this too: there is
the neediness and extremity of prayer: 'Perhaps if she had been a religious woman . . .? She wondered sometimes about Roman Catholics,
whether the Virgin Mary . . .'. A great deal is made to hang on an ellipsis or suspension here, as it does in *The Last September*; and in envis-
aging the most crucial and intimate moments between parents and
children, or surrogate parents and surrogate children, Elizabeth
Bowen, Anglo-Irish Protestant, gives, in both *Friends and Relations*
and *The House in Paris*, an altogether unexpected, perturbed, fascinated, and compelled inflection to the most exclusively Roman Catholic
image of all, that of the Madonna and Child.

V

In various ways we are encouraged to read Leopold as a second Max,
and when Mme Fisher meets him, 'She re-read a known map of thought
and passion in miniature' (201). He is a child whom it is also feasible
to imagine being impelled to self-destruction by his upbringing, or
conceivably to something even worse, since Bowen very subtly
insinuates—Henrietta notices and is repelled by—a driven, almost
Napoleonic, autocracy in him, the self-dramatizing arrogance of the
unspeakably lonely, baffled, and damaged child, which may culminate
in fantasies destructive of others as well as, or instead of, himself. The
obverse of this, however, is Leopold's radical refusal to accept his lot;
and in *The House in Paris* the subjected or subjugated child insists on
his release.

But in this Leopold requires assistance; and here Bowen plots a further symmetry into the novel by making his experience rhyme with his
mother's. Karen's relationship with Max is, at least in part, prompted
by her desire to break free from the constrictions of her apparently
amiable, decent, moneyed, liberal, Regent's Park-metropolitan family,
and especially from her mother. There comes a point in Karen's

relationship with Max when, in an act of self-preservation, she must lie to her mother, as we have seen: in a characteristically Bowenesque piece of moral revisionism, she thinks, regarding Naomi's lack of privacy, that 'Never to lie is to have no lock on your door, you are never wholly alone' (133); and Naomi, as I have already said, literally has no lock on her door in the house in Paris. When Karen realizes that her mother knows she has been lied to yet refuses to acknowledge it, their hitherto very affectionate and, it has seemed, intimate, relationship disintegrates. In a moment almost bruisingly affecting for the reader, Karen puts her arm around her mother 'as she used to do when she was small', but her mother is 'like a statue moving', an image which, of course, recalls the way Mme Fisher appears to Max to be like a stone madonna. 'Nothing was said' (172), we are told, in a sentence which opens and then, repeated, closes a long paragraph describing strategies for avoiding communication; and then, devastatingly split across a paragraph break, we are told emphatically that 'Nothing was to be said'. This 'deadly intention not to *know*' on the part of Karen's mother is the obverse of Leopold's hunger to know and, as we have seen, the whole of Part II is, precisely, what might be 'said' by his mother to Leopold, what he might be encouraged to 'know'.

This is the major example—several others are given in the novel too—of the deep emotional reserve and repression of the Michaelises who are, in this, clearly representative of their class but also, almost equally perhaps, of their time; and there is a generalizing tendency in their portrayal, notably when, in her stoical reaction to the news of her sister's death, Mrs Michaelis is said to behave 'as she behaved in August 1914': that is, 'nobly'. Not saying and not knowing in the domestic context therefore have their clear political dimension: they are collusive with the machinations of power, and in this novel of the 1930s, in which Karen is pregnant with the child of a Jewish person, this has manifest contemporary significance. Unlike her mother, indeed in a way opposed to everything in her mother's *haut-bourgeois* standards, Karen knows that 'Love is obtuse and reckless; it interferes' (174). This is to make love necessarily dangerous since, in this novel, passionate jealousy and hatred also 'interfere' and so too, in Ray's final decision about Leopold, does passionate concern. Karen's affair with Max is her commitment to risk, to the obtuse recklessness of interfering and of being interfered with. Her lie and its result find out in her mother a 'worldliness beginning so deep down that it seems to be the heart' (174); and this is indeed what Bowen's next novel will call, in its

very title, 'the death of the heart', a death against which Karen pits herself, despite the fact that the effort eventually causes her emotional
breakdown.

So the sharpest symmetry in the novel is Karen's struggle to extricate
herself from a home which is no home at all, and Leopold's struggle to
find a true home, as opposed to the one he has with the Grant Moodys:
'They keep trying to make me be things. Have they bought me, or
what?'(204) Karen will not 'be' what her family keep trying to make her
be, and this is one significance of her early, abandoned career as a
painter: 'They keep me away from everything that has power; they
would be frightened of art if I painted really well' (161).[10] In the very
important section of the novel set in Ireland at the beginning of Part II,
during which Karen realizes that she wants to break off her engagement, she is compelled to recognize that the life of her dying Aunt
Violet has not been the satisfactory hidden woman's life that she
had condescendingly assumed it to have been. Her aunt's tiny but
immensely powerful complaint, when Karen hears it, is, unforgettably,
'like hearing a picture you had always loved . . . sigh inside its frame'
(83). So there is a real sense in which Karen's understanding of her
aunt's unfulfilment is an impulsion to her affair with Max; and her
refusal to be what they wish her to be is most emphatically focused
through Max's Jewishness, since it makes him, she knows they will
think, 'a person who would not do'.

In a very delicately designed moment in the novel we see how the
social and cultural liberalism of the Michaelises, which has appeared
virtually ideal, does not save them from the casually presumptive
upper-middle-class anti-Semitism of their period. Hermione Lee thinks
that Max's Jewishness is, in fact, intended by Bowen to make him
appear 'suspect', and she presumably therefore believes that Bowen
herself shared the prejudice; and Jane Miller, enthusiastically celebrat-
ing Bowen's work, nevertheless maintains the reservation that suspect
characters in it are likely to turn out to be Jewish.[11] I cannot at all see
the force of Miller's caveat, since Max is, in fact, the only Jewish character in Bowen's novels, and I also think Lee mistaken. To me there is
no taint whatever of anti-Semitism in the portrayal of Max: quite the

---

[10] It is probable that Karen is named after the Danish novelist Karin Michaelis, whose
Den Farlige Alder (1910), translated in 1912 as *The Dangerous Age*, is a novel about an
erotic crisis in the life of its heroine, and was hugely popular in its day.

[11] See Hermione Lee, *Elizabeth Bowen* (1981; revised edn., London: Vintage, 1999),
92, and Jane Miller, 'Re-reading Elizabeth Bowen', *Raritan*, 20: 1 (2000), 17–31.

contrary, he is there precisely to define the anti-Semitism of the
Michaelises and, through them, of upper-class educated English liberal
culture.[12] In this respect Leopold (who shares his forename with the
most famous literary Jew written by a gentile—and, like Elizabeth
Bowen, an Irish gentile—in the twentieth century, Joyce's Leopold
Bloom in *Ulysses*) is also a second Max, a Jewish child living, now, in
continental Europe in the mid-1930s. In an excellent essay, Jean
Radford has written persuasively about the historical dimension of
The House in Paris, and she notes with historically alert precision that,
in fact, neither Max nor Leopold is Jewish according to Jewish law,
since neither has a Jewish mother: but, under the anti-Semitic
Nuremberg Laws introduced in 1935, the year in which *The House in
Paris* was published, both are deemed to be Jewish, and would there-
fore have been deprived of citizenship in that year, had they been
German citizens. In the light of this she reads *The House in Paris* as 'a
historical novel which reflects upon England and Europe between the
wars and on the political history of Paris since 1789'—by which she
means that the treatment by the French of the 'other', in this case the
Jew, is a failure of the obligations taken on as a consequence of the
French Revolution. The result, she memorably says, is that the nervous
Leo 'has something to be nervous about.'[13]

Even though Henrietta, in a taxi at the beginning of the novel, strikingly remembers 'how much blood has been shed in Paris', I think
myself that this is to read rather too much into this nevertheless very
prominent element in the book: Radford's verb 'reflects' proposes a
more analytic treatment than I think these matters receive, and she
appears to suggest a more substantially articulated historical critique
than I think Bowen actually offers, or would be interested in or moved
to. Despite her admiration for Stendhal, she is not a Stendhalian novelist. Yet I sympathize with the tendency of Radford's argument here;
and at the end of *The House in Paris* it is hard not to think of the child
whom Ray considers 'this brittle little Jewish boy' (215), carrying his
suitcase at the Gare de Lyon, without recalling all those other brittle little Jewish boys who would, only a few years after the contemporary
date on which this novel is set, also stand on European station

[12] As we shall see in my chapter on *The Heat of the Day*, Bowen is sensitive to Irish
anti-Semitism during the Second World War.
[13] Jean Radford, 'Late Modernism and the Politics of History', in Maroula Joannou,
Women Writers of the 1930s: Gender, Politics and History (Edinburgh: Edinburgh
University Press, 1999), 33–45, 39, 42.

platforms, but not in order to be returned to their mothers. In this context, as in several others—as we shall see—it is significant that Bowen's wartime novel, *The Heat of the Day*, opens with the fall of France.

I would not wish to claim prescience for Elizabeth Bowen, although there is, at the very beginning of *To The North*, that other novel of the 1930s partly set in continental Europe, a remarkable passage in which Cecilia, halted in a train outside Chiasso, 'began to feel she was in a cattle truck shunted into a siding . . . She sent one wild comprehensive glance round her fellow travellers, as though less happy than cattle, conscious, they were all going to execution'(5). But that a sense of the political disruptions of the 1930s is present to Bowen's imagining of both Max and Leopold is piercingly apparent in this climactic episode. There is the sudden intrusion of a large, quasi-metaphysical question, as if from the narrative itself, 'Where are we going now?'; and there is the comparably metaphysical figuration of the 'soul stand[ing] still like a refugee, clutching all it has got, asking: "I am where?" ': 'refugee' is, of course, a word prominent in the discourse of the day and, as we shall see, prominent also in *The Death of the Heart*. There is also the utterly unanticipated desire of Ray himself, now a successful cosmopolitan businessman, to become like one of the tramps he sees lying on the concourse of the Gare de Lyon. This has a sudden jaded relish for inertia which implies a critique of the restless and perhaps pointless activity of the time, inherent in the Parisian station itself: 'The tramp inside Ray's clothes wanted to lie down here, put his cheek in his rolled coat, let trains keep on crashing out to Spain, Switzerland, Italy, let Paris wash like the sea at the foot of the ramp (237)'. Rather than by analysis or reflection, Bowen's historical imagination works through such unpredictable disjunctions, obliquities, and foreshadowings, through what Valentine Cunningham calls, accurately, moments of 'unnerving threshold clairvoyance'.[14] They are to be valued as highly as anything else in her.

VI

We can read out of *The House in Paris*, then, a mordantly undeceived view of history, whose apparent coldness may well be self-protective, a shield against emotional stress or even disintegration, a damming-up of

[14] Valentine Cunningham, *British Writers of the Thirties* (Oxford: Oxford University Press, 1988), 365.

feeling where the greater danger would be the giving way to it, a strat-egy—in other words—of survival. And this may be the most profound reason for the novel's linking of an Irish with a French setting. The Ireland Karen visits at the opening of Part II is the genteel Ireland of the post-revolutionary settlement in which, unforeseeably, the new state has generously compensated Irish landowners for the loss of their properties during the 1920s: Rushbrook, above Queenstown, now renamed Cobh, harbour, just outside Cork, is where Karen's aunt and her husband stay on in some tranquillity and economic ease, having exchanged their destroyed house Montebello for the comfortable villa, Mount Iris. In this setting of an Ireland that 'did not look like a coun-try subject to racking change' (72), Karen nevertheless looks forward to 'the Revolution': 'I wish the Revolution would come soon; I should like to start fresh while I am still young, with everything that I had to depend on gone . . . I feel it's time something happened' (86)—even though she will, of course, work against it, she says 'rather grandly'. That phrase ironizes her callowness; but Karen's sexual behaviour is congruent with such a politics, and genuinely 'revolutionary'. But Karen also thinks that 'People must hope so much when they tear streets up and fight at barricades. But, whoever wins, the streets are laid again and the trams start running again. One hopes too much of destroying things. If revolutions do not fail, they fail you' (152); and Elizabeth Bowen is unillusioned enough as a writer to show us the ways in which Karen's private revolution fails her too: and the failure focuses on the figure of Ray.

Karen rejects Ray for Max partly because Ray is her family's choice for her. She objects to her mother's 'well-lit explanation of people', favouring the 'blur' of modern photography, its 'effort to apprehend'; and, of course, Ray is, in his very name, well-lit, a ray of light. But he has shadings which Karen does not suspect. He does marry her, despite her 'ruin', although she has assumed that he will not, and although it costs him his chosen career; and he behaves unpredictably too in the decision he makes about Leopold, whereas Karen, in the novel's most devastating irony, now, in 'The Present', wants 'most of all to live like her mother' (218). She has disapproved of Ray's timidity and calcula-tion, his 'liking for going over things carefully twice' (78), but his final decision is the product of instinct, impulse, and the certainty that he is right, that Karen's abandonment of Leopold must be ended. In this, he steps so far out of Karen's characterization of him as to entertain a willingness to break the law: since, to take Leopold away from his adoptive parents without their permission would entail precisely that, even if the novel is a little hazy on the exact legal implications of his act. Ray's undauntedness in the face of the accumulated debts and deficits of the past makes possible a new arrangement for the future, the one Leopold needs to become whole, and the one Ray knows Karen needs too, although she does not yet know it herself. Ray thereby becomes the potential liberation of the past into a future, the new orientation that is a contemporaneity beyond the mores of the Michaelises.

This may be a future in which words like 'ruin' will no longer be used of women, and in which mothers and sons will be able to speak to one another in something at least approximating the ideal of Karen's address to Leopold, which is still, in the novel's historical moment, possible only on the plane of Heaven or art. The characterization of Ray must also give us pause in any decision that Elizabeth Bowen is politically an essentially conservative novelist: his responsibility is exercised by the breaking of social constraint and taboo, by an act of transgression. No blood relation of Leopold's, he becomes with his decision a kind of surrogate male mother for the child, acting for him in a way Karen is herself incapable of doing. Indeed, Leopold's intake of breath at the Gare de Lyon may be read as a figurative rebirth, in which the womb is now Ray's, not Karen's: 'No, he was not cold; he had been someone drawing a first breath' (238). In such strange revisions of convention and gender Elizabeth Bowen's extraordinarily profound meditations on the relations between mother and child fetch up in *The House in Paris*.

VII

The old forms of these relations may be about to undergo a sea change, and Leopold's relationship with Karen and Ray may be a pre-figuring emblem for this; but *The House in Paris* balances any such uplifting cadence with the desperation of Naomi's return to the confinement and violation of her own relationship with Mme Fisher. The novel prominently and persistently includes an imagery of human hands touching and separating, notably, as we have seen, in the empathetic encounter between Leopold and Henrietta, but notably too in the erotic encounter between Karen and Max when they first make clear their feelings for each other in a Twickenham garden, where the word 'hand' is almost mesmerically repeated within the agonizingly slow rhythm and assonances of the passage:

Max put his hand on Karen's, pressing it into the grass. Their unexploring, consenting touch lasted; they did not look at each other or their hands. When their hands had drawn slowly apart, they both watched the flattened grass beginning to spring up, again, blade by blade.   (120)

The melancholy of this resides in the fact that what they are watching, when they do watch, is their own absence from the physical action which the grass now makes as a consequence of their consenting touch, the first mobilization of sexual desire; and when subsequently the lovers have consentingly touched much further, Karen conceives of Leopold, at the moment of his conception, as 'the mark our hands did not leave on the grass' (153), the inscription of their signature on the absent space.

  Now, however, as the novel nears its end, and Naomi takes her leave of Leopold, an imagery of hands figures again, in the context of what is to be, for her, a further and probably permanent absence. The gesture is, again, melancholy; and it is also piercing, even desolating. Its inscription of human desire, loss, tenderness, and generosity is Elizabeth Bowen at her finest as a poetic novelist. The deeply damaged woman, and daughter, approaches the damaged son who is, as I have said, the incarnation of the damage done to her:

When Leopold walked into view, politely holding his hand out, she started and looked down at him. Instead of shaking hands or bending down to kiss him, she put out her right hand gently to touch his face. The act seemed so natural that he stood with his face up, as though her expected fingers were so much rain. Her touch passed delicately across his forehead, down the line of one cheek. She looked into his eyes that were still to see so much, and at his lips, consideringly and gently, as though she could be no enemy of anything they could say.   (231)

5

Motherless Child:
The Death of the Heart (1938)

I REFUGEES

The Death of the Heart was published only three years after *The House in Paris* and, while in some ways thematically related to it, it is formally entirely distinct from it. Where the mode of the earlier book is purely that of the tragic-melodramatic, sustaining itself at a constant level of fraught emotional epiphany, the predominant, although not the only, mode of the latter is the comic-satirical. Its social settings in upper-middle-class Regent's Park London and in the version of Hythe which Bowen calls here, as elsewhere in her work, Seale-on-Sea, are the vehicles of an analysis of England in the 1930s which has affinities with the work of Evelyn Waugh, Henry Green, and even D. H. Lawrence. The analysis most often remains at the level of the inexplicit, carried by character, psychology, and incident, but it rises to the explicit too in the character of Thomas Quayne, who sometimes acts almost as chorus: he is the upper-middle-class Englishman, whose money nevertheless comes from the new industry of advertising, profoundly conscious of social discontinuity, keeping up the game even as he realizes that the game is up.[1] His jaded lugubriousness is a comically understated but also chilling study in a 1930s malaise of privileged paralysis, expressed nevertheless in sometimes witty near-aphorism: 'You can't get up any pace when you feel right at the edge' (32); 'We are minor in everything but our passions' (37); 'I suppose there is nothing so disintegrating as competitiveness and funk, and that's what we all feel' (97); 'The most we can hope is to go on getting away with it till the others get it away

---

[1] The powerful sense in Bowen's work of a finger very firmly taking the pulse of the period is sometimes reinforced by the jobs people do as a consequence of 1930s mobility and leisure: advertising in this novel, and Anna Quayne's (failed) attempt at a home decoration business; the travel agency in *To The North*.

from us.' (94) Notably, too, in the character of Matchett, Bowen now also includes, as Green does in some of his work, the world of the working-class servant; and Matchett is in many ways made to carry the ethical weight of what is, as its melancholy title dramatizes, an ethically instructive novel.

Yet, for all its treatment of surface, its taking of the temperature of its time, it also lurches, or shelves, into depths of character and psychology which are products of impulses comparable to those at work in *The House in Paris*. These are primarily to do with its heroine, the orphaned, 16-year-old Portia Quayne, and her relationships with her guardians (Thomas, her elder half-brother, and his wife, Anna); her desultory suitor, Eddie (who is never dignified with a surname); the servant, Matchett (who is never honoured with a forename); and the 'family friend', Major Brutt, whose military rank does duty for a forename ('In so far as the Quaynes were a family, Major Brutt was the family friend' (13)). The crucial first moment when the slippage from social satire to interior psychology occurs concerns Portia's memory of her recently dead mother, Irene. Before this we have learned that Thomas and Anna are keeping Portia, the daughter of Thomas's father's adulterous relationship with Irene, on the merest sufferance, under the duress of the dying father's request that they house her for a year in their Regent's Park home before sending her on to what they call 'some aunt . . . abroad'. We already know that Anna loathes Portia and we also know, from the novel's brilliantly realized opening scene between Anna and her friend the novelist St Quentin Miller, that Anna has been reading Portia's diary, in which she is herself extensively disparaged: this is to become the motif central to the design of the plot of *The Death of the Heart*. Anna is of course to be judged adversely for this, as she is also for her snobbishly contemptuous attitude to Portia's mother —'a scrap of a widow, ever so plucky, just back from China, with damp little hands, a husky voice, and defective little tear ducts that gave her eyes always rather a swimmy look' (17)— where the repeated 'little' is the emphatic index of class condescension. However, in one of the strengths of Bowen's always ambivalent characterization, Anna is also highly intelligent and witty, and our judgement is complicated by the delight we take—as St Quentin, who knows she is performing for him, does—in the brilliant bravura of her invective.

To say that our reactions are further complicated by the passage in which Portia remembers Irene is understatement. Portia has been telling Thomas, a little too brightly, about her economically straitened life with her mother, after her father's death, in various cheap European hotels. Bowen's first novel was called *The Hotel*, and is exclusively set in one, and *The Death of the Heart* ends in another; and Portia's exclusively hotel existence as a child makes her the paradigm of a character constant in Bowen, the restless or rootless transient. She may even be considered an incarnation of Joseph Conrad's view of modernity, in the opening sentence of *Victory*, as 'the age in which we are camped like bewildered travellers in a garish unrestful hotel'. In this scene Portia, as usual, is not receiving much of Thomas's attention, and when he says, glibly, that she must 'miss all of that', she withdraws into an 'overcome silence' in which, he realizes, she no longer sees him:

What she did see was the *pension* on the crag in Switzerland, that had been wrapped in rain the whole afternoon. Swiss summer rain is dark, and makes a tent for the mind. At the foot of the precipice, beyond the paling, the lake made black wounds in the white mist. Precarious high-upness had been an element in their life up there, which had been the end of their life together. That night they came back from Lucerne on the late steamer, they had looked up, seen the village lights at star-level through the rain, and felt that that was their dear home. They went up, arm in arm in the dark, up the steep zigzag, pressing each other's elbows, hearing the night rain sough down through the pines: they were not frightened at all. They always stayed in places before the season, when the funicular was not working yet. All the other people in the *pension* had been German or Swiss: it was a wooden building with fretwork balconies. Their room, though it was a back room facing into the pinewoods, had a balcony; they would run away from the salon and spend the long wet afternoons there. They would lie down covered with coats, leaving the window open, smelling the wet woodwork, hearing the gutters run. Turn abouts, they would read to each other the Tauchnitz novels they had bought in Lucerne. Things for tea, the little stove, and a bottle of violet methylated spirits stood on the wobbly commode between their beds, and at four o'clock Portia would make tea. They ate, in alternate mouthfuls, block chocolate and *brioches*. Postcards they liked, and Irene's and Portia's sketches were pinned to the pine walls; stockings they had just washed would be exposed to dry on the radiator, although the heating was off. Sometimes they heard a cow bell in the thick distance, or people talking German in the room next door. Between five and six the rain quite often stopped, wet light crept down the trunks of the pines. Then they rolled off their beds, put their shoes on, and walked down the village street to the viewpoint over the lake. Through torn mist they would watch the six o'clock steamer chuff round the cliff and pull in at the pier. Or they would attempt to read the names on the big still shut hotels on the heights opposite. They looked at the high chalets stuck on brackets of grass—they often used to wish they had field-glasses, but Mr Quayne's field-glasses had been sent home to Thomas. On the

way home they met the cows being driven down through the village—kind
cows, damp, stumbling, plagued by their own bells. Or the Angelus coming
muffled across the plateau would make Irene sigh, for once she had loved
church. To the little Catholic church they had sometimes guiltily been, afraid
of doing the wrong thing, feeling they stole grace. When they left that high-up
village, when they left for ever, the big hotels were just being thrown open, the
funicular would begin in another day. They drove down in a fly, down the
familiar zigzag, Irene moaning and clutching Portia's hand. Portia could not
weep at leaving the village, because her mother was in such pain. But she used
to think of it while she waited at the Lucerne clinic, where Irene had the
operation and died: she died at six in the evening, which had always been their
happiest hour.

A whir from Thomas's clock—it was just going to strike six. Six, but not six
in June. At this hour, the plateau must be in snow, and but for the snow dark,
with lights behind shutters, perhaps a light in the church. Thomas sits so fallen-
in, waiting for Anna, that his clock makes the only sound in his room. But our
street must be completely silent with snow, and there must be snow on our balcony. (34–5)

The now orphaned Portia is here evoking a life 'precarious' in more
than just its topographical altitude, since her father is already dead, and
her mother dies; and the passage, with its black wounds, its torn mist,
its familiar zigzag, its muffled Angelus and its stolen grace, is a *paysage
moralisé*. But against precariousness Portia and Irene make a lovingly
communal culture from a nowhere, comfort from discomfort, a 'dear
home' out of a temporary, foreign, dingy, ill-heated, thin-walled, out-
of-season room; and the portrayal of mother and daughter 'arm in arm
in the dark' casts its harshly judgmental light back on the cruelty of
Anna's description of Irene's 'damp little hands' and the grubby lubricity of her thoughts elsewhere in the novel about Irene's affair. Anna
objects to Portia's 'animal' inability to keep her room tidy, and at school
she is mocked for her 'hotel habit'. In this passage, however, we see her
more than capable of making a loving existence, a kind of eager, almost
animally instinctual shelter out of physical togetherness, which is a 'tent
for the mind' too, and one under which the withdrawn Portia clearly
still acutely misses sheltering. Elsewhere, Portia and Irene are described
sleeping in the same bed, 'overcoming, as far as might be, the separation
of birth'; but there is no overcoming, of course, the separation of death.
The authority invested in Portia by this sense, very early in the novel, of
her experience of deep suffering, leads us to view her subsequently as
moral arbiter as well as suffering victim: and, like Leopold in *The
House in Paris*, she is ultimately the victim who refuses the role.

The plot of *The Death of the Heart* is a distant relative of James's in *What Maisie Knew*, and concerns Portia's sentimental education, as she acquires knowledge of various kinds of heartlessness from Anna and Thomas, St Quentin, Eddie, and the Holcombes in Seale, to whom she is farmed out while Thomas and Anna holiday in Capri. At various points in this plot Portia weeps, and the image of the homeless, weeping child is as desolating here as it is in *The House in Paris*—perhaps in some ways even more so, since Portia is older than Leopold and Henrietta. We never know Maisie's age in James's novel: although we assume that she gets a lot older as the narrative progresses, we can never be sure what she should know, or when she should know it, and the uncertainty makes for a profound ethical insecurity on the reader's part. The fact of Portia's age, 16, is crucial to *The Death of the Heart*: it is an ambivalent age and an age of ambivalence, an awkward age (although Nanda in James's novel *The Awkward Age* is, in fact, 18). It is the age of consent, but Portia nevertheless frequently appears younger; and, partly as a consequence of her upbringing, she is naively unformed and immature. She is the Bowen child on the verge of adolescence, the child as *ingénue*. This is clear throughout in Portia's relationship with Eddie, but it becomes particularly acute at the novel's climax, when, as the consequence of what she regards as her betrayal by Eddie and by the Quaynes, she absconds from the house in Windsor Terrace and attempts to take refuge with Major Brutt in his hotel, the Karachi, in Kensington. Portia therefore ends in the novel where we are told she began: in yet one more poky, cheap, and, of course, temporary hotel room. And it is much to the point of the novel's historical contingencies, as the Pakistani name of Brutt's hotel insinuates, that both Brutt, recently returned from Malaysia, and Irene, the returnee from China, are refugees of a kind from the last phase of the British Empire. In the sad constriction of his hotel room, Brutt explicitly figures Portia too as a refugee:

Unhappy on his bed, in this temporary little stale room, Portia seemed to belong nowhere, not even here. Stripped of that pleasant home that had seemed part of her figure, stripped too of his own wishes and hopes, she looked at once harsh and beaten, a refugee—frightening, rebuffing all pity that has fear at the root. (293)

In various ways *The Death of the Heart* rhymes Brutt with Portia as an outsider, and, in fact, in this episode Portia makes the relation explicit when she disabuses him of his view of the Quaynes' opinion of

him: 'You are the other person that Anna laughs at . . . You and I are
the same' (288). Almost a walking entropy, a 'born third', Brutt is a
decorated survivor of the First World War, a superfluous man: 'Makes
of men date, like makes of cars. Major Brutt was a 1914–18 model:
there was now no market for that make' (90). It is Brutt's intense solitude that draws him to the Quaynes; but it is his tender solicitude for,
and generosity to, Portia that draws her to him when she has no one
else to turn to. In doing so, she is, as Brutt realizes perfectly well, yet
once more putting herself at risk. *The Death of the Heart* makes this
clear even as it explicitly attempts to make it clear that there is no risk.
Anna knows Brutt only through one long-ago contact, when he spent
an evening with her and her then-boyfriend, Robert Pidgeon, and she
has newly encountered him only accidentally and recently. Brutt is said
to keep returning to Windsor Terrace partly because of Portia, 'that
dear little kid', whom he regards with 'fervent, tender, quite sexless
desire' (86). Yet she is also called a 'dear little kid' by both Eddie and
by a would-be seducer in Seale, and she recognizes and objects to the
condescension, with its covertly erotic insinuations. And, although we
are told that Brutt's 'desire' for Portia is 'sexless', we also know that his
loneliness has its sexual dimension, since we at one point discover him
a long way from the Regent's Park drawing-room while he 'hesitates
round the West End about midnight—not wanting to buy a girl, not
wanting to drink alone, not wanting to go back to Kensington, hoping
something may happen' (45).

He does nevertheless acquit himself well when something does happen, when Portia embarrasses him by turning up at his hotel. When, at
her insistence, they move from the hotel's foyer to his tiny, cheap-rate,
attic room, he is conscious only that he must do the right thing, and
contact Thomas and Anna. However, this does not prevent the scene
from having its decidely sexual tenor. Portia, after sitting on the bed,
stands up to approach him sitting down:

Deliberately, with her lips tight shut, she got off the bed to come and stand
by him—so that, she standing, he sitting, she could tower up at least a little
way. She looked him all over, as though she meant to tug at him, to jerk him
awake, and was only not certain where to catch hold of him. Her arms stayed
at her sides, but looked rigid, at every moment, with their intention to move
in unfeeling desperation. She was not able, or else did not wish, to inform
herself with pleading grace; her sexlessness made her deliver a stern summons:
he felt her knocking through him like another heart outside his own ribs.
(295)

The prose here is, to some degree, opaque—miming, I think, the opacity of Portia's feeling, which is tentative, exploratory, undecided, but still intensely physical. But the word 'sexlessness' returns to the word in which Brutt has formulated his desire for Portia, reminding us of sex even as it apparently wishes to negate the possibility; and the sexual connotations of the word 'jerk', given its close proximity to the word 'rigid', are disturbingly activated in such a context. The final richly metaphoric statement of Brutt's feeling , which echoes the empathetic physical posture adopted by Henrietta and Leopold in *The House in Paris*, would seem, outside this context, an exact evocation of being riveted by sexual desire, not least because literalizing the metaphor would place in the closest possible physical proximity her heart and his ribs, as they might be placed in the act of love.

Then—not out of nowhere, exactly—Portia proposes marriage, yearningly opposing to the lonely transience of their mutual existences the fragility of the desired repose: 'I could do things for you: we could have a home; we would not have to live in a hotel' (295). And she lies under his eiderdown on his bed. This is a register of her abjection, of her desire, in the crisis of her life, for self-obliteration; but it inevitably has a sexual connotation too, and it is clear that Brutt is tempted, even as he turns a marriage into a mirage:

The preposterous happy mirage of something one does not even for one moment desire must not be allowed to last. Had nothing in Major Brutt responded to it he would have gone on being gentle, purely sorry for her—As it was, he got up briskly, and not only got up but put back his chair where it came from, flat with some inches of wall, to show that this conversation was closed for good. And the effort this cost him, the final end of something, made his firm action seem more callous than sad.   (296)

It is the 'final end'—that emphatically double *finis*—not only because, after this, he can, of course, never see Portia again, but also because his knowledge of Thomas's and Anna's contempt for him makes this also the end of his relationship with Windsor Terrace, which has been 'the clearing-house for his dreams', with its entirely illusory 'holy family' (88). There is a real sense, therefore, in which *The Death of the Heart* is more the tragedy of Major Brutt than it is that of Portia—since she, after all, may eventually find a home, whereas Brutt will be forever excluded; and all the indications are, in this 1930s novel acutely sensitive to the economic situations of its characters, that he is probably on the way to something like destitution.

This concluding episode brings to prominence, then, what has to a large extent been occluded, but which is nevertheless permanently present in the novel: Portia's sexuality. That she is far from 'sexless', as the text tells us, twice, Major Brutt's reaction proves; that she is at risk his reaction also proves, since his choosing to behave well inevitably raises the possibility that he might behave otherwise: desire is inchoate and sometimes uncontrollable, as *The House in Paris* has already shown us very well indeed; and provocation, in a tiny, enclosed space, can easily induce behaviour out of character, as numerous novels of sexual relations prove. This element of *The Death of the Heart* is glossed by what James Kincaid says in his book *Child-Loving: The Erotic Child and Victorian Culture*: that, 'Making the child's sexuality a central problem, we have married them [that is, the child and sexuality], even when we deny that they are on speaking terms.'[2] In Portia they are indeed on speaking terms; and if the novel's plot looks back to *What Maisie Knew*, it also makes us read James with a difference: since—and it is the one aspect of that great novel which may leave the reader incredulous—Maisie, whatever she knows, never herself seems at risk. Portia does: and *The Death of the Heart* may even seem to lean forward towards another novel in which a girl-child is devastatingly damaged. In Vladimir Nabokov's *Lolita* more than the heart has died: Dolores Haze, whose childhood has been taken away from her by her sexual predator, Humbert Humbert, herself dies in childbirth.

This novel of Elizabeth Bowen's also describes a childhood being taken away; and it is by no means certain, in this exceptionally open-ended novel, that Portia's decision to pose a test for Thomas and Anna before she will agree to return to them will result in any permanent change in her circumstances. The test itself, however, is the register of her outraged refusal to put up with her lot; and, if *The Death of the Heart* is intertextual with *What Maisie Knew*, here surely is one way in which Bowen advances beyond James in psychological penetration, since it has seemed to many readers of James's novel that Maisie's lack of anger, and her apparently resilient lack of any damage, as a consequence of her unspeakable upbringing—which includes, as Portia's does not, physical abuse—is incredible. 'Even his children are, in their fineness, mature', says Bowen herself, discussing what she calls his 'promotions in age'.[3] I read *The Death of the Heart*, then, as occupying a

[2] James Kincaid, *Child-Loving: The Erotic Child and Victorian Culture* (London: Routledge, 1992), 183.

[3] Elizabeth Bowen, *English Novelists* (London: William Collins, 1942), 42.

point on the trajectory between *What Maisie Knew* and *Lolita*: it is the novel of the child, or young adolescent, at risk of too great a knowledge of adult heartlessness, and it also brings significantly into range, as *What Maisie Knew* does not, the specifically sexual risk. For, what if Major Brutt had been Humbert Humbert? What if Major Brutt had been a brute?

II SURVIVOR

But *The Death of the Heart* is not *Lolita*; and the essential movement of the novel's plot is a bathetic or anti-climactic one, in which dangerous possibilities are opened only to be foreclosed. Major Brutt is not Humbert Humbert, and we are led to believe that, after the final page, he will hand Portia over to Matchett, who has been sent to fetch her as a consequence of his telephone call to the Quaynes. Eddie is duplicitous and an apparently expert seducer, but he does not seduce Portia, although he has easy opportunities in scenes during which we are led to anticipate it: in a deserted boarding house; in woodland; in his flat. And neither does anything sexual, apart from flirtation, happen to Portia with the Heccombe crowd in Seale, although it might well have done. Similarly, the titles of the novel's three parts have a certain bathos, since even though what figures in them is certainly moral corruption, this lacks the metaphysical dimension suggested by 'The World', 'The Flesh', and 'The Devil'. Nevertheless, the bathos is also a means of ethical judgement, subtly managed, in which, in particular, Eddie and Anna are closely scrutinized, and in which Matchett, the servant, joins Major Brutt as an ethical counterweight. The plot, we might say, is like one of the jigsaw puzzles which Brutt has given Portia and which we frequently see her doing, but never see her finishing, since the plot is the callow, naïve, or innocent Portia's opportunity to puzzle out the way this world actually works. Like the jigsaw, too, the plot suggestively refuses closure, when Portia puts the Quaynes to the test. They must find a way of behaving well to her finally—and only she will judge its merits—as the price of her agreeing to return; but we never actually see this judgement being made. In her insistence, Portia is as adamant and heroically single-minded as Leopold in his demand that he see his mother in *The House in Paris*; and the final point of Portia's sentimetal education in the novel is this newly acquired purposiveness and refusal of instrumentality. In the end, her 'startling authority', which is the authority of despair, makes her 'ruthless as a goddess' (290). And the agency of judgement, notably of Eddie and Anna, is Portia's sexuality.

The subtlety of Bowen's characterization of Eddie lies in his lack of self-knowledge. Egotistical, self-flatteringly Byronic, self-regardingly petulant, and extremely attractive to both Anna and Portia—as, we are given to understand, to many other women, since his life is busy with adventure and intrigue—he is nevertheless not at all a conventional seducer. 'The brilliant child of an obscure home', his social perform-ances in Windsor Terrace are motivated by knowing himself the recip-ient of charity, and resenting it, and knowing also that what is being bought is a *nostalgie de la boue*, his 'proletarian, animal, quick grace' (62), his lithely Lawrentian sexual presence in the drawing rooms of Regent's Park. His inexplicit, ambiguous relationship with Anna, whom he has once tried to seduce, makes him both her 'troubadour', although one who must sing for his supper, and, when she organizes a job for him in Thomas's firm, 'bought goods, with "Quayne and Merrett" pasted across his back' (70). Money matters in *The Death of the Heart*, as it does, realistically, elsewhere in Bowen, too: she is as alertly sensitive to, and unsentimental about, the economic bases of relationships as Jane Austen and Henry James; and Eddie, like Portia, has no money.[4] Anna's privileged incomprehension of the difference this makes is slyly conveyed in her sudden silences and disengagements, and Eddie has to insist, rebukingly, on his alternative knowledge. When Anna says, 'To be right or wrong with people is the important thing', Eddie responds, 'I expect it would be if you had got money' (69). Portia, as the consequence of her hotel upbringing, also knows that 'wherever anyone is they are costing someone something, and that the cost must be met' (189). The sharp knowledge of the economic basis of morality is one of the several intermittencies of self-knowledge which Eddie does display in the novel, but elsewhere he is a remarkable demonstration of self-opacity. The combination is lethal to the 16-year-old Portia, since the instability of Eddie's class position makes him, in one sense, like her, an outsider to the world of Windsor

---

[4] Czeslaw Milosz would appreciate this. 'Novelists', he writes, 'who once were very concerned with the so-called struggle for existence, have escaped into the regions of deep inner experience, as if it is obvious that their characters have somewhere to live and food to eat, but I find such prose, where no mention is made even of money, to be suspect, and I am grateful to my life experiences for my skepticism.' See *To Begin Where I Am: Selected Essays,* ed. and with an introduction by Bogdana Carpenter and Madeline G. Levine (New York: Farrar, Straus and Giroux, 2001), 439. In Bowen the surface of economic necessity combines with the depth of 'inner experience'.

Terrace, tolerated but never necessary: so there is the attraction of similarity. But Eddie's age, 24, and his apparently large sexual experience, place him at a serious remove from the much younger and utterly inexperienced Portia. Her age is important here also, of course, so that the potential violation of her inexperience is always an issue, and their dialogues are masterpieces of mismatching degrees of sophistication.

Inevitably, then, we ask what Eddie is doing with Portia, how far his relationship with her is a game played with Anna, or just a game of his own. The point is, I think, that Eddie genuinely doesn't know himself, even though he readily makes himself available to Portia's fantasy conception of him. Her baffled loneliness and longing can, she thinks, be filled by him—'You make me not alone' (108), she says, pathetically—but he is, in fact, a moral void filled with oscillating forms of self-love, self-doubt, and self-contempt, all of which he turns into an endlessly nervous self-performance and self-display. So Portia is 'disturbed, and at the same time exhilarated, like a young tree tugged all ways in a vortex of wind' (105). But if Eddie's violation of Portia is not a sexual one, it is a violation none the less, when, in the crucial moment of their relationship, he betrays her trust during her time in Seale-on-Sea.

Seale is one of those marginal, maritime locations so significant in Bowen, where the action of her novels moves, as it were, into another register; and it may recall Katherine Mansfield's 'summer colony' in her story 'At the Bay' (1921).[5] Portia is summarily despatched there because Anna and Thomas want a holiday in Capri without her, and she is to stay with 'a Mrs Heccombe', who, as 'a Miss Yardes', was once Anna's governess: the indefinites seem constitutive not only of her virtually invisible social status but of her altogether indefinite or incapable personality. Mrs Heccombe's house, Waikiki, where she lives with her stepchildren, Dickie and Daphne, is a kind of mirror image of Windsor Terrace: not cruelly cold as that is, and even, indeed, too warm in its constant chaotic flurry of flirtatious parties, cinema trips, walks, sports, and social drinking, but still, neverthless, a house that is not a home for Portia. This section of the novel has a more than usually broad kind of satire for Bowen, in which the coarseness of Waikiki life commands an appropriately unfastidious style. The result is a kind of buoyantly zestful mockery not so much of vulgarity as of the almost

---

[5] Mansfield was very important to Bowen, and she writes about her at length—although, peculiarly, not at her best—in an essay of 1956, 'A Living Writer: Katherine Mansfield', reprinted in *The Mulberry Tree: Writings of Elizabeth Bowen*, selected and introduced by Hermione Lee (London: Virago Press, 1986), 69–85.

entire absence of any interior life: 'when these young people stopped doing what they were doing they stopped all through, like clocks' (177).

Portia is also moving forward from her initially intense grief for her mother, but this serves only to heighten the sense that she has no more valuable a maternal representative in the careless, imprudent, and cowardly Mrs Heccombe than she has in Anna. So Eddie is allowed to visit Portia at Seale and to stay with the Heccombes, although Mrs Heccombe feels uneasy when she actually meets him: it 'struck into her heart its first misgiving for years—a misgiving not about Portia but about Anna' (189), and it is a misgiving connected, as we shall see, with Anna's early, definitive, affair with Robert Pidgeon. The morally opaque Mrs Heccombe is here given a moment of insight; and Eddie's betrayal of Portia occurs during a visit to the cinema, where, while a group of Heccombes and friends sit in a row, Portia sees, in the 'jumping light' of a cigarette lighter, Eddie holding Daphne's hand.[6] The harshness of its illumination of Eddie's deceit is the lurid light in which the rest of the novel is bathed; and in this light Portia is the agent of a condemnation of Seale life just as she is of Windsor Terrace. She challenges Daphne out of a profoundly hurt inexperience, but Daphne assumes, in her cynicism, that Portia intends only sarcasm: 'there was a pause in which slowly diluted Portia's appalling remark. In that pause, the civilization of Waikiki seemed to rock on its base (203)'. Portia is, in her quietly naïve way, a rocker of civilizations which do not, of course, deserve to be saved. In this sense, Portia's innocence has, indeed, its own victims; but some criticism of the novel makes rather too much of this, in my view. Despite some interpretative directions from the narrative voice itself, damage in the plot of *The Death of the Heart* seems to me to be very centrally done to Portia, not by her.

Given that Eddie is presented in the cinema scene almost as a moral vacuum, he subsequently behaves far better in explaining himself, and not explaining himself away, to Portia. There is a stratum of his being at which he is genuinely capable of better, and here, unpredictably, he manifests it. Alone in woodland with Portia, he tells her, 'I've been as true to you as I've got it in me to be' (214–15). This is desolating for her, but we believe it of Eddie. The explanation for tawdry human behaviour is accompanied by a moment of extreme tenderness in which

---

[6] This is one of the several places in Bowen's work where not only is the cinema taken as setting but where narrative style itself is influenced by cinematic technique, as in the work of those other novelists writing in the 1930s, Evelyn Waugh, Henry Green, and Graham Greene.

Portia suddenly seems like a lost or hunted woodland animal, since a 'form' is also the home of a hare:

Portia, lying in her form in the grass, looked at the crushed place where he had lain by her—then, turning her head the other way, detached two or three violets which, reaching out, she picked. She held them over her head and looked at the light through them.   (213–14)

Although Eddie responds to the moment by calling her Primavera, he later loses the violets from his buttonhole in a drunken incident. We may find this lurch from the mythical into the reductively mundane a further beat in that rhythm of bathos which is the ground of the novel; and, although Portia goes briefly to Eddie towards the end of the book, on horrifiedly discovering that Anna reads her diaries, this is effectively the end of their relationship. What we remember of Seale is, finally, Eddie's drunken sobbing and Portia's newly quickened and wise knowledge that 'Someone sobbing like that must not be gone near' (222). And what we recognize in this is someone now on the verge of something worse than the lack of self-knowledge: disintegration. What we are beginning to realize is that Portia, not Eddie, will be the survivor of this relationship, and that Eddie may well end up as hopelessly destitute as Major Brutt appears on the way to becoming.

III DOUBLES

Why does Anna behave so badly to Portia? This is not a question Portia herself ever asks: her resignation is as desolately absolute as Maisie's in *What Maisie Knew* when she says 'Mamma doesn't care for me. Not really': 'Child as she was, her little long history was in the words; and it was as impossible to contradict her as if she had been venerable.'[7] But we, as readers, do ask the question; and the novel answers it, I think, in a way that uncovers the permanent adult consequences of suffering exactly the kinds of experience in adolescence from which Anna is doing nothing to save Portia.

Anna's affair with Pidgeon in her early youth has been disastrous. We learn few details of it, but its intensity is apparent in Anna's constant preoccupation with it even now, much later in life; in her sudden vividly erotic memory of his war-wounded body; in the intimation the

---

[7] Henry James, *What Maisie Knew* (1897; London: Penguin, ed. with an introduction and notes by Paul Theroux with additional notes by Patricia Crick, 1985), 86.

novel gives us of some kind of possibly sadistic perversity in him; and in an eventual outburst of hurt and disgust to Major Brutt ('He thought nothing of me at all' (263)). At her first meeting with Brutt, during a discussion of Pidgeon, Anna feels Portia looking at her:

Had the agitation she felt throughout her body sent out an aura with a quivering edge, Portia's eyes might be said to explore this line of quiver, round and along Anna's reclining form. Anna felt bound up with her fear, her secret, by that enwrapping look of Portia's: she felt mummified.

'Portia', we hear, 'had learnt one dare never look for long. She had those eyes that seem to be welcome nowhere, that learn shyness from the alarm they precipitate' (49). The alarm precipitated in Anna by Portia's female gaze here is the fear that her most interior life—she calls the period of Pidgeon her 'closed years'—has been instinctively recognized; and the word 'mummified' offers a cruel, cutting-both-ways pun, since Anna should, of course, be acting as Portia's surrogate mother, should be her 'mummy', but, in fact, cannot bear even to catch her eye.

And indeed the disaster of her relationship with Pidgeon has led to her subsequent emotional mummification, since although she is passionately loved by Thomas she cannot return his love: the one bedroom scene between them in the novel finds them 'friendly unfriendly' and leaves him in a state of intense marital loneliness.[8] Eddie is, we are given to understand, one in a series of intimacies, rather than sexual liaisons, of Anna's, which Thomas tolerates. She feels known and judged by Portia; Portia is the revelation to her of her own self-doubt. She has failed in this relationship with Pidgeon; she has also failed to have children of her own, although she wants them (she has had two miscarriages); and she has failed in a career she initiated. It is as if Portia is the return to Anna of these repressed failures: which is why she is drawn to her as well as repelled by her, and why, in that act of odious intrusion and voyeurism, she reads the diary. Anna succumbs to the temptation to attempt to destroy in Portia—by inertia rather than direct action—the purity she knows she has herself lost: it is as though she can prove Portia's fragility only by crushing her. This is, in fact, the impulse which, in more extreme forms, becomes paedophilia or child abuse: so, if I want to place *The Death of the Heart* on an arc curving

---

[8] Hermione Lee describes the Quaynes' relationship as 'one of the great studies of an inhibited English marriage, to be set beside the Goulds in *Nostromo*, the Brookenhams in *The Awkward Age*, or the Ashburnhams in *The Good Soldier*'. See *Elizabeth Bowen* (1981; rev. edn., London: Vintage, 1999), 111.

from *What Maisie Knew* to *Lolita*, it is largely because of Anna in actuality as well as Major Brutt in potentiality. That the highly intelligent Anna knows all of this herself is apparent when she says of Portia that 'Everything she does to me is unconscious: if it were conscious it would not hurt' (246). But this is the kind of intelligently penetrating self-knowledge which lacerates even more; it is a deeper wound rather than the beginning of a cure.

That Anna may in a sense be doubled with Portia, that we may read her as what Portia, unprotected from men who may not share what is, in the end, Eddie's sexual scruple, may well become, is intimated too by a further crucial event during Portia's time at Seale. She gazes here at a portrait of Anna in her childhood made by Mrs Heccombe: 'a pastel drawing of Anna, Anna aged about twelve, holding a kitten, her long soft hair tied up in two satin bows' (207). Mrs Heccombe had, in fact, been a general factotum and companion rather than a governess to Anna, since her mother died when Anna was even younger than Portia: so Anna too has been a motherless child. In fact, Anna, we learn, used to call Mrs Heccombe 'poor Miss Taylor', which is, although *The Death of the Heart* does not explicitly say so, what Jane Austen's Mr Woodhouse calls Emma's former governess after her marriage to Mr Weston; so there is the suggestion about Anna not only of maternal loss but also of a version of the kind of paternal weakness and incompetence of which Mr Woodhouse is virtually the paradigm in English fiction. This emotional and ethical vacuum is then filled by Pidgeon, whom we guess to be a seducer and betrayor of the adolescent Anna. Gazing at the portrait, Portia reads in it 'the urgent soul astray in the bad portrait . . . She saw the kitten hugged to the breast in a contraction of unknowing sorrow' (207). As we shall see, the phrase 'a soul astray' also figures significantly in *The Heat of the Day*; and on both occasions it is, I think, one of those instances of high emotional intensity in which Elizabeth Bowen slips into a Hiberno-English idiom. 'Astray' has something of the force here which it does in the title of Seamus Heaney's *Sweeney Astray*, which translates the Irish 'buile', and hence means not only lost but wild or mad; and so Portia is recognizing in Anna the profound damage done by childhood grief, and the need it creates for the solace even of a Pidgeon—just as Portia herself has felt the intense need for the unworthy, incapable, and irresponsible Eddie.

So in this affecting moment of *The Death of the Heart* Portia is, it may be said, gazing at herself and at her own sorrow. This is an effect reinforced when the word 'astray' appears again during the episode in Brutt's hotel room, figuring Portia in one of the many animal and bird images attached to her during the novel, images opposite in spirit, it may be, to the comically deflating but nevertheless minatory suggestiveness of the name 'Pidgeon': 'she was terrified here, like a bird astray in a room, a bird already stunned by dashing itself against mirrors and panes' (287). In the relationship between Anna and Portia there is a dark hint of the *doppelgänger*, as I have suggested there is in the relationship of Gerald and Daventry in *The Last September*, and as there is also in an arrestingly strange moment towards the end of *Friends and Relations* when Laurel senses a figure interposing between herself and her sister, 'a grotesque, not quite impossible figure . . . an unborn, shameful sister, travestying their two natures' (122).

At the end of *The Death of the Heart* we discover that Thomas is well aware of the psychology of Anna's behaviour, since he tells her that she is jealous of Portia's 'extraordinary wish to love'; and although Anna denies this—'she and I are hardly the same sex'—we know it to be, at some level to which she perhaps no longer even has access, the truth. Anna's intelligence is elsewhere in the novel a moral intelligence too: when, for instance, she witheringly rejects the cant of a couple called the Peppinghams during an excruciating lunch which she hosts in an attempt to put a job in the way of the unemployable Brutt: she is bravely caustic about the self-interested hypocrisy of their concept of '*instinctive* respect' ('I should so much rather just pay people, and leave it at that' (258)). But her moral intelligence stops at Portia, and stops at, precisely, the point of the sexual. It is not only snobbery but something closer to lubricity which compels her to focus on the moment of Portia's conception:

What is she, after all? The child of an aberration, the child of a panic, the child of an old chap's pitiful sexuality. Conceived among lost hairpins and snapshots of doggies in a Notting Hill Gate flatlet. (246)

The warping of her own sexual nature, and of what, we realize, may well have been her own instinctively good nature, makes us doubt that, whatever test Portia puts her to, whatever ultimatum she is offered, she will ever attempt to undo the damage she has done; since she is emotionally and psychologically disabled from making any such attempt. At the end of the novel the now self-recriminatory Thomas tells Anna that Portia has not 'created' a 'situation' but is 'just acknowledging it. An entirely different thing. She has a point of view' (308). But that is the very last thing Anna would wish her to have, since a point of view would hold her in its purview and would find her wanting. Anna must always distrust a point of view in anyone with Portia's 'enwrapping look', anyone with eyes which are the wraps that embalm the mummy.[9]

IV SERVANTS

Servants are often significantly present in Elizabeth Bowen, as they are not in other modern novelists of the liberal tradition in whom their ministrations nevertheless also sustain the relatively leisured and cultured life which is the primary subject-matter of such fiction. In Henry James and E. M. Forster, for instance, servants certainly exist but they do so without speaking. Servants are more significant, and more audible and visible, in some Bowen novels than in others, however. In *To The North*, for instance, they are 'the downstairs machinery' which 'goes into action again' when soup is required late, in a dehumanizingly mechanistic metaphor which implicitly criticizes the person— Markie—making the request. But in *The Death of the Heart* they step much more prominently to the fore, and it is appropriate that they should do so in a novel of the decade which would witness the end of the social structures dependent upon them. When Portia's domestic space literally contracts with her removal from Windsor Terrace to Waikiki, the servant's mechanism takes on unignorable flesh, with 'the many sensory hints that Doris was human and did not function in a void of her own' (158); where the all-purpose lower-class name— T. S. Eliot uses it too in 'Sweeney Agonistes'—is nevertheless as much as we ever learn of her. With the Windsor Terrace servant Matchett, however, the presentation amounts to the recognition in her of a moral authority nowhere else available to Portia. And this is precisely what Thomas, Anna, and St Quentin are forced, humiliatingly, to realize when deciding how to respond to Portia's ultimatum, even though, prior to this, St Quentin has taken so little notice of Matchett's social

---

[9] Charles Ritchie, once a lover of Bowen's, and a significant figure in her later life, notes in his published diaries that he sees 'the two women . . . as the two halves of Elizabeth.—Portia has the naiveté of childhood—or genius. She is the hidden Elizabeth. The other woman is Elizabeth as an outside hostile person might see her. But this is my own surmise and not what she told me.' See Charles Ritchie, *The Siren Years: Undiplomatic Diaries 1937–1945* (London: Macmillan, 1974), 127.

existence that he wonders, when he hears her name, if she's the woman he has occasionally encountered on the staircase, looking 'like a caryatid' (312).

Matchett is present in *The Death of the Heart* from the very beginning, when we hear Anna complaining about her to St Quentin. She has moved to Windsor Terrace on the death of Thomas's mother, 'along with the furniture'; and Matchett does, indeed, articulate a virtually mystical or occult sense of how furniture can be 'knowing'. Her relationship to the household in which Portia's father lived prior to his adultery—that is, her relationship to a past of which Anna and Thomas never speak—is the cement in her relationship with Portia, who longs to know about the past, and, in particular, about the day of her own birth. Matchett's discussing this with her may be thought to have an analogue in the imaginary conversation Karen has with Leopold about the moment of his own conception; and, like that, it offers Portia the vestige of an identity she would otherwise lack, even though this is far from consolatory. Matchett's association with an order of domesticity other than the one operating at Windsor Terrace also allows her the vantage of judgement: 'In this airy vivacious house, all mirrors and polish, there was no place where shadows lodged, no point where feeling could thicken' (42). The authority of her judgement is also the product of her integrity: she makes out of servility something resolutely unservile: 'She gave, in return for hire, her discretion and her unstinted energy, but made none of those small concessions to whim or self-admiration that servants are unadmittedly paid to make' (41).

If her access to a point of thickened feeling makes her the only conceivable alternative maternal figure for Portia in the novel—and it is she, uniquely, who worries about the emotional and sexual dangers to Portia of her unchaperoned existence—there is also something very like erotic feeling between them. When Matchett puts Portia to bed, for instance, Portia senses 'the musky warmth from her armpit [that] came to the pillow'; and Eddie thinks of Matchett, with his customary coarseness, as 'a jealous old cow' (102). The combination of the quasi-maternal and the erotic is a striking one, and makes Matchett, as Richard Tillinghast has said, 'one of the most serious portraits of a servant in fiction since Proust's Françoise' (although I would also instance the many portraits in Henry Green's *Loving*).[10] There is certainly a

---

[10] Richard Tillinghast, 'Elizabeth Bowen: The House, the Hotel and the Child', *New Criterion*, 13: 4 (1994), 24–33, 30.

deeply conservative element in this portrait. It is hard to know, for instance, what irony, if any, should be read into the view we are offered, in the narrative's third person, of Matchett's bed-making: that 'The impassive solemnity of her preparations made a sort of altar of each bed: in big houses in which things are done properly, there is always the religious element. The diurnal cycle is observed with more feeling when there are servants to do the work' (73). Yet Bowen's surrendering of the third-person narrative to the first person of Matchett's monologue at the very end of the book is a radical gesture indeed, making this kind of reflection suddenly seem to belong to a gone world. Hermione Lee has memorably said that the monologue is 'startling, as though a sphinx had broken silence'; although, of course, Matchett is far from literally silent during the rest of the novel.[11]

But the monologue is indeed startling, appearing suddenly to come out of nowhere into a narrative itself about to culminate in the completely unexpected. It occurs in the taxi which Matchett has taken to the Karachi hotel on Thomas's instructions, since sending Matchett is the solution which he, Anna, and St Quentin have found to Portia's ultimatum: she has said, through Major Brutt, that what she does next will depend on what they do; and it is a brilliant ethical challenge, charged with all the newly acquired authority of her refusal of victimhood. Even at this pitch of exacerbation, however, and even in his newly acquired capacity for self-recrimination, Thomas is so discourteous to Matchett as not to let her know where she is going: so that her taxi ride, in gloved hands behind glass, at a disadvantage with the vague menace of an impudent driver, is an index of what it is to be a mere 'servant' in such a society, and also seems proleptic of the uncanny taxi ride which Mrs Drover will take in the wartime short story 'The Demon Lover'.

The monologue has been criticized as a rather poor imitation of working-class speech, and it does, it is true, have its uncertainties. Nevertheless, it is undoubtedly in part a bow to Molly Bloom's monologue at the end of *Ulysses*; and it seems to me an appropriate and skilful adaptation of the mode as a mechanism of narrative termination. What it appears to propose is that the 'big house' (that Irish rather than English locution), in its coldness, disdain, and heartlessness, may be saved from itself, if it is to be saved at all, only by the agency of the class whose labour it exploits. Matchett does, indeed, in the end, prove a

---

[11] *Elizabeth Bowen*, 125.

match for Thomas and Anna, and has (virtually) the last word. She is, Portia thinks, 'the person who sees what really happens' (291): which is the highest compliment from one whose eyes are as keen as Portia's. If Matchett is one of the best serious portraits of a servant in fiction since Proust's Françoise, then, she is also the last serious portrait of a servant in fiction in which any positive value at all is accorded to the role. And in the irritation of Matchett at Thomas's behaviour to her and in the fact that she, as it were, commandeers the ending of this upper-class English novel, we can, I think, read the first faint inkling of the servant's fate in future English writing and culture: the table-turning of Raunce, the English butler in wartime Ireland, in Henry Green's *Loving* (1945); the far more sadistic table-turning of Dirk Bogarde's butler in Harold Pinter's screenplay (from a Robin Maugham novel) for Joseph Losey's movie *The Servant* (1963); and the portrait of repressed self-delusion that is Stevens, the emotionally cauterized interiorizer of his own victimisation, in Kazuo Ishiguro's historical, and historically ramifying, novel *The Remains of the Day* (1989).

V WRITERS

On her first night in Waikiki, after looking at Anna's portrait, Portia has a dream:

Portia dreamed she was sharing a book with a little girl. The tips of Anna's long fair hair brushed on the page: they sat up high in a window, waiting till something happened. The worst of all would be if the bell rang, and their best hope was to read to a certain point in the book. But Portia found she no longer knew how to read—she did not dare tell Anna, who kept turning pages over. She knew they must both read—so the fall of Anna's hair filled her with despair, pity, for what would have to come. The forest (there was a forest under the window) was being varnished all over: it left no way of escape. Then the terrible end, the rushing-in, the roaring and gurgling started—Portia started up from where they were with a cry—

'*Hush, hush,* dear! Here I am. Nothing has happened. Only Daphne running her bath out.' (140–1)

The bathos of the conclusion here acts as a foil to the luminously unsettling oneiric moment. This dream, I think, seals the relationship of, as it were, empathetic damage between Anna and Portia which I have tried to define. In a Magritte-like surrealism, the potentially verdurous forest

hardens into constriction and confinement, glazes with rejection; but initially, had they been the same age, they would have been friends, or even,
perhaps, something rather more, since that 'bell' suggests a schoolroom,
and the notation of the hair brushing the page has a marked erotic quality. This makes the atmosphere of the dream not unlike that of Bowen's
erotically charged school story 'The Jungle', which prominently figures
two much more obviously symbolic erotic dreams.[12] We may think, too,
that the fantasy of their being the same age is a brief evocation of the
kind of ideally 'contemporary' relationship between Karen and Leopold
in the art or 'Heaven' of Karen's address to him in Part II of *The House
in Paris*. Clearly, this dream is framed to reveal to Portia something
about the nature of Anna's envy of her.

But it does something else too: it makes the act of reading crucial in
the relationship, as it is, of course, in the novel's plot. At this point
Portia has not yet discovered that Anna reads her diary, the act which,
when she does discover it, she regards, as well she might, as 'betrayal';
but we, as readers of *The Death of the Heart*, of course know this from
the beginning of the novel, in a kind of sustained, and cruel, dramatic
irony. We are also put in Anna's position, as it were, at the end of the
first two parts of the novel, which both culminate in lengthy sections
from the diary: so to read *The Death of the Heart* is also to become the
illicit reader of another's private writing. There are literal dangers
associated with the act of reading for Portia, since Eddie's first letter to
her is discovered in the schoolroom by her teacher, Miss Paullie, and
discovered also beneath Portia's pillow by Matchett, as she puts Portia
to bed. There are other references to reading in the novel too: Daphne
in Seale reads nothing, almost on principle, although she is a librarian,
and Waikiki has a very well-shut bookcase. Eddie condescends to
Portia by telling her she does not read, whereas we, in fact, see her
reading Tauchnitz novels aloud with her mother in their Swiss hotel
room, and she elsewhere reads *Great Expectations*, which has an
appropriately analogous plot of childhood orphanage, imperilment,
and sentimental education. It is a novel, like others of Dickens's, too,
in which no child seems ever safe—which is a major reason for Bowen's
continuing fascination with Dickens, which reaches a climax, as we
shall see, in *Eva Trout*. So the dream in which Portia figures herself for-
getting how to read, while Anna reads on, may be the register of her

---

[12] 'The Jungle' appeared in *Joining Charles and Other Stories* (1929). It is reprinted in
Bowen's *Collected Stories*, 231–41.

intense fear both of having her privacy violated by, precisely, the act of reading, and also of being condescended to in a way unappreciative of her intellectual ability.

That Portia has such ability is not in doubt, partly since the extracts from the diary also, of course, present us with Portia as writer, in this novel which prominently includes novelists as characters: St Quentin is a famous one of, I imagine, a vaguely post-Jamesian kind, and Eddie has published a satirical *roman-à-clef* which has cost him his job on a newspaper, although he has now lost any faith he had in writing: 'I hate writing', he says, 'I hate art—there's always something else there' (109). During the scene in which St Quentin tells Portia that Anna reads her diary, he counsels her against keeping one: 'It is madness to write things down' (248); and when Portia taxes him with writing things down himself, as a novelist, he offers an account of the virtues of fiction as against fact, with a Proustian gloss on the blandishments of false memory. But *The Death of the Heart* works a sophisticted irony here, since Portia's diary, with its combination of vulnerable childishness and brilliant perceptiveness, is, in fact, alive with the virtue of written record. When Anna reads aloud to St Quentin a sentence from it—'So I am with them, in London' (11)—he praises the placing of the comma. As well he might: the flatness of the cadence, which the punctuation not only points but manages, hesitates between the mournfulness of resig-nation and the defiance of animosity. Which is, of course, why Anna hates it, discovering herself disparaged with perfect writerly finesse.

Portia is, in the diary entries we see, a comparably exquisite placer of a lethal comma—that mark of separation—on three other occasions also: the knowing imputation of 'Then we sat in the drawing-room, and they wished I was not there' (115); the enforced boredom of 'Tomorrow is Saturday, but nothing will happen' (115); the sigh of dereliction in 'I am back here, in London. They won't be back till tomorrow' (228). Elsewhere in the diary too it is visibly the act of writ-ing itself which reveals to Portia what she feels; we witness the way writing is a growth in consciousness and in self-consciousness: 'This house makes a smell of feeling' (111); 'I like a day when there is some sort of tomorrow' (111); 'All Thomas's looks, except ones at Anna, are at people not looking' (113). And we also see her simply practising the art, with self-delighted aptitude, as when, for instance, she writes of fog in a brilliant simile that 'it was not like night, but like air being ill' (114) and when she notices of another kind of weather, with an almost haiku-like delicacy, that 'Today it is not raining but quite dark, black is all through the air though the green looks such bright green' (225). In the lonely solitude of Portia's diary, we may think—and with mixed feelings—that the death of the heart may be about to be the birth of the writer, that the artist will emerge as heroine when the family collapses into ruin.[13]

VI PORTIA

In the opening chapter of *The Death of the Heart* St Quentin asks Anna, understandably, 'But why was she called Portia?' 'I don't think we ever asked' (21), replies Anna. So this becomes another Shakespearean aporia in Elizabeth Bowen, of the kind I have already identified in *The Last September*, and am about to identify in *Eva Trout*. But if we never know why her parents called her Portia we might guess—and this dialogue invites us to—why Elizabeth Bowen called her that. Because the quality of mercy is not strained, I suppose: it is so 'strained' throughout this novel, which presents us with the emotionally devastating results of such strain. It also allows Portia a little intertextual pre-emptive strike at Eddie, who, at his most preposterous moment of ecstatically egotistical self-dramatization, tells Portia that 'The whole of Shakespeare is about me' (101–2). But Portia has her name also, surely, because she finally puts people to the test, as Shakespeare's Portia puts her would-be suitors, and acts in the quasi-courtroom of her own creation in the closing scenes of the novel; and because her experience has finally educated her into the necessity for such forensic behaviour.[14] In Portia spontaneity has schooled itself into trial and judgement: and if this is loss, it is also necessity, since Portia

---

[13] Phyllis Lassner also considers Portia as a writer, as part of an argument about Bowen's engagement with, and combating of, 'domestic fiction'. See *Elizabeth Bowen* (London: Macmillan, 1990), ch. 5.

[14] Ann Ashworth's ' "But Why Was She Called Portia?": Judgment and Feeling in *The Death of the Heart*', in *Critique: Studies in Modern Fiction*, 28 (Spring 1987), 159–66, is an interesting essay on the judgements Portia makes, but it presses the analogies between novel and play further than I would. William Heath says that Henry James may have been a mediating factor in Portia's naming: in the preface to the New York edition of *The Portrait of a Lady* James writes of Shakespeare's Portia as 'the very type and model of the young person intelligent and presumptuous'. See *Elizabeth Bowen: An Introduction to Her Novels* (Madison: University of Wisconsin Press, 1961), 17. For Maud Ellmann, Portia is a portion, 'a floating fragment of the past washed up into the present', and she is also 'portable'. See *Elizabeth Bowen: The Shadow across the Page* (Edinburgh: Edinburgh University Press, 2003), 137.

simply could not live without such knowledge and the capacity it brings for self-preservative aggression. Yet the openness of the novel's ending, which leaves Portia waiting for Matchett in Brutt's hotel, also leaves it open whether it can ever be exactly 'Portia' who goes on living. To know that the quality of mercy is very strained indeed, and that the only response to this knowledge is emotional combat, is sadly corrosive knowledge, leaving little space for the ingenuousness we have deeply admired in Portia. There are dead hearts in *The Death of the Heart* when the novel opens, but a heart certainly dies a little in it too. If there is necessity in this there is also shame. 'From all the deceits of the world, the flesh, and the devil, Good Lord, deliver us' is the liturgical prayer echoed by the titles of the three sections of *The Death of the Heart*, a novel in which the phrase of the title nowhere itself appears: but the novel knows that there is no such deliverance, at least not in the world.

6

Childless Mother:
The Disfigurations of *Eva Trout*
or *Changing Scenes* (1968)

I

At the end of Part I of *Eva Trout* its eponymous, childless, vastly wealthy heroine visits Chicago in order to acquire a child. Before doing so, she unexpectedly encounters an old schoolfriend, bizarrely called Elsinore, in yet another of the Shakespearian aporias I have already described in Bowen; Eva is seeing her for the first time since they were at school together as very young children.[1] We know that Elsinore has meant a great deal to Eva, because during a feverish illness in Part I of the novel, at a time of 'enormous sadness' for her, she remembers the school and Elsinore's attempt to drown herself there, after which Eva devotedly watched over her in their shared bedroom, which she calls a 'marriage chamber'; and she also remembers someone saying, 'Who is my darling?':

[1] On her first appearance she is described as 'a fairylike little near-albino who had for some reason been christened Elsinore' (52). One might suggest a reason or two for the name Elsinore (who is elsewhere in the novel referred to as 'the Juliet' and 'Ophelia's illegit'), but with no great conviction: that *Hamlet* is full of spies, and Eva feels spied upon and betrayed; that *Hamlet* is a play much preoccupied with performance itself, as *Eva Trout* is; that *Hamlet* is a play much taken up with the relationship between a mother and son, as *Eva Trout* is, sort of. But these are, I admit, reasons why Elsinore might more properly be called Hamlet, or Ophelia (particularly since she nearly drowns); it is the irresolvability of these aporias itself that is of interest. Patricia Coughlan says that the *Hamlet* allusion is 'a false trail' but does not speculate about why Bowen might wish to lay such a trail. See 'Women and Desire in the Work of Elizabeth Bowen', in Eibhear Walshe (ed.), *Sex, Nation and Dissent in Irish Writing* (Cork: Cork University Press, 1997), 103–31, 129. In Vladimir Nabokov's *Bend Sinister* (1947) there is a discussion about *Hamlet* between the characters Ember and Krug during which Ember says that 'Elsinore' is an anagram of 'Roseline', as it is. Is it possible that Bowen is encoding a secret personal meaning in her use of the name?

To repose a hand on the blanket covering Elsinore was to know in the palm of the hand a primitive tremor—imagining the beating of that other heart, she had a passionately solicitous sense of this other presence. Nothing forbad love. This deathly yet living stillness, together, of two beings, this unapartness, came to be the requital of all longing. An endless feeling of destiny filled the room. (56)

Now, years later and on another continent, Elsinore still seems, as she did then, a tiny, elfin child, even though she is now herself a mother. During their meeting Eva again remembers their time in school. This school was in a castle by a lake, and is much described and returned to during the novel: indeed its opening chapter is set there, as Eva drives back to it in maturity. It is at least as much a primal scene as it is an educational establishment (which it is, in any case, only in the most approximate, louche, and chaotic sense). The narrative of Eva's memory now, as she meets Elsinore again, is italicized to represent what is virtually an hallucination:

The tower room in the castle, the piteous breathing. The blinded window, the banished lake. The dayless and nightless watches, the tent of cobwebs. The hand on the blanket, the beseeching answering beating heart. The dark: the unseen distance, the known nearness. Love: the here and the now and the nothing-but. The step on the stairs. Don't take her away, DON'T take her away. She is all I am. We are all there is.

Haven't you heard what is going to be? No. Not, but I know what was. A door opening, how is my darling? Right—then TAKE her away, take your dead bird. You wretch, you mother I never had. Elsinore, what happened? Nobody told me, nobody dared. Gone, gone. Nothing can alter that now, it's too late. (133)

After an episode which deftly traces Elsinore's present sickeningly torpid and debased life in the United States, as part of a Greek-American community, in which she seems a silenced and even menaced automaton, Eva and Elsinore part once more—this time for ever:

No one was in the lobby. Elsinore ran ahead, to the glass doors, to make certain the avenue still was there. She came back and flung herself against Eva: the bottomless, nocturnal sobbing began. '*Take me with you, Trout!*' The ungainly tear-wetted fur slithered and heaved between their two bodies. '*You never left me, you never left me before!*' The despairing clutch upon Eva, round Eva, was not to be undone till, most of all despairingly, it undid itself. 'No,' reasoned Elsinore, 'you can't have me come with you, and I can't go. No, however could I?' She buried her forehead in Eva, then pulled it back—looking down, Eva saw the purple, membraneous eyelids, the cast-out fledgling's. The terrible, obstinate self-determination of the dying was felt also. Eva cried out: 'Elsinore, *don't—don't*, will you?' Both of them froze together. (144)

These moments of childhood memory and of the desired but impossible later relationship have a very strong erotic element: the wet, slithering, heaving fur is literally that of Eva's coat, but the intensely carnal verbs suggest another kind of fur, or hair, altogether; and the phrase 'come with you' is hardly unaware of itself in such a context. But the moment also has an emotional authenticity which is hardly ever apparent elsewhere in a novel deeply preoccupied with, and plotted around modes of, the inauthentic. The Romantic form of individual identity transcended by, while also constructed out of, erotic love, which recalls *Wuthering Heights* in its tremulous intensity ('Nelly, I *am* Heathcliff!' | *'She is all I am. We are all there is.'*) confronts everywhere else in the novel a fundamental insecurity about personal identity. This is sometimes so underminingly severe as to make the novel's modes of characterization congruent with radical postmodern conceptions of the hollowing-out of subjectivity, as characters—and Eva herself in particular—are virtually devoid of all continuity, becoming sites traversed by the endless mobilities of desire.[2] The rendering of the one authentic relationship in the novel as homosexual—if, of course, pre-pubic—brings into its foreground the lesbian element which is often present but partly submerged in the earlier novels: in, as we have seen, Lois and Marda in *The Last September*; in Theodora Thirdman in *Friends and Relations*; in the sad comedy of frustration and misunderstanding that is Miss Tripp's relationship with Emmeline in *To The North*; in Louie and Connie, and Louie's attitude to Stella, in *The Heat of the Day*.[3] Indeed, in a study of homoeroticism in modern fiction Patricia Juliana Smith refers to the novel's 'revolutionary accomplishment' in this regard: it manages, she says, 'the

---

[2] For Andrew Bennett and Nicholas Royle in *Elizabeth Bowen and the Dissolution of the Novel: Still Lives* (London: Macmillan, 1995), some such hollowing-out is a *donnée* of all Bowen's novels. Even so, they also think that 'In chronological terms, this dimension of Bowen's work becomes increasingly articulate and explicit.' (66). For Maud Ellmann in *Elizabeth Bowen: The Shadow across the Page* (Edinburgh: Edinburgh University Press, 2003), the novel 'both anticipates postmodernism and diagnoses its deficiencies' (21), by asking, as she puts it later, 'how far fiction can go without ethics, or without forsaking any aspiration for the truth' (204).

[3] Patricia Coughlan regards this new foregrounding of lesbian desire as itself constitutive of 'the tongue-tied, halting utterance not only of the characters but sometimes of the narrator' in *Eva Trout*; which is a striking observation, although it would be difficult to prove. See 'Women and Desire in the Work of Elizabeth Bowen', 12.

thorough displacement of the romance plot, the de-essentialization of heterosexuality as a social or narrative norm, and the establishment of lesbian panic as a narrative in and of itself'.[4] This makes *Eva Trout* seem rather more single-minded than I find it, less baffled by its own adventurous procedures; but the novel does certainly also include a male homosexual relationship, the one Eva's father, Willy Trout, has with Constantine Ormeau, who becomes Eva's guardian, and an apparently chaste but homoerotically coloured one between Constantine and a young Anglican priest, Fr. Clavering-Haight. Above all, the relationship between Eva and her English teacher and sometime mentor, Iseult Smith, which is at the centre of the novel's plot, is one with a strong homosexual dimension, although it is never explicitly sexual.

Further, these passages raise what is, for Eva, who is on the verge of acquiring a child in an uncommon, and perhaps unlikely, manner, the crucial issue of personal identity and its crises: that is, as it was in *The House in Paris* too, the issue of maternity. Whereas in Part 1 of *Eva Trout* we assume that it is Eva herself who cries out, in her fever, to the sick child, 'How is my darling?', we learn from the passage in Part 2 that it is, in fact, Elsinore's mother who has come to take her away from Eva's protective and amatory, but also quasi-maternal, care. 'You mother I never had' is a cry of desolation but also of recrimination: it is Eva's blaming of Elsinore's mother, but also the blaming of her own mother, who died when Eva was only a few months old, for not existing, for making her a motherless child. The question of maternity is prominent in this episode also since, when Eva meets Elsinore again, Elsinore is wearing her mother's clothes. So Elsinore is figured in Part 2 as child, lover, and mother, and she reappears just as Eva is about to acquire a child. We must, therefore, read this child, Jeremy, as Eva's ultimate attempt to replace a first authentic love; but her way of doing so—she appears to pay for a kidnapped child, although the novel is darkly inexplicit on this—is, of course, utterly inauthentic, and also immoral and illegal. The subtitle of *Eva Trout* has various

---

[4] Patricia Juliana Smith, *Lesbian Panic: Homoeroticism in Modern British Women's Fiction* (New York: Columbia University Press, 1997), 102. For this critic the novel's lesbianism is also an index of its postmodernism: 'As a bizarre congeries of gender and sexuality confusion, fetishism, consumerism, and contemporary culture rendered through non-linear plotting, *Eva Trout* is perhaps the ur-text of postmodern lesbian panic upon which such works as Beryl Bainbridge's *Harriet Said*, Emma Tennant's *The Bad Sister*, and Fay Weldon's *The Heart of the Country* subsequently expand' (123).

ramifications, as I shall suggest: but here the scene to which the novel changes is the scene of a crime.

In all of these ways *Eva Trout* is a deeply problematical but also, to me, an absorbingly experimental fiction—even if one has to learn, over the course of several readings, how to be absorbed by it—which both inherits and deviates from Bowen's earlier fictions of motherless children. It is as though the co-ordinates of the earlier novels have been thrown out of alignment, or as though some of the essential elements and attributes of plot, theme, and characterization in the earlier novels are here placed in front of a set of distorting mirrors. There they undergo processes of anamorphosis in which characteristic kinds of poignancy and pathos are supplanted by sheer emotional weirdness; in which lucidities of plot and epiphany are exchanged for abruptions and over-determinations; in which characterization can seem shorthand, off-hand, sometimes close to caricature, a matter more purely of surface than of depth; and in which style itself can sometimes seem disconcertingly almost artless or even whimsical, a mode of obfuscation rather than clarification, or at least the register of a baffled narrative uncertainty. Narrative method is occasionally even interrogative, as though we, as readers, may have as good an idea of motivation as the novel's writer.

This distorted-mirror anamorphosis reminds me of the photographer André Kertész's sudden, unpredictable nude portraits in distorted mirrors of 1933, that one-off experiment which similarly, with both a challenge to the viewer and an ironically self-directed scepticism, calls into question any assumptions about the transparency of realism in the rest of his work.[5] I can hardly claim that Bowen would have had any such analogy in mind, although her novels do, as we have seen, frequently refer to photographs and photography, and, as we have also seen, Antonia in *A World of Love*, who may be partly an authorial self-representation, is a photographer. Nevertheless, what *Eva Trout*, Bowen's last completed book, seems to involve is the reconfiguration, or even disfiguration, of some of the obsessive preoccupations of her earlier work, in a way which suggests a bravely resilient pushing against the boundaries of her own narrative structures but also a

---

[5] See, for instance, Pierre Borhan, *André Kertész: His Life and Work* (New York: Bullfinch Press, 1994). The description of Eva crying, for the first time ever in her life, towards the very end of the novel, reminds Maud Ellmann (*The Shadow Across the Page*, 222) of the famous Man Ray (surreal) photograph, 'Glass Tear'.

radically unsettling dissatisfaction with them. The novel is a comedy, up to a point, but it is also a tragedy; or, it is a comedy containing its own opposite—as the restaurant in which Eva lunches alone towards the end of the novel does when she thinks, 'Here was a table for two: something was suddenly trying to sit down opposite her at it: tragedy' (190). It is a novel in which all sorts of things suddenly try to sit down opposite us. It is a black comedy and a black farce, a fairy tale, a melo-drama, and then, suddenly, a novel of the most heartbreaking sadness. It sometimes seems a parable, but one not to be restated in any terms other than those it offers us. A generic *mélange adultère de tout*, its system of representations is wildly unstable, even self-contradictory. It is an utterly unpredictable end to Elizabeth Bowen's career as a novel-ist; and it is a novel which, in every weave of its texture, forgoes serenity.

II

It is characteristic of *Eva Trout* that it provides terms we might find useful for its own critique. One of the characters, Henry Dancey, with whom Eva falls in love, for instance, describes the novel's own con-cluding episode, before it happens—as it were, preparing us for it, telling us how to read it—as a '*comédie noire*' (239); and his father, the Revd Dancey, whose extreme form of hay fever is frequently evoked, as a kind of grotesque Dickensian tic, is said at one point to undergo a 'disfiguration' when affected by it. Elizabeth Bowen uses a similar word elsewhere too, very arrestingly, with an emotional rather than a physical implication, when, in an autobiographical reminiscence, she discusses the grief consequent on her mother's death when she was a child of 13: 'I had', she says, 'what I see can go with total bereavement, a sense of disfigurement.'[6] While not wishing to establish too inevitable a psycho-biographical motive here, I think it is possible to read Eva as a kind of physical and psychological disfiguration too, a kind of incarnate damage—and the word 'damage' figures prominently as a definiton of what Eva then, in her turn, inflicts on others. Henry thinks of her as 'a sort of Pippa—though in reverse' (179), who brings

---

[6] Elizabeth Bowen, 'Pictures and Conversations', in *The Mulberry Tree: Writings of Elizabeth Bowen*, selected and introduced by Hermione Lee (London: Virago Press, 1986), 265–98, 289.

disintegration and chaos where Browning's young girl in 'Pippa Passes' revises everything towards the good or the just.

Physically, Eva is grotesque in a way recalling the sexually thwarted Valeria Cuffe in Bowen's culturally ramifying 1930s Irish short story of misunderstanding and ill-connection, 'Her Table Spread', who is also 25, the age Eva attains during the novel, at which she comes into her immense inheritance.[7] She is large, awkward, and outrageously dressed; and, as Bowen says elsewhere with cruelly aphoristic wit, 'An unsuccessful appearance is more than a pity; it is a pathological document.'[8] As a child her schoolmates wonder if she's hermaphroditic or handicapped; and, as in Valeria Cuffe, there persists in Eva an element of that 'infantilism' which Bowen finds 'sublimated' in Sheridan Le Fanu and regards as characteristically Anglo-Irish.[9] She stammers, and, in what we might regard as a kind of negative distortion of the weeping done by Leopold and Henrietta in *The House in Paris* and by Portia and Eddie in *The Death of the Heart*, she is unable to cry. One of the most vivid physical descriptions of her is provided by the estate agent Denge, whom she terrifies when she looks for a house near Broadstairs: in her furs she appears to him 'less feline than paramilitary: she brought to mind Russian troops said to have passed through England in the later summer of 1914, leaving snow in the trains' (76–7); and this comedic but also awe-inspiring gigantism inheres in many of the novel's descriptions of its bizarre heroine. Yet she is still notably attractive to men; and a large element of the plot is taken up with Eva's influence on men who are attracted to her.

Psychologically, the absence of a mother—she is 'motherless from the cradle' (39), according to Constantine, and, in fact, Eva's mother was killed in a plane crash two months after her birth—is complemented by the inadequacy of a father, who, having fallen in love with a man, more or less ignores Eva as he treks around the world, leaving her with paid minders, including, in San Francisco, 'some relations of his chropodist' (57). This passage of the novel, describing the cynical

---

[7] John Coates reads Eva as 'an analogue of those Jamesian heiresses, especially Milly Theale in *The Wings of the Dove*, who are "conscious of a great capacity for life but early stricken and doomed"'. See 'The Misfortunes of Eva Trout', *Essays in Criticism*, 48: 1 (1998), 59–79, 77. This essay mounts a perceptive, sturdy, and persuasive defence of the novel's ethical meanings against some poststructuralist views of it.

[8] 'Dress', in Elizabeth Bowen, *Collected Impressions* (London: Longmans Green & Co., 1950), 112.

[9] Elizabeth Bowen, '*Uncle Silas* by Sheridan Le Fanu', in *The Mulberry Tree*, 100–13.

nonchalance of Willy Trout's child-minding arrangements, plays a kind of mad black scherzo on the themes of abandonment and topographical mobility in Bowen's earlier work; and *Eva Trout*, a deeply restless novel, has, in fact, far more locations, more 'changing scenes', than the others: it moves between Worcestershire, North Foreland, the American Midwest, New York, London, Richmond, Cambridge, Paris, and Fontainebleau. When Mrs Dancey goes for a drive with Eva at the opening of the book she says, 'Wherever this was, it was soon to be somewhere else' (15); and the reader of *Eva Trout* may well feel the same combination of anxiety and exhilaration about the book's wild, almost lurching, career; and we might regard this too as a kind of disfigured version of the social and cultural restlessness of Bowen's novels of the 1930s.

Eva internalizes these external discontinuities, and at her first school she cannot feel homesick: 'for, sick for where?' (50). And when she passes into Constantine's distracted and slightly suspect guardianship, she is 'a legacy', as Portia is to the Quaynes in *The Death of the Heart*. In compensatory reaction to these derelictions, Eva becomes an inveterate fantasist and a liar. Her fantasy of a honeymoon opens the novel; the histrionic imposture of a marriage closes it; and Eva encourages Iseult in the belief that the child she, Eva, acquires in the States has, in fact, been fathered by Iseult's husband, Eric. This inverted reaction to her plight—which we may think of as a form of prophylactic infantilism, the withdrawal into a fantasy world as a protection against a shatteringly painful reality—is the opposite of Leopold's and Portia's refusals of the role of victim. So we may regard Eva too as an anamorphic variant, a disfiguring, of the orphan children of the earlier novels; and, just as Portia is called a 'refugee' when she flees to Major Brutt, so Eva is described as 'a displaced person' (17), the post-war equivalent of the pre-war term.

A further disfiguring of the repeated figure is Eva's vast wealth, and this brings the question of money into the foreground in Bowen's work where, like the lesbian motif too in the earlier fiction, it has previously, as we have seen in relation to *The Death of the Heart*, been present but unemphasized. Before she comes into her inheritance Eva lives for a while with Iseult and her husband, Eric Arble: but she stays with them as a paying guest; and, as she is well aware, this is to be far more a payer than it is to be a guest. Eva is a source of income, and in return the Arbles spy on her for Constantine, which is the destruction of all trust between Eva and Iseult, on whom she has previously been hopelessly and adoringly dependent; and this inevitably leads to Eva's split with them. So Eva is the final spied-upon person in Bowen, a last victim of surveillance. And the novel is, among other things, a study in extreme, corrosive loneliness, as Eva is walled up in her wealth. The image that persists for this is Eva meticulously collecting skulls and shells from the beach at Broadstairs, and constructing them into a 'little marine museum' (102) at her temporary home, Cathay, where she lives on her own for a while, in the final evocation in Bowen's work of an obscure seaside location. The image of the manufacturing of the little museum has isolation, grief, misery, and tenderness in it all at once, and also, prominently, the displacement of pain. In all of these ways it is a reca-pitulation of Portia's making of Major Brutt's jigsaw in *The Death of the Heart*; but Eva is, of course, far older than Portia. She becomes therefore the persistent Bowen figure of the isolated child grown to a fragile, anxious, and incompetent maturity. So *Eva Trout* is, I would argue, intertextually anamorphic. A novel of subsequence and succes-sion, it explores the fate of the suffering child at a point at which, when revolt or revenge are no longer options, the damage is far too deeply done.

In this sense the plot of *Eva Trout* too may be considered a disfigura-tion of the plots of the orphan child in the earlier books. Eva's search for a mother figure and her desire for an education focus initially on Iseult: Eva is 16, Portia's age, when she first becomes involved with her teacher. Iseult's own childlessness is a central psychological factor for her, as it is for Anna in *The Death of the Heart*, and Eva's living with Iseult and her husband makes her an interruptor of settled domestic and sexual routines, in a way that also recalls the interruption Portia makes in the Windsor Terrace household: Eva is, we might say, a big woman in a small house, where Portia is, of course, the reverse, and very much made to feel so. Jeremy, the child Eva acquires, or steals, is deaf and dumb, which we may read as a reverse image of the hyper-volubility of all other children in Bowen, notably Leopold. Despite his handicap, however, Jeremy is also the ultimate wise child in Elizabeth Bowen, his unnerving silence the register of a 'somehow unearthly per-spicacity' (158). (I have also sometimes wondered whether Jeremy is not, in his silence, a kind of comment on the children in Virginia Woolf: although childhood is central to Woolf's conception and representa-tion of life, children hardly ever actually speak in her novels. This is not what they do, exactly, in *The Waves*.) When, in one of the novel's many strange and unpredictable twists of plot, Iseult comes to believe that she has some kind of occult bond with Jeremy and in turn kidnaps him from Eva, she is acting out an anamorphic version of Ray's benevolent kidnapping of Leopold from his foster-parents in *The House in Paris*. And when Eva falls in love with the far younger Henry (she is 32; he is 20), whom she has known since he was 12, it is a disfiguration of the age difference between Portia and Eddie in *The Death of the Heart*. Finally, the tragic dénouement of the novel, when Jeremy shoots Eva dead just as she is departing for her fake marriage, may represent the child's ultimate exaction of a terrible revenge for the adult's behaviour, a more intense version of the table-turning effected by Portia in *The Death of the Heart*. Further, its tragedy inheres in the fact that, at the last moment, Eva's artificial marriage would have become a genuine one, had she lived, since Henry finally realises that he does actually wish it; and the realization that her love is reciprocated causes Eva to weep, for the first (and last) time in her life.

Interpretation of this material is not easy, and criticism of *Eva Trout* is more than usually divided on the novel's meanings; but what is clear, I think, is that it is a final return, with a difference, to the material of Elizabeth Bowen's earlier fictions of childhood: a return in which the relationships between parents and children, men and women, men and men, women and women, and adults and children are all now destabilized in a way productive of panic rather than release. In the death of Eva at the hands of her surrogate son, Elizabeth Bowen's work ends with a sense of the utter inexorability of wrong beginnings. 'I suspect victims, they win in the long run' (92), says Iseult of Eva, disguising her envy and fear in glib analysis; and, in fact, victims, while not exactly winning in the end, may well be on the verge of doing so in both *The House in Paris* and *The Death of the Heart*. But no, they do not win in the long run, says the astonishing final moment of *Eva Trout*, the culmination of Jeremy's very long run down the station platform at Waterloo.

Jeremy's shooting of Eva is unnervingly unclear in its motivation; it is even unclear whether it is the product of accident or design, and the complicated plotting which delivers him a gun—that almost risibly phallic appendage—seems to have dropped in from a different kind of novel altogether.[10] But if this is calculated matricide, a major

---

[10] Victoria Glendinning, in *Elizabeth Bowen: Portrait of a Writer* (1977; London: Phoenix, 1993), 226, remarks that 'the idea of the child with the gun—the supreme illustration of the lethal potential of innocence—had been there for a long time', noting its

motive would be Eva's failure to provide him with the much longed-for 'home' which she has promised him. In this, she is doing to him what she has had done to her, and she realizes her guilt, which is phrased as blankly and flatly, even childishly, as the impossibility of its assuagement demands: 'Eva had broken a pact, which was very grievous' (190). Jeremy's antagonistic feelings towards her are grimly figured in the maquette he makes of her head when he is sent to sculpture lessons: its eyes are pushed virtually right through the skull, and Eva is appalled when she confronts this representation of herself: 'Out of their dark had exuded such non-humanity that Eva had not known where to turn' (190). Jeremy, in recognizing the inhumanity that has first of all stolen him, then failed to provide him with a home, and is now, finally, marrying without letting him know, is revealing a true Eva to herself: but in the act he commits as a consequence—if it is as a consequence—he is, of course, with a terrible irony, sealing his own fate as one final orphaned child in the work of Elizabeth Bowen.

III

Where then was to be the promised land, the abiding city?

Eva Trout, 163

The plot of *Eva Trout*, crowded and frenetic as it is, is ghosted by the structure of an organizing metanarrative: the narrative of traditional Christianity. 'Genesis' is the title of the novel's opening section, and Eva's first name makes her an Eve, a first woman, a first mother, a temptress, 'cast out from where I believed I was' (185), and there are explicitly symbolic apples in her vicinity: Jeremy's sculpture teacher is called Miss Applethwaite; and, in the quite extraordinary 'Interim' chapter of the book, in which an American academic philosopher becomes infatuated with Eva in the plane taking her to the States to acquire Jeremy, he introduces himself to her when his apples roll under

---

presence literally in *The Little Girls*, where the children bury a gun in a coffer, and metaphorically—and very appositely indeed—in *The House in Paris*, which asks, apropos of Leopold, 'The child at the back of the gun accident—is he always so ignorant? I simply point this thing, it goes off: *sauve qui peut.*' There is also, of course, a gun—and, perhaps, a comparably phallic one—in the ruined mill episode of *The Last September*.

her seat. Eva may also be seen as the figure of what Catholic theology has called the 'second Eve', the Virgin Mary, since she is, in a sense, and remains, a virgin mother. Her second name, 'Trout', makes her a fish; and the fish, or 'icthus', was the symbol for Christ among the first communities of Christians in Rome.[11] Biblical associations are prominent in some sections of the book too, notably when, towards its conclusion, Eva returns to the castle school with Henry where, in an otherwise idyllic passage, he warns her not to catch herself on thorns. In fact, she does exactly this, and bleeds: Henry tells her that she is like Abraham's ram caught in the thickets. When Eva meets Iseult, we are told, there was in her 'something of Nature before the Fall. There was not yet harm in Iseult Smith—what first implanted it?' (61). Their subsequent doing of harm or damage to each other is to be read therefore as one instance of how the Fall may happen in human affairs, one instance of the perverting of love or affection by the desire for dominance or the implantation of envy.

During a significant early encounter, in which Iseult teaches Eva what adequate reading might be like, the unnamed text is the final three stanzas of George Herbert's metaphysical poem 'Even-song', whose Christian paradoxes ('But thou art light and darkness both together') may also be read as a commentary on the stresses and tensions which are to follow in this human relationship, just as its final line, 'And wake with thee for ever' cannot but have a sexual reverberation, given Eva's desire for Iseult and Iseult's apparent encouragement of it.[12] Eva aquires Jeremy at Christmas time, and there are hints of his Christ-like status; but just before she does so she puts her thumb in her hotel's Gideon Bible, perhaps in a version of the fortune-telling serendipity of the *sortes Vergilianae*, and reads Leviticus 7: 37 on 'the law of the burnt offering . . . and of the trespass offering', which puts what she is doing under the shadow of the judgement of the law of the Old Testament, since the acquiring of Jeremy is certainly an ethical 'trespass'.

When Constantine's new friend, the Anglican priest Fr Clavering-Haight, appears in Part 2 of the book he introduces a language of Christian sacramentalism and confessionalism which offers further

---

[11] It also makes her, in the sexist slur of previous times, 'an old trout', which the OED defines as 'a derogatory term for an old woman'.

[12] The poem is one of two quite different poems by Herbert to bear this title, and the much less well known of the two, since it did not appear in *The Temple*.

judgmental interpretations of both Iseult's and Eva's cases, bringing prominently to bear the concepts of grace, penance, absolution, forgiveness, retribution, salvation, resurrection, and eternal life. Through his agency also Constantine undergoes some form of *metanoia* and, although this is hard to credit in terms of consistency of characterization, he consequently exchanges his earlier heartlessness, cynicism, and self-satisfaction—which may be thought to make him a kind of anamorphic version of St Quentin in *The House in Paris*—for a new social concern and 'spiritual content' (174), and he certainly develops a new affection for, and intimacy with, Eva. And when Henry falls out with his father, the vicar, as a consequence of his relationship with Eva, he faints in church during his father's sermon on the text, 'I hate the sins of unfaithfulness, there shall be no such cleave unto me.'

In that very striking episode, in a way which may offer a pastiche of the famous passage in Bede's *Eccesiastical History* in which life is likened to the flight of a sparrow through a meadhall, a thrush enters the Revd Dancey's beautiful Perpendicular church, blunders about in panic, and eventually kills itself by crashing into a window just at the moment Henry faints. We might regard this as a kind of interruption, from the margins, of the central Christian-theological narrative of both the Perpendicular church itself and of its vicar's sermon. In this, the thrush is emblematic of the narrative of *Eva Trout* as a whole, in which the kinds of theological or metaphysical modes of interpretation I have outlined here are opened up only to be ultimately foreclosed. In a plot whose suddennesses and abruptions occasionally recall Daniel Defoe's at the beginning of the history of the novel, or E. M. Forster's in *The Longest Journey*—'Gerald died that afternoon. He was broken up in the football match.'—the metaphysical elements lead nowhere and are never resolved. They remain as merely attenuated traces of redemption, conversion, fulfilment. The metaphysical depth which they might suggest or affirm in a different kind of novel—probably a Victorian one, but possibly, also, one by Bowen's friend Graham Greene, or one by an admired post-Flaubertian French writer such as Francois Mauriac—is everywhere fractured by perceptions of surface hollowness. The narrative or myth which might once have brought interpretative and redemptive succo[ur] simply left hanging, bereft of its traditional value or weight. L[ike] the façade of the castle school which always appears to have nothin[g behind it,] the Christianity of *Eva Trout* is only façade; a matter of ges[ture ...] remembered citation, a tissue and a trace, without the [value or force] of human attachment.

This foreclosure of the metaphysical, the unavailability of its grand narratives to the actual contingencies of the novel's plot, is one measure in *Eva Trout* of its fundamental sense of the instability of identity. 'What a performance', thinks Eva of Iseult's telephone conversation with her before she kidnaps Jeremy; and the idea of the self as a performance rather than a morally or theologically responsible entity is central to the conception of character in the novel, whose subtitle, 'Changing Scenes', gestures, in one of its meanings, towards the idea of the theatrical, and perhaps to the conception of the novel itself as a piece of manipulated stage machinery. Henry, in addition to proposing that the scene which concludes the novel will be a *'comédie noire'*, also predicts that it will be a 'burlesque', although he does not, of course, foresee that what it will actually be is a tragedy. It is also the converging, as it were for a final curtain-call, of most of the novel's major characters and some of its minor ones—of what Henry, again, calls 'the entire cast'—in a way disruptive of the norms of realistic verisimilitude, which, for, all its strangenesses, *Eva Trout* never entirely abandons previously. And when Jeremy rushes forward with his gun, the other travellers on the platform assume that he is taking part in a film: 'he sped like a boy on the screen towards the irradiated figure, waving his weapon in salute' (268). Elsewhere in the novel too life is figured as a movie: Paris is one to Jeremy ('At this hour, it exhausted the resources of Technicolor, and exceeded them' (204)), and Eva's life with him is, in its silence, said to be a 'cinematographic existence' (188). The novel is also replete with the technologies of representation, notably when Eva furnishes Cathay with 'outstanding examples of anything aur-visual on the market this year, 1959' (118), including a tape-recorder, which we see Eva trying out—duplicating, of course, and then listening to, her own voice in reproduction.

The figuration of the unstable self in performance in *Eva Trout* is accompanied by Eva's own figuring of identity as emptiness when she says of Constantine that 'Nothing authenticated him as a "living" being. A figure cut from some picture but now pasted onto a blank screen. To be with him was to be *in vacuo* also' (45); and she subsequently reflects explicitly on identity itself, fearfully and anxiously doubting its existence, a Trout reflecting on a fish: 'What a slippery fish is identity; and what *is* it, besides a slippery fish?' (193). She is as profoundly affected as she is by what she regards as Iseult's betrayal of her because she had relied on Iseult to provide an identity for her: she explains to Constantine that 'She sent me back again—to be nothing. . . . I remain gone. Where am I? I do not know—I was cast out from where I believed I was' (185)—where 'cast out' has, of course, a further Biblical resonance. In an almost dreamlike episode, Eva visits the National Portrait Gallery to discover if the historically famous and powerful people represented there display any more authoritative certainty about their identities than she can muster about hers. She finds, however, in a superb phrase, only 'the twilit arrestedness of history', and discovers in the portraits 'nothing but a pack of cards' (195), the *Alice*-like hallucinatory transformations of what can never be retrieved. She expresses this to herself as a kind of hollow, echoing, and entrapping chiasmus: 'There was no "real life"; no life was more real than this' (196). This episode immediately precedes the kidnapping of Jeremy; and, since whatever identity Eva does possess is so intimately bound up with her 'performed' maternal relationship with him—what Eva herself calls the 'mimicry' of maternity (222)—this is the moment at which a terminal defeat of her selfhood is threatened: 'If he *is* in the past, there is no future. He was to be everything I shall not be' (199). But the tragic irony of *Eva Trout* is that it is Jeremy, in the present, who terminates all future and all identity for Eva, by killing her.

IV

In a novel so preoccupied with representation and performance, and with the radical instability of the self, it is unsurprising that Iseult is working on a translation of a French critical book on Dickens called *Le Grand Histrionique*; and Dickens, whom Portia is reading in *The Death of the Heart*, figures notably in *Eva Trout*, in which Iseult is herself a failed novelist.[13] We have seen how novelists, quasi-novelists and nascent novelists figure in the earlier novels, and it seems peculiarly in tune with what I am calling the 'disfiguration' of this book that it should so prominently include someone who cannot write a novel. *Eva Trout* is also full of the names of other writers, and of references to, and quotations from, them. In this sense by far the most fore-groundedly literary of Bowen's works, it summons, on my count (and

---

[13] Adam Piette tells me that in 1926 J. B. Van Amerongen published a book called *The Actor in Dickens: A Study of the Histrionic and Dramatic Elements in the Novelist's Life and Works* (New York, 1926). I suspect that Bowen knew this book; but one would not need to, of course, to decide that the concept of the histrionic might be usefully applied to Dickens.

in addition to Dickens), Lawrence, George Eliot, James, Browning (a great deal of Browning), Proust, Chekhov, Flaubert, Herbert, Pater, Descartes, Keats, Wordsworth, Ibsen, and Lewis Carroll.

It also includes many more instances of the characters' own writing, in the form of letters, than the earlier books; and 'Interim', the chapter to which I have already referred, represents a long letter from the self-obsessed and deeply unengaging Portman C. Holman, a letter which is never, in fact, delivered. In it Holman—from whom Eva has clearly made her escape on landing, although he cannot quite believe that this is indeed what she has done—offers testimony to the awed fascination which Eva can command. In the prolixly self-qualifying prose of this letter, Holman also makes explicit the connection, and the difference, between literary and maternal creativity. It seems to me that this nexus lies deep in the interior structure of *Eva Trout*, and that an unresolved stress and pain to do with it, on the part of the novelist herself, may account for at least some of the peculiarities of the novel. In *Eva Trout*, Bowen's final book, co-ordinates are thrown out of alignment, anamorphisms distort perspective, because a will to articulation or dramatized confession encounters resistance from an instinct of self-preservation or a profound, distressed habit of reticence. The novel may be read as the seismograph of this disturbance. Eva has told Holman yet another one of her lies: that she is a mother. He tells her in his letter, presumptuously enough but perhaps not altogether unfairly, that she differs entirely from 'the mother-image hitherto entertained by me' (123). It is entirely characteristic of this novel that such thematically significant material is introduced in an undelivered letter in a chapter entitled 'Interim':

I myself am debarred from knowing what it must be other than figuratively to have given birth, to have brought forth. There is, there can be, no intellectual analogy. Bring into being that which was not, one can. Bring into being that which of its own volition proceeds onward from what when brought into being it first was, one cannot. You have the better of me. Let me give the full weight it has for me to the statement: *You have offspring.*   (123)

Elsewhere, when the also unhappily childless Iseult tells Constantine that she has failed to write her novel, she does, however, draw what she calls the frequently drawn 'intellectual analogy' when she says that 'It was born dead' (228).

It is in this context of the association between literary and uterine creation, between the writing of a book and the production of a child, that the episode of *Eva Trout* set in Dickens's house, Bleak House (previously called Fort House), in Broadstairs in Kent has its importance. It was here that Dickens wrote *David Copperfield*, that supreme, partly autobiographical novel of childhood, and where he 'gestated'—*Eva Trout* says—*Bleak House*; and it was Dickens who first imported the Romantic child and the Romantic conception of childhood from early nineteenth-century poetry into the novel; the child was consistently, of course, at the very heart of Dickens's imaginative interest. Bowen herself, in *English Novelists*, says something slightly different and more striking, in addition, when she says that 'There was something superbly childish . . . about his imagination.'[14] Iseult, erstwhile English teacher, translator of a French critical book on Dickens, and failed novelist, has chosen to meet the estranged Eva here, in Dickens's study, because Dickens has become so real to her that she feels, comfortingly, 'in the presence of a third person (virtually)'(110). Iseult's reflection on Dickens has a more than merely local weight in the work of Elizabeth Bowen, a writer so deeply influenced by Henry James, since Iseult thinks, 'What, now one came to think of it, *had* James, that Dickens really had not? Or if he had, what did it amount to?' (113). What Dickens amounts to is: 'a literature—of what? Longing. The lyricism of forgetfulness. The nightmare of the frustrated passion. The jibbering self-mockery of the "comic". The abasements of love . . .'. (113) It is, of course, a self-reflexive statement of what *Eva Trout* itself amounts to: and Bowen's last novel is written very deliberately—and, here, explicitly—under Dickens's sign, and in contradistinction to James's.

Iseult heightens the sense of Dickens's presence by reflecting on memorized quotations from his letters, and by musing enviously on Ellen Ternan, the young actress with whom he had a presumptively sexual relationship. 'Who knew better', she reflects of the novelist, 'what one can come to, or be brought to?' (113). And then, in a kind of trance of possession by the spirit of Dickens, she thinks, 'he took our nature upon him' (113). This is to impute rather more to Dickens than even he merits, since it is, in yet another of the novel's theological allusions, what God did by becoming man in Christ, according to the theological prescription. So Iseult is here, out of too idealistic a regard for literary art, making, as it were, a category error by confusing

---

[14] Elizabeth Bowen, *English Novelists* (London: William Collins, 1942), 30. For Dickens's 'importation' see, for instance, Peter Coveney's enduringly excellent study, *The Image of Childhood* (Harmondsworth: Penguin, 1967).

aesthetics and theology. She has made a similar error in her marriage to Eric, far her intellectual inferior but physically extremely attractive, because she has read D. H. Lawrence: she has made a Lawrentian marriage, and it ends in disaster (at least until virtually the novel's conclusion, when it appears to be reviving). She also accounts for her bad behaviour to Eva by telling Constantine that she, Iseult, is *'capable de tout'*: 'I am soiled by living more than a thousand lives; I have lived through books' (92–3); but she is also brought to the realization that 'All had been nothing. Life is an anti-novel' (206).

However, when Eva enters the study in Broadstairs, she sits in Dickens's writing chair behind his desk, the 'empty chair' of Luke Fildes's famous painting, done on the day of Dickens's death.[15] Eva is, of course, emphatically not a novelist: indeed, prominent in her attraction to Iseult had been the fact that she, Eva, lacked all education and literary ability, which she thought Iseult might inculcate in her. But Eva is a novelist of a kind, nevertheless: she is a maker of fictions, a fantasist, a liar ('she has a passion for the fictitious for its own sake', says Iseult), for whom lying is the only feasible way of arranging for the world to match her longing and desire; and, when she inherits her fortune, she uses it to make her fantasy, or fiction, a reality, by buying herself a child. Jeremy is, therefore, the impossible thing: in Portman C. Holman's terms, he is not 'the bringing into being of that which was not', or at least he is not Eva's bringing such a thing into being, but he certainly is 'that which of its own volition proceeds onward from what when brought into being it first was'; and as Jeremy discovers the desire to speak, and (while he is being taught to do so by doctors in Fontainebleau) begins, necessarily, to separate himself from Eva, he is, of course, proceeding onwards; as he must.

We may, therefore, I think, read his killing of Eva, whether it was done by accident or design, as the catastrophe of his human rejection of Eva's imaginative figuring of him as her son, his violent release from her now utterly unwanted fiction of maternity. So we may also read in Jeremy an anamorphic version of Leopold's plight in *The House in Paris*, when he says of the Grant Moodys, his adoptive parents, that 'They keep trying to make me be things. Have they bought me, or what?' (204), and when he considers Ray's removing him from them as 'this theft of his own body' (223), even as he is grateful for it. If, as I

---

[15] The painting is reproduced in, for instance, Peter Ackroyd's *Dickens* (London: Sinclair-Stevenson, 1990).

claimed earlier, *Eva Trout* appears to be a kind of parable which we cannot retell in any terms other than those it offers us, it nevertheless insinuates, very powerfully and provocatively, in its sometimes extreme clashings of register, that the categories of living and of making fictions are confused only at our greatest peril. To turn our fantasies into reality in anything other than written fictions is to court destruction. Great as your need might be, you may write a child, but you may not force one to take your nature upon him. It is hardly necessary to say that the lesson is an urgent one for the childed as well as the childless; but that it should be written as Elizabeth Bowen's last word on the matter also suggests that, for her at least, there was no consolation whatever to be taken from the putatively assuaging fiction that a writer may substitute a book for a desired baby, that writing a child is in any sense emotionally equivalent to gestating one in actuality. In the book's sometimes heavy sadness this has its unrelentingly bleak element; but nevertheless the reader is given by *Eva Trout* a new knowledge about the capacity of the empathetic imagination, the imagination which, in a childless writer, may recreate with such overwhelming energy and inwardness the experience of both mothers and children.

And yet that knowledge stays deeply mysterious too, as endlessly unfathomable as one truly astonishing sentence which Elizabeth Bowen writes about her own mother in *Seven Winters*. That mother died, as we have seen, when Bowen was only 13, and *Seven Winters* is, in part, a memorial recreation of the mother's feelings for the very young Elizabeth: feelings which can be recovered, of course, only by the empathetic imagination. But what principle of empathy is at work when the mature woman writer of *Seven Winters*, published in 1942, imagines her mother looking at her when she is a very young child and then tells us, in her own person, 'I know now the feeling with which she stood on the bridge, looked along the lake till she came to my scarlet coat, then thought "That *is* my child!" '?[16] This writer is childless, she has never been a mother: so she cannot 'know' this feeling by experience. So how can she 'know now' what her mother, or any mother, ever felt? But no adequate reader of Elizabeth Bowen will doubt, nevertheless, the perfect truth of the claim she is making.

---

[16] Elizabeth Bowen, *Seven Winters* (Dublin: The Cuala Press [1942], repr. 1971 for the Irish University Press, Shannon), 29.

III

War

7

Words in the Dark: *The Demon Lover and Other Stories* (1945)

There is no place for it in human experience; it apparently cannot make a place of its own. It will have no literature.

'Sunday Afternoon'

Owing . . . to the thunder of those inordinate years, we were shaken out of the grip of our own pathos.

Elizabeth Bowen, postscript to the US edition of *The Demon Lover*

I

The Demon Lover and Other Stories, which Elizabeth Bowen published in the final year of the war in Europe, and which is, for me, her finest single volume of stories, is a book of many unhappy returns. It begins, in 'In the Square', with a military man returning to London to visit a woman with whom he has had an indeterminate pre-war relationship, who has herself recently returned to this bomb-ravaged square from rural evacuee seclusion; and it ends, in 'Mysterious Kôr', with a girl returning with her soldier lover after a long, frustrating night out, and in brilliant moonlight, to the tiny Regent's Park flat she shares with a girlfriend. Between these stories 'Sunday Afternoon' presents an Anglo-Irishman temporarily returned to neutral Ireland from a London where his flat has been bombed out; and the Sunday afternoon's superficially genteel conversation in the Wicklow mountains outside Dublin, which is the material of the story, shelves into a lethally exacerbated portrayal of the perturbing emotions of attachment and detachment, of loyalty and desertion, among the Anglo-Irish during wartime. In one of the volume's many significant interweavings of, or shifting hesitations between, the literal and the figurative, 'Something less than a wind, a breath of coldness, fretted the edge of things' (17). Three further stories, 'The Inherited Clock', 'Songs My Father Sang Me', and 'Ivy Gripped the Steps', the longest story in the book, involve adults returning, either literally or in memory, and under wartime inducement, to the scenes of childhood crisis, primal scenes; and we may remember Bowen's view that not only does the form of the short story essentially centre on one crisis only but that 'one might call it, almost, a crisis in itself'.[1]

Another group of stories, 'The Cheery Soul', 'Pink May', 'Green Holly', and, outstandingly, 'The Demon Lover', concern that more ultimate form of returnee, the revenant or ghost; and, indeed, both the volume's opening and closing sentences include ghosts of a kind: the atmospheric 'ghost of the glare of midday' in the former, a white light eerily leaking towards the unearthly; and the ghost city of Andrew Lang's and Rider Haggard's 'mysterious Kôr' in the latter, a city not of this earth at all. And one of the finest stories in the volume, 'The Happy Autumn Fields', involves the mysterious return, in a kind of waking dream, or, it is hinted, in some form of metempsychosis, of a woman in a bombed-out London flat, to the scene of a Victorian family house and estate. This is a return enabled, we are to understand, by her being an unexpected survivor, someone who has just avoided being killed by the fall of her ceiling during a raid: the merging of identities across time is effected by the sudden abject loss of identity for this 'woman weeping there on the bed, no longer reckoning who she was.'[2] Where in 'The Demon Lover' someone returns from the past, in 'The Happy Autumn Fields' someone returns to it; but both returns of the dead should also be read, I think, as figuring the actual dead of the Blitz, who nowhere appear literally in these stories. They nowhere appear literally, that is to say, but their presence is, nevertheless, everywhere.[3]

Most readers instinctively feel that, although this is never explicitly stated, the Victorian part of 'The Happy Autumn Fields' is set in

---

[1] Elizabeth Bowen, *Afterthought: Pieces about Writing* (London: Longmans Green & Co., 1962), 78.

[2] In *Afterthought*, 96, discussing this volume in the postscript to the first American edition, and therefore describing its sources in the Blitz for a readership which had never experienced aerial bombardment, Bowen comments on 'the strange, deep, intense dreams' people had in wartime London. This is corroborated by Tom Harrison in *Living through the Blitz* (1976; Harmondsworth: Penguin, 1978), 317, his fascinating and superbly written study based on the files of Mass Observation, where he says that 'Raid dreams were shared by old and young, but experienced more vividly by women.'

[3] Harrison says that 13,596 people had been killed in London by the end of 1940.

Ireland, not only because of the descriptions of the landscape but also because of the quasi-feudal landlordism which its social system appears to suggest; and this perhaps makes it Elizabeth Bowen's own version of the syndrome she identifies in Sheridan Le Fanu's *Uncle Silas* when she calls it 'an Irish story transposed to an English setting'.[4] It is also of interest that nineteenth-century Ireland should figure, perhaps especially in this unidentified or invisible way, as an element of quasi-visionary or hallucinatory retrospect in a collection of stories whose supernaturalism and quasi-supernaturalism, and whose whole preoccupation with returnings and hauntings, inherit that strain of Protestant gothic endemic to Victorian Anglo-Irish literature, and which I have already discussed in relation to the haunting in *Bowen's Court* and 'The Back Drawing-Room' in my opening chapter.[5] 'Dislocation' is a word prominent in both 'The Demon Lover' and 'The Happy Autumn Fields', to convey a sense of numbness, dissociation, alienation; and Bowen's discovery in *The Demon Lover and Other Stories* is that a mode of writing inherently appropriate to the circumstances of marginalized Irish Protestants may also fit the devastated lives of bombed-out London where, exactly, and as these stories again and again insist, people were feeling pushed to the side of their own former lives—and, furthermore, pushed aside by fire, that threat which also lay in wait for the agrarian landlord society evoked in the retrospect of 'The Happy Autumn Fields'. In this context it is more than merely apposite that in *The Heat of the Day* Bowen defines the London of the blackout as a 'garrison society'; which is, of course, the way Anglo-Ireland was defined and, indeed, the way it thought of itself for much of its history.

II

Other kinds of return are prominent in the stories too. One is the literary return which is allusion or intertext. 'The Demon Lover' takes its

---

[4] Bowen's remark on *Uncle Silas* is made in *The Mulberry Tree: Writings of Elizabeth Bowen*, selected and introduced by Hermione Lee (London: Virago Press, 1986), 101. In the preface to a volume of her stories, *A Day in the Dark and Other Stories* (1965), Bowen says that the setting is 'unshakeably Co. Cork' (9).

[5] For an excellent account which links Bowen to the tradition of Protestant gothic, see R. F. Foster's essay 'Protestant Magic: W. B. Yeats and the Spell of Irish History', in *Paddy and Mr Punch: Connections in Irish and English History* (1993; London: Penguin, 1995), 212–32.

title from an old Scottish ballad (sometimes known as 'The Carpenter's Wife') and, with eerily chilling brilliance, the story makes contemporary the ballad's tale of someone returned from the dead to redeem a promise from a one-time lover: it is, in particular, a masterstroke to have made the ballad's otherworldly ship, on which the lover carries off the woman, the London taxi from which there is no exit.[6] The title of 'The Happy Autumn Fields' is an allusion to 'Tears, idle tears', one of Tennyson's integral lyrics in his long poem 'The Princess' (1847). The empathetic and nostalgic desolation suffered by Mary, the story's heroine, is presumably developed from the lyric persona's condition:

> Tears, idle tears, I know not what they mean,
> Tears from the depth of some divine despair
> Rise in the heart, and gather to the eyes,
> In looking on the happy Autumn-fields,
> And thinking of the days that are no more.
>
> 'The Princess' IV, 22–5

Christopher Ricks has said that the poem is 'about the most potent of absences', and so is the story: so potent, in fact, that the absence becomes present again to the heroine.[7] But the nostalgia of 'The Happy Autumn Fields', its crossing of the historical and the contemporary, is also itself crossed with the peculiar condition of the narrator-prince in 'The Princess', who endures the 'weird seizures' of his 'waking dreams' in which 'I seemed to move among a world of ghosts, | And feel myself the shadow of a dream', a situation strung between the febrility of epilepsy and the ecstasy of vision. Similarly, the intense youthful sexual jealousy of the story's dream-narrative may also have been caught up from the lyric's evocation of the sweetness of kisses 'by hopeless fancy feigned | On lips that are for others; deep as love, | Deep as first love, and wild with all regret.' And the volume's final story, 'Mysterious Kôr', alludes in its title to a poem of the 1920s by Andrew Lang, dedicated to his friend H. Rider Haggard, and evoking the city of the dead which figures prominently in Haggard's novel *She* (1887). Lang's sonnet interiorizes or psychologizes Kôr as the name for ineradicable or ineffable human longings and desires; and the story's heroine, Pepita, in a state of intense sexual frustration, moulds her own personal fantasy further out of the sonnet's invitation: lines from the poem are

---

[6] The text of the ballad may be read in, for instance, *The Oxford Book of Ballads*, chosen and ed. by James Kinsley (1969; Oxford: Oxford University Press, 1989), 83–5.

[7] Christopher Ricks, *Tennyson* (London: Macmillan, 1972), 199.

quoted prominently, and poignantly, in the story, and the poem itself is discussed by the characters.[8]

More incidentally, 'Sunday Afternoon' ends when the Anglo-Irishman Henry Russel insists, twice, on calling the young girl of the story not by her actual name, Maria, but by the name of the daughter on Prospero's island in Shakespeare's *The Tempest*, Miranda. Utterly certain of his own responsibility to return to wartime London from the peace of neutral Ireland, and realizing how offensive such a decision is to the valetudinarian Anglo-Irish society he is leaving, with its 'fastidious, stylised melancholy', he nevertheless understands Maria's desire to leave too as a dereliction of her true responsibility. We are, therefore, to read his rechristening of her, I think, as his irony against her neutrally islanded and callow sense of the brave new world awaiting her on the other side of the Irish Sea, when he is so painfully, even exacerbatedly, aware of the decaying but still not despicable ethos of the old world which she is so anxious to escape. The nominal change is also complicated by Henry's erotic feeling for Maria: so that when he calls her Miranda it is almost as though he is both Prospero, the father, and Ferdinand, the lover, in relation to her. (If we read the Shakespearean reference so, then this is a Shakespearean allusion of almost transparent, although still inexplicit, significance, which we may set against the various Shakespearian aporia which I have described elsewhere in this study.)

In a similarly glancing but more recondite way, Proust is quoted in 'Ivy Gripped the Steps'. Its hero, the middle-aged, deeply isolated, and, it is implied, voyeuristic and alcoholic Gavin Doddington, revisits the scene of the definitive traumatizing events of his childhood—a kind of seduction and a kind of betrayal by a middle-aged woman—and thinks of his fate as 'l'horreur de mon néant'. No more is said in explication, and the phrase, although in French, is not, perhaps, a particularly distinctive one; but to recognize or identify its source, which is the episode in *A L'Ombre des jeunes filles en fleur* in which Marcel is ignored by the Balbec lift-boy, is to discover in it not just the metaphysical terror it appears to suggest but also a tremor of the farcical:

---

[8] The novel haunted Bowen, who read it as a child. See 'Rider Haggard: *She*', in Elizabeth Bowen, *The Mulberry Tree*, 246–50. It also fascinated Freud: 'A *strange* book, but full of hidden meaning', he says in *The Interpretation of Dreams*, where it is also invoked as the origin of a very strange dream indeed of his own. See *The Interpretation of Dreams*, trans. by Joyce Crick with an introduction and notes by Ritchie Robertson (Oxford: Oxford University Press, 1999), 293.

which is as unfortunately appropriate to the neurotically self-preoccupied Gavin as it is to Proust's narrator at this point in the novel. Bowen who, as the inspired use of this quoted phrase makes plain, was very deeply immersed in Proust indeed, knew as well as he does the contingency of tragedy and farce.[9]

I think it is worth saying that this kind of literary allusiveness is not entirely characteristic of Bowen, although it does, of course, occasionally figure elsewhere in her work too. It could be read as the writer's attempt to draw corroborative strength from some fragments of a literary tradition when engaged on the representation of an experience which was considered by many to lie beyond the capacity of 'literature', as Bowen slyly and self-challengingly makes plain in her character's observation in my epigraph from 'Sunday Afternoon' ('It will have no literature'); and indeed in her postscript to the American edition of the book she observes, in a way clearly of most relevance to 'Mysterious Kôr':

People whose homes had been blown up went to infinite lengths to assemble bits of themselves—broken ornaments, odd shoes, torn scraps of the curtains that had hung in a room—from the wreckage. In the same way, they assembled and checked themselves from stories and poems, from their memories, from one another's talk.[10]

In bending her literary sources to the challenge of the apparently unwritable in her own act of assembling and checking, her form of literary bricollage, Bowen is extremely resourceful, and the stories of *The Demon Lover and Other Stories* genuinely answer to the peculiar wartime combinations of distress and apathy, in which resignation is liable at any moment to lurch into terror, in which devastation is combined with adjustment.

In fact, Bowen occasionally foregrounds the intertextual nature of her writing in these stories. For instance, she repeats the word 'story' itself in 'Ivy Gripped the Steps', where it is said of Gavin that 'from his tour of annihilation nothing out of the story was to be missed' (129), an observation which cruelly plots him into his own long-since written narrative, and makes his 'tour'—his journey—a 'retour' too in which,

[9] Scott-Moncrieff and Kilmartin translate the phrase as 'the horror of my own nonentity': see *Remembrance of Things Past*, Vol. 1 (London: Chatto & Windus, 1981), 715. I am indebted for this reference to Geoffrey Wall. It is inevitable, however, that the word 'néant' will also strike the contemporary ear with the connotations given to it by Sartrean existentialism.

[10] *The Mulberry Tree*, 97.

far from annihilating his past, which might have been his expectation of this return, he is himself annihilated by it. In this story that foregrounded 'tour' is accompanied by a reflexivity in which the literary term is, as it were, made to precede the human experience, in a kind of serial nightmare: in relation to the constricting ivy of the story's title, we are told that the house 'had the air of reserving something quite of its own. It was then perhaps just, or not unfitting, that it should have been singled out for this gothic fate' (115); and it is conceivable that an ultimate precursor of the story is indeed the very gothic tale of a poisonous plant which intertwines human hopes and desires quite literally in Nathaniel Hawthorne's gruesome story 'Rappacini's Daughter' (1844).

Many of the earlier works of literature alluded to or transformed in *The Demon Lover and Other Stories* are also, however, prominently preoccupied with gender. The plot of 'The Princess' is designed to voice various attitudes to nineteenth-century feminism; *She*, with its eponymous amazonian *femme fatale*, is a 'pivotal' text of turn-of-the-century imperial and sexual politics; 'The Demon Lover' is, on one level, a ballad about the power relations implicit in promissory acts between the sexes; and the figure of Miranda in *The Tempest* gathers about itself many aspects of the relationship between amatory games and public political power games in the English seventeenth century.[11] In all of these ways the earlier literary texts adapted in this volume may be thought to imply an undermining of public, official, attitudes to the war: these are prominently stories of women, and stories of betrayal, isolation, hallucination, sexual thwarting, jealousy, manipulation, profound anxiety. Their emotions are a very long way indeed from the official narratives of the Blitz, with their testaments to solidarity, courage, resilience, and so on—which were, at best, only a very partial truth. If literature is corroborative in *The Demon Lover and Other Stories* it corroborates the darker, more distressing, tale, and it also complexly intricates human sexuality, and more particularly sexual neurosis, and war. 'The Happy Autumn Fields' includes a sudden, disconcertingly self-reflexive sentence about its cross-temporal correspondences: 'We surmount the skyline:

---

[11] Sandra Gilbert and Susan Gubar, in *No Man's Land, Volume 2: Sexchanges* (New Haven: Yale University Press, 1989), 21, say that *She* is 'a pivot on which the ideas and anxieties of the Victorians began to swivel into what has come to be called "the modern" '. It is also noteworthy, and perhaps not merely coincidental, that they read it in the light of 'The Princess': in both works 'three dauntless male explorers penetrate the secret fastness of a female country' (6).

the family come into our view, we into theirs' (100); and this is the way earlier literature works in these stories too: as these texts come newly into our view, so we come into theirs, and the ensuing judgements are deeply unsettling. Or, in another definition of intertextuality in that story, 'Everything one unburies seems the same age' (103). Referentiality is both a way of staying the present against hopeless confusion, and also a reminder of the besetting nightmares of the past from which the present cannot break free.

III

Prominent in many of these returns, as I have inevitably suggested simply by describing them, is social and sexual disruption. What wartime produces in *The Demon Lover and Other Stories*—notably the wartime London of the Blitz—is a world of social and sexual mobility, displacement, and transgression, in which the traditional relationships between masters (and mistresses) and servants, and between the upper- and the lower-middle classes, are destabilized in a sometimes erotically provocative way. 'Who would think this was the same world?' (10), asks Magdala on her return to London in 'In the Square'; and hitherto private, domestic, spaces are, quite literally, when walls are knocked down and interiors become visible, exposed and intruded upon by bombing. 'In the Square' defines it as a time of 'functional anarchy . . . fittings shocked from their place' (8). And if fittings no longer know, or keep to, their place, neither do people. When Travis, in 'The Happy Autumn Fields', feels vulnerable and threatened by the 'jaqerie' [*sic*] playing Tchaikovsky, badly, on the piano of a bombed-out flat, it is as though the fear of social revolution is as deep-seated as the fear for one's personal physical safety. The volume is full of vehicles, which both literally enable topographical mobility and also figure its emotional and psychological consequences: notably the 'democratic' bus which takes Henry Russel away from the pre-democratic, dying social world of the Anglo-Irish in 'Sunday Afternoon'; the taxi which opens the volume in 'In the Square', returning Rupert to the utterly changed world of his pre-war experience, and that other unforgettably ominous taxi of the dead which closes 'The Demon Lover'; and the bicycle of 'The Cheery Soul', on which the young girl makes her painfully awkward and lengthy rural ride towards a deeply disconcerting Christmas visit.

Within this context of literal physical mobility, marriages collapse under the strain of separation and affairs, but affairs too are sometimes extraordinarily difficult to manage in the cramped conditions of wartime London, with its newly, and necessarily, shared social spaces, with the permanent menace of the blackout—when Clara walks through it in 'The Inherited Clock', she 'seemed to pass like a ghost through an endless wall' (39)—and with the immediacy, for military and civilian alike, of the threat of violent death. In the volume's major stories it is as though, just as the interiors of London are being opened up by the bombs, human psychology is being opened up to its formative psycho-sexual patternings or stresses; and the revealed sexuality is usually of an inhibited, dispirited, or even atrophied kind. In 'The Inherited Clock' Clara, a woman in her thirties in a hopeless relationship with a married man, gradually discovers the source of her sexual dependency in her sadistic treatment in childhood by both her aunt and her cousin. During the course of the story, in which the sadism is concentrated on the skeleton clock of the title—in childhood Clara's fingers are forced into its mechanism, and bloodied—we are given to understand that her 'inheritance' from this childhood involves far more than just the clock; and the story is an almost literal realization of the Freudian return of the repressed, with the clock also acting as an emblem of Clara's entrapment in the past. In 'Songs My Father Sang Me' the woman's experience of her father's desertion in childhood, and of the unhappy marriage which led to it, is to be understood as a cauterizing of her own affective impulses, since she appears incapable of emotional generosity, trapped into a kind of narrative and sexual, or asexual, seriality by the circumstances she once endured. In this disconsolate story she understands herself as written by the script of her father's desertion of her, almost physically formed by the cancer of its wound: 'his actual words are gone as though I had never heard them, but his meaning lodged itself in some part of my inside, and is still there and has grown up with me' (75).

In 'Ivy Gripped the Steps' the central character literally returns to the scene of his quasi-seduction, between the ages of 8 and 10, by a middle-aged woman, and the story uncovers the patterns of his emotional and sexual life which were set, or frozen, then, first by his longing and subsequently by his hurt and abjection: both are conveyed, with a kind of intense delicacy, in the story's focus on the fetishistic. Although the figure is never made explicit, the ivy of the story's title grips the steps of the house in which Gavin came to painful knowledge of adult sexual behaviour just as the poisonous ivy of that knowledge has gripped his own sexuality since: and, in a volume in which, as I have said, the literary also returns, it is hard to believe that this story was not itself influential on the great modern English novel written to this theme—a novel sometimes condescended to by critics—L. P. Hartley's *The Go-Between*.[12] Bowen's story is as unsettling an exercise in 'the intensity of a person who must think lest he should begin to feel' as Hartley's, even though the sexual consequences are diametrically opposed: the hero of *The Go-Between*, Leo, becomes incapable of any sexual life; Gavin becomes, it is heavily implied, a cynically manipulative serial seducer.

In 'The Happy Autumn Fields' Clara, the dreaming woman of the contemporary wartime moment, appears to have a less than satisfactory relationship with her lover, Travis, for whom she feels only 'indifference', and from whose touch she flinches. She is emotionally wholly given over to the past, not the present; and the Victorian scene she enters is the site of extreme, it appears more than merely sibling, affection between two sisters, compounded by their extreme sexual rivalry over the same man. This story of sexual extremity and identification ends in a putatively supernatural moment, when Eugene, the male object of desire, is conceivably willed to death by one of the sisters: he dies in an otherwise unaccountable fall from his horse. In 'Mysterious Kôr', a story poised with ironic delicacy between farce and pathos, sexuality is also prominently the issue, since the lovers, Pepita and Arthur, are foiled in their attempt to make love—first by the brightness of the moonlight, which makes Regent's Park an impossibly public space, even at midnight, and then by the prudish or innocent friend Callie, who has resisted all hints that she might leave the flat to the lovers alone; and there are also intimations of a perturbedly unselfknowing lesbian sexuality in Callie herself, a 'more obscure trouble'.

In both 'Songs My Father Sang Me' and 'Ivy Gripped the Steps' the entrapments of sexuality, and the obsessional return to its sources, are accompanied by reminders of, or returns to, the First World War. In the former, a girl at a club tells her partner about her 'father', who disappeared from her life on her seventh birthday; and her monologue makes her appear obsessive about her story, a kind of female ancient mariner in relation to it. Although she calls him her father, the story

---

[12] Douglas Brooks-Davies adduces the story in a footnote to his edition of the novel (London: Penguin, 1997), 276 n. 14, comparing the story's ivy to the novel's deadly nightshade.

makes it plain that the man she is remembering was not biologically that, since she is, in fact, the product of an affair her mother had while her father was at the Front. Like Major Brutt in *The Death of the Heart*, he is 'one of the young men who were not killed in the last war', and her memory of his constrained, supernumerary, post-war existence is at the centre of her story, with its portrayal of a marriage disintegrating under the strain of his ex-officer joblessness. The larger cultural resonance becomes explicit when, just before he disappears, he evokes for his daughter the forever lost idea of the England he thought he was fighting for, now inextricably intertwined with the idea of the lost woman he once deeply loved: ' "I've lost her," he said, "or she's lost me; I don't quite know which; I don't understand what's happened' (74); and the story—now, in another war—compounds his baffled incomprehension with his daughter's own, as she obsessively narrates her loss but never comes any closer to comprehending it or to overcoming its traumatic results.

In 'Ivy Gripped the Steps' the contemporary month of September 1944, when Gavin returns to a Southstone newly opened up to visitors after its wartime sequestration, is crossed with the year of his defining visit there to his mother's friend Mrs Nicholson in 1912; and the Edwardian calm is unsettled by the First World War's imminence, notably in Admiral Concannon's efforts on behalf of the Awake Britannia League. He says of Gavin that 'What may come is bound, before it is done, to be his affair' (140), although, in fact, a further reason for Gavin's feeling the 'horreur de son néant' is that he was too young to fight in that war, and is too old to fight in this. What was to come was certainly, however, as he wanted it to be—'his alternative to love'—the Admiral's own 'affair', since we eventually learn that he was killed in that war; and a further, tacit crossing of the two wars in the story is Bowen's placing the initial meeting between Edith Nicholson and Gavin's mother in Dresden—one of the German cities, of course, which bore the brunt of Churchill's response to the Blitz of British cities. There is, I think, some suggestion in these explicit references that the First World War persists under the surface of the Second in something of the way in which the origins of sexual neurosis persist in these stories too, a suggestion that the culture itself, as well as individual psychologies, is trapped in a repetitive or serial pattern: the 'affair' of war is made to rhyme with the 'affair' of sex, and the admiral, in a way that puzzles the uncomprehending Gavin, is having some kind of an affair with Mrs Nicholson.

The volume's title story, in which the eponymous revenant is one of the 'missing' of the First World War, 'presumed dead' but never actually found—so that his return may, just about, be susceptible to rational explanation—makes the equation at its most disturbing.

IV

> She tugged at a knot she had tied wrong.
> 'The Demon Lover', 86

'People don't, on the whole, come back, and I've never blamed them', says the obsessive daughter of 'Songs My Father Sang Me', with reference to her father: but in the story immediately following this one someone does indeed come back, with a vengeance; and 'The Demon Lover' stands as the brilliantly economical paradigm of the book's themes and motifs of return.

Mrs Drover is herself returning from her family's evacuee rural retreat to her shuttered, bomb-damaged, Kensington house in order to collect some remaining household items. Naming her in its opening sentence as 'Mrs Drover', the story is both identifying her with her role as wife and mother and also, as it were, nominally locking her into her eventual fate, since this is a story in which a 'Drover' ends up being terrifyingly driven, sealed behind a taxi's soundproof glass.[13] The domestic space of the house has been defamiliarized for her, estranged from her, by her absence and its dereliction; and the story, a tale of two Augusts, is very much preoccupied with—in fact pits in radical opposition—domesticity and its other. 'In her once familiar street . . . an unfamiliar queerness had silted up' (80); and that queerness enters the house itself when Mrs Drover discovers an impossible letter on the hall table, a letter that no one could have put there. This is probably the most unsettling of the many letters in the long catalogue of them in Bowen's work; and when Mrs Drover reads it, and the story quotes it,

---

[13] Paul Muldoon finds another significance in the name: 'The "D" of "Demon" and the "over" of "Lover" are built into "Drover". It is fated that Mrs. Drover meet her demon lover at the hair-raising end of the story.' See Paul Muldoon, *To Ireland, I* (Oxford: Oxford University Press, 2000), 19. W. J. McCormack, in *From Burke to Beckett: Ascendancy, Tradition and Betrayal in Irish Literary History* (1985; Cork: Cork University Press, 1994), 402, says that the name Kathleen Drover 'strongly suggests an Irish provenance'. 'Kathleen' is, as we have seen, the name of the cook in *The Last September*, and 'Kathie' that of the one in *A World of Love*.

it both exposes the now defamiliarized present to a long-distant past and also appears ominously poised in relation to a putative future. It reminds her that today is the day of 'our anniversary', about which she has made a 'promise', and it notifies her that she may 'expect' its writer 'at the hour arranged'. The letter addresses Mrs Drover as 'Kathleen', making her more familiar to us than she is as 'Mrs Drover', and it is signed 'K': so that writer and addressee appear complicit in their sharing the initial letter of their forenames, even as the virtual anonymity of the writer's initial (and the accident—or is it that?—that it is shared with the eerily almost anonymous protagonist in Kafka) renders it disturbingly minatory. The letter appears as a disruption of legitimate privacies of a kind, as we have seen, endemic to the wartime existence described in other stories in the volume too, but now with an added personal animosity: 'she felt intruded upon—and by someone contemptuous of her ways'.

As Mrs Drover, 'a woman whose utter dependability was the keystone of her family life', continues her packing, evocations of her present familial, and familiar, life, are crossed with her memories of the past she once shared with K. Her present circumstances are deftly evoked as, under the pressure of the dawning knowledge of what the letter means, she examines her face in a mirror, contemplating what she has become:

She was confronted by a woman of forty-four, with eyes starting out under a hat-brim that had been rather carelessly pulled down. She had not put on any more powder since she left the shop where she ate her solitary tea. The pearls her husband had given her on their marriage hung loose round her now rather thinner throat, slipping into the V of the pink wool jumper her sister knitted last autumn as they sat round the fire. Mrs. Drover's most normal expression was one of controlled worry, but of assent. Since the birth of the third of her little boys, attended by a quite serious illness, she had had an intermittent muscular flicker to the left of her mouth, but in spite of this she could always sustain a manner at once energetic and calm.   (82)

The pathos of self-recognition is managed wonderfully here. The faintly *distraite* loneliness of her ageing; the loyalty she maintains by continuing to wear her marital pearls (even though—we are subsequently told—her marriage has been, for her, one of convenience, made late in her life); the sense of domestic constriction implied by the presence of a sister as well as a husband, a member of the first as well as the second family, in the domestic space; the slight dowdiness exuded by that home-made 'pink wool jumper'; and, above all, the grimly affecting detail of the 'intermittent muscular flicker' which has been the result, possibly, of more childbirth, and later in life, than she should have been made to bear: all are powerfully suggestive of a life lived under control, in check, unspontaneously, subserviently; and lived for others, not herself, a driven life.

Mrs Drover is then described 'turning from her own face as precipitately as she had gone to meet it'; and there is in this, I think, a fleeting memory of T. S. Eliot's early poetry—of the narrating persona of 'Portrait of a Lady' feeling 'like one who smiles, and turning shall remark | Suddenly, his expression in a glass', and of the persona in 'The Love Song of J. Alfred Prufrock' anxiously advising himself that 'there will be time | To prepare a face to meet the faces that you meet'. In the following episode of the story, which I describe below, there is another fleeting memory of Eliot: the young Kathleen Drover's question, 'What shall I do, what shall I do?' is clearly reminiscent of the vividly panicky repetition in 'A Game of Chess' in *The Waste Land*: 'What shall we do tomorrow? | What shall we ever do?' And Bowen's story shares several elements with this early poetry of Eliot's: the preoccupation with what 'Portrait of a Lady', alluding to Matthew Arnold, calls 'the buried life'; the minatory and anxious turnings and returnings, of cultural as well as personal history, consequent on being haunted by the post-1914 war dead; and the deeply perturbed and repetitive sexuality neurotically incarnate in the figure of Tiresias in *The Waste Land*, who has 'foresuffered all | Enacted on this same divan or bed'. 'The Demon Lover', returning to such motifs, feeds the distresses of an earlier twentieth-century post-war period into its own Second World War fiction of repetition.

That sense of Mrs Drover's driven life is intensified by the phrase 'sustain a manner'. Mrs Drover is an actor in the domestic space; and the intrusive letter from K, with its talk of the 'promise', is the return to her of what she has repressed in order to maintain the domestic role. What this is appears in a flashback—and the story is, in several ways, prominently cinematic in technique—in which we learn that Kathleen has been engaged to K, a soldier about to return to the Front in August 1916. The flashback is to their leavetaking in her family garden, outside—and this is emphasized—the lit-up interior space in which her mother and sister await her return:

The young girl talking to the soldier in the garden had not ever completely seen his face. It was dark; they were saying good-bye under a tree. Now and then—

for it felt, from not seeing him at this intense moment, as though she had never seen him at all—she verified his presence for these few moments longer by putting out a hand, which he each time pressed, without very much kindness, and painfully, on to one of the breast buttons of his uniform. That cut of the button on the palm of her hand was, principally, what she was to carry away. (83)

Principally, then, what she was to carry away, from this space beyond the familial and domestic, was a wound, the physical impression of a sadistic impulse. But she was to carry it further than she thought, it was to be far-fetched indeed: since, although the promise she makes to him is never specified in the story, its nature is terrifyingly clear to her, and it is, of course, this which returns to haunt her in his letter. The scene in the garden ends like this:

Only a little more than a minute later she was free to run up the silent lawn. Looking in through the window at her mother and sister, who did not for the moment perceive her, she already felt that unnatural promise drive down between her and the rest of all human kind. No other way of having given herself could have made her feel so apart, lost and foresworn [*sic*]. She could not have plighted a more sinister troth.   (83–4)

In the ballad which supplies the story's title the lover returns from the dead after seven years to demand that the now married 'dearest dear' renew her promised 'former vows': so, for him, it is her subsequent marriage which makes her forsworn. In Bowen's story the promise is a kind of ellipsis or aporia; but the being forsworn is, for Kathleen, not the consequence of her marriage, but the immediate consequence of the promise itself. What is the promise? That she will wait for him whether she hears that he is 'missing, presumed dead' or not? Or that she will meet him 'at the hour arranged' even though she may, in fact, believe him to have been killed? We are not told; and neither are we told why she promises, although we are almost told. As Mrs Drover completes her packing and tries to allay her growing apprehension with the solace that she can take a taxi away from the house, she reflects on what had compelled her:

He was never kind to me, not really. I don't remember him kind at all. Mother said he never considered me. He was set on me, that was what it was—not love. Not love, not meaning a person well. What did he do, to make me promise like that? I can't remember—But she found that she could.

She remembered with such dreadful acuteness that the twenty-five years since then dissolved like smoke and she instinctively looked for the weal left by the button on the palm of her hand. She remembered not only all that he said and did but the complete suspension of *her* existence during that August week. I was not myself—they all told me so at the time. She remembered—but with one white burning blank as where acid has dropped on a photograph: *under no conditions* could she remember his face.   (86)

'But she found that she could.' The 'dreadful acuteness' of her memory here makes the memory itself an implicitly but powerfully erotic one; and it is combined with the reiteration of his sadism: 'she instinctively looked for the weal left by the button on the palm of her hand', which seems a kind of erotic stigma, a token of her subjection to him. In this figure we may, I think, understand that her promise has been extracted as the consequence of her attraction to, precisely, this kind of sadism. What K's letter has returned to her is her own long-repressed sexual desire, desire of a sado-masochistic kind, and a desire which seems so terrifyingly, guiltily, perverse to this dutiful, conscientious, 'prosaic' woman that even in memory she cannot name it. Only such desire could extract a 'promise like that' from her; and, for her, real desire bears no relation whatever to the 'love' she can recognize, or has had to endure: a love, it appears, not passionate at all, one adequately defined by the drained banality of 'meaning a person well'.

For Mrs Drover, however, the repressed does not return to aid release but to enforce entrapment. In the superbly effective concluding paragraph, which is indeed, as Paul Muldoon says, 'hair-raising', the taxi which she is about to enter initially appears, to the first-time reader, as it does to Mrs Drover, as the true solace of release from apprehension, despite the story's cumulative tension as the 'hour arranged'—the time appointed—approaches. But then comes the reversal of all expectation, as the various enclosed spaces of 'The Demon Lover', familiar and defamiliarized, now concentrate themselves into one final familiar space, become terminally unfamiliar and claustrophobic; and a Drover fatally commits herself to a driver:

The driver braked to what was almost a stop, turned round and slid the glass panel back: the jolt of this flung Mrs. Drover forward till her face was almost into the glass. Through the aperture driver and passenger, not six inches between them, remained for an eternity eye to eye. Mrs. Drover's mouth hung open for some seconds before she could issue her first scream. After that she continued to scream freely and to beat with her gloved hands on the glass all round as the taxi, accelerating without mercy, made off with her into the hinterland of deserted streets.   (87)

Mrs Drover has earlier examined, with her eye, her own face in the mirror; and she has failed to remember his, in a way reiterated in the story. Now it is revealed to her, as they are thrust face to face and eye to eye. Bob Dylan in 'We Better Talk This Over', a postmortem on a love affair, sings, 'You don't have to be afraid of looking into my face | We've done nothing to each other time will not erase'; but here the lovers have done something to each other which time will never erase, and the recognition of this when she also, in terror, recognizes his face gives time the aspect of eternity.[14] What is eternal also takes on the infernal, quasi-theological, resonance of that 'without mercy'. We may read this as precisely the opposite of that 'compassion that was timeless and without mercy' at the end of William Golding's *Pincher Martin*, since in 'The Demon Lover' no metaphysic of compassion obtains, even one terribly beyond the humane rationale of mercy; and what is eternal is this woman's terrified panic before the persistent violence of this man, which she may once have desired, of which she is now in mortal dread.[15] What is also eternal is that he 'made off with her'—drove her off in the taxi, of course, but also decamped with her in his possession, dispossessing her of a self. Driving her.

V

Even under enormous pressure Mrs Drover has persisted with the collection of household items which has been the purpose of her return to London; and 'The Demon Lover' is, in a sense, a story about the relationship between possession and self-possession. When she wrote a postscript for the first American edition of *The Demon Lover and Other Stories*—and was therefore writing about the circumstances of the London Blitz for a readership which had had no experience of civilian aerial bombardment—Elizabeth Bowen prominently advertised this relationship, although she phrases it differently and strikingly. Included among the various elements comprising what she identifies as a state of 'lucid abnormality' is the sudden lack of possessions: 'Now there was not what you liked, and you did not choose'; whereas deciding what you liked, and choosing, had previously been the way 'you

---

[14] Bob Dylan, 'We Better Talk This Over', in *Lyrics 1962–1985* (London: Paladin, 1988), 577.

[15] William Golding, *Pincher Martin* (London: Faber & Faber, 1966), 201.

used to know what you were like'.[16] This very effectively phrases the relationship between 'what you liked' and 'what you were like', between commodity and identity, possession and self-possession; and this was precisely the relationship disrupted by the Blitz, partly since you were, in an air-raid, likely to be killed by your own possessions, by the exploding components and commodities of your own home. The disruption allows the re-emergence of hitherto repressed memories and desires, and 'The Demon Lover' knows this all too well:

The desuetude of her former bedroom, her married London home's whole air of being a cracked cup from which memory, with its reassuring power, had either evaporated or leaked away, made a crisis—and at just this crisis the letter-writer had, knowledgeably, struck. (84)

The leaking away of domestic memory, and the re-surfacing of contingent memory, is Mrs. Drover's condition; and it is noteworthy that the scene of this knowledge is her 'former bedroom'. 'But she found that she could.' Could remember, that is: remember what had once happened in, presumably, another bedroom.

Given that for Bowen, as we have seen, the short story was itself crisis, the form had unerringly found its moment and its occasion, since the Blitz, we might say, forced the moment to its crisis; and 'The Demon Lover' is an almost textbook demonstration of what we might think of as the moment forced to its ultimate crisis, the moment which Freud, in his famous paper published in the aftermath of the First World War, calls the 'uncanny': 'something which is familiar and old-established in the mind and which has become alienated from it only through the process of repression'.[17] But since the virtually anonymous, sadistic, K is also a soldier from the First World War, the story has a historical and cultural resonance beyond Mrs Drover's psycho-sexual being: he is the culturally repressed which returns, with extreme violence, bringing death once more in its wake; he is the unexorcised and unassimilated other, the '*unheimlich*' which intrudes on the space of the '*heimlich*'; and the presence of Mrs Drover's sister in both her girlhood home and her mature, married, home is a very delicate and subtle indication of the persistence in her life of a constraining 'homely' only just managing to protect her, temporarily as it transpires, from the vortex of the 'unhomely' revealed by the story. 'She felt intruded

---

[16] *The Mulberry Tree*, 97.
[17] Sigmund Freud, 'The "Uncanny"', in *The Penguin Freud Library*, Vol. 14: Art and Literature, ed. by Albert Dickson (London: Penguin Books, 1985), 335–76, 363–4.

upon—and by someone contemptuous of her ways' applies literally to Mrs Drover's home, but it applies also, figuratively, to the British homeland. So these stories write a kind of history too; and it is notable that when she writes of them in her 1945 postscript she defines them formally in metaphors drawn from the aerial bombardment itself: they are, she says, 'flying particles of something enormous and inchoate that had been going on. They were sparks from experience—an experience not necessarily my own'.[18]

And, in fact, the volume does include the word 'history' prominently, if ironically, on several occasions. In 'Sunday Afternoon', for instance, Maria is told that the war she wants to become involved in is 'not like a war in history'; to which she replies, 'It's not in history yet.' For Mrs Nicholson in 'Ivy Gripped the Steps', denying, in 1912, the very possibility of another war, history is something she did at school, and is now at an end: her fey whiggery—'I suppose there *is* one reason for learning history—one sees how long it has taken to make the world nice' (128)—is about to be terribly repudiated, and in any case she is guilty of deep moral myopia, since she is being anything but 'nice' to Gavin, whose life she is cynically, or just carelessly and self-absorbedly, destroying. That story is also a tale of two Englands: her genteel suburban south-coast resort; and Gavin's virtually defunct, quasi-feudal, squirearchy, which brings him a historical understanding the opposite of hers: 'This existence had no volition, but could not stop; and its never stopping, because it could not, made history's ever stopping the less likely' (129). At the end of the story, nevertheless, he reaches a rather different conclusion: 'On the return through the town towards the lip of the plateau overhanging the sea, the voidness and the air of concluded meaning about the plan of Southstone seemed to confirm her theory: history, after this last galvanized move forward, had come, as she expected, to a full stop. It had only not stopped where or as she foresaw' (146). Such apocalyptic sentiments do inhere in these stories, as they do in other literature of the war. Figuring the end of history is to figure the most intense feelings of powerlessness and loss of identity; which is also why the stories return to the past, where Mary in 'The Happy Autumn Fields' nostalgically locates a value utterly lost to the disinherited present:

How are we to live without natures? We only know inconvenience now, not sorrow. Everything pulverizes so easily because it is rot-dry; one can only wonder that it makes so much noise. The source, the sap must have dried up, or the

[18] *The Mulberry Tree*, 95.

pulse must have stopped, before you and I were conceived. So much flowed
through people; so little flows through us.   (112)

The ennui of supersession in this passage is intended to be met by
what Bowen calls, in her American postscript, those hallucinations
which are 'an unconscious, instinctive, saving resort on the part of the
characters'.[19] In the book's superb concluding story, 'Mysterious Kôr',
the sexually frustrated Pepita, who is also terrified that her soldier lover
will be killed, makes her 'hallucination' out of a deeply inward, almost
mesmerized transformation of Andrew Lang's sonnet.[20] Pepita's reinvention of the sonnet's dead city of Kôr as the scene of oneiric togetherness with her lover does indeed figure an imaginative possibility in
fact denied by the almost unbearable constraints of her present history.
And yet, in a way epitomizing Bowen's coldly affronting realism amid
all the hallucinatory hyper-realism of these stories, it is hard to see that
'saving' is quite the right word for this, despite its author's assertion. In
this story too, we might well feel, something repressed also, just about,
returns: since in *She* the *femme fatale* of the title, Ayesha, is in the end
horrifyingly consumed by the fire which she believes will renew her.[21]
Such knowledge is elided in Pepita's consciousness of the story as it is
mediated by the poem: but it is a knowledge which seems, nevertheless, to insist itself, in this London consumed by fire, in her final
reflection, which is also the final paragraph of *The Demon Lover and
Other Stories*, where what is being invoked is, it seems to me, indeter-
minably sexual love or death. Pepita's lover, Arthur, has earlier been
overheard by Callie mumbling to himself in the early hours of the
morning 'words in the dark, words to the dark'. In these culminating
sentences, with their mesmeric rhythms and repetitions, and their con-
juration of a mysteriously almost De Chirico-like cityscape, Elizabeth
Bowen has found, we might claim, as she has in all the major stories of
this volume, words in the dark and words to the dark of wartime civilian disruption and devastation:

---

[19] *The Mulberry Tree*, 96.
[20] Deborah Parsons interestingly suggests that Pepita corresponds to a literary type:
that of the female wanderer or *flâneuse* of wartime London. See 'Souls Astray: Elizabeth
Bowen's Landscape of War', in *Women: A Cultural Review* (Spring 1997), 8: 1, 24–32.
[21] It is instructive that, when Bowen writes about her childhood obsession with the
novel, she tells us that part of her terrified fascination was that Ayesha 'had entered fire
(the thing of which I was most frightened)'. See *The Mulberry Tree*, 112.

She still lay, as she had lain, in an avid dream, of which Arthur had been the source, of which Arthur was not the end. With him she looked this way, that way, down the wide, void, pure streets, between statues, pillars and shadows, through archways and colonnades. With him she went up the stairs down which nothing but moon came; with him trod the ermine dust of the endless halls, stood on terraces, mounted the extreme tower, looked down on the statued squares, the wide, void, pure streets. He was the password, but not the answer: it was to Kôr's finality that she turned.   (189)

8

War's Stories: *The Heat of the Day* (1948) and its Contexts

But what story *is* true?
Cousin Nettie

I STORIES

'History', then, is the resounding word which *The Demon Lover and Other Stories* does not shirk, but it is the word 'story' that echoes through Elizabeth Bowen's wartime novel rather than through her collection of wartime stories. *The Heat of the Day*, a story about entangled loyalties and treacheries—in war, in love, and in relationships across the generations—is itself generated out of a radical sense of the destabilizations or erosions of identity consequent on wartime displacements and disorientations. In this novel the familiar Bowen preoccupation with the tenuousness of identity now becomes the generative element of an extensively ramifying plot. The paradigm for the terror caused by the erosion of identity is the heroine's, Stella Rodney's, anxiety about her son who, at 19, has become a soldier: she thinks that 'the Army was out to obliterate Roderick. In the course of a process, a being processed, she could do nothing to stop, her son might possibly disappear' (49). 'Disappear' is Stella's fearful euphemism for 'die'; but it also registers the terror that what 'Roderick' has meant to her will vanish too, transformed by a uniform, an ethos, a set of traumatizing circumstances. In the process, the 'being processed', that is modern warfare the potentially obliterated self becomes what Bowen, in her postscript to *The Demon Lover* calls 'the uncertain "I" '.[1] *The Heat of*

---

[1] *'The Demon Lover'* (1945 postscript to US edn.), in Elizabeth Bowen, *The Mulberry Tree: Writings of Elizabeth Bowen*, selected and introduced by Hermione Lee (London: Virago, 1986), 94–9, 98.

the Day is a novel in which the panic of possibly losing identity, and of others deceiving you about their identities, operates not only as the agency of plot but as the very texture of style. It is a style fraught, intimate, and urgent: its pitch is so high, and its syntactical distortions and dislocations sometimes so arrestingly peculiar, because the pitch of the potential panic is so acute. The wartime world of *The Heat of the Day* is one in which, it sometimes seems, anyone can be, or can become, anything.

In these contexts of panic and threat the word 'story' reverberates insistently. Whereas much criticism of the novel has focused, under-standably, on its accounts of treachery, Bowen's interest is also in where the truth of any story might lie in a universal wartime discourse of story-telling; and this aspect of the book has been very illuminat-ingly contextualized by Adam Piette in his chapter on propaganda in an excellent study of wartime literature, *Imagination at War*.[2] In a novel of, essentially, a very simple plot and sub-plot, the crucial 'story' of the main plot is one of political treachery. Stella is told what she herself calls a 'story' about her lover, Robert Kelway: 'somebody . . . came to me with a story about you', she eventually tells him, the story that he is an enemy agent. She is told the story by the enigmatically unsettling Harrison, who uses it as an attempt to blackmail her into having an affair with him: Harrison himself refers to it, prominently, as 'that par-ticular story'. When, a long way into the novel, Stella finally tells Robert about the accusation and, after first denying it, he confesses and attempts to justify his treachery, he also refers to it as a 'story': 'What was to stop you turning the story in?' (281), he asks Stella, in a way that peculiarly almost personifies 'the story' as though it is itself capable of treachery and impeachment. Finally, with everything revealed between them towards the very end of the novel—which culminates in Robert's death—Stella thinks that his then telling the truth 'had come as the end, or rather the fading-out, of so many stories at the end of so many days; or, as a sort of confession as to why many stories, now that she came to tell them, had no ending' (285). And indeed this story itself, *The Heat of the Day*, has, as we shall see, no certain ending at all.

Woven into this central, self-reflexive, story are 'many stories' which people tell about themselves to one another, or even, more poignantly sometimes, which they tell about themselves to themselves, in order to

---

[2] Adam Piette, *Imagination at War: British Fiction and Poetry 1939–1945* (London: Papermac, 1995), ch. 5.

maintain identities in peril. Stella has told Roderick an untrue story about her marriage, allowing him to believe that Victor, his father, rather than she herself, was the abandoned party. She does so partly to protect Roderick's sense of his dead father's merit, but also out of a perverse willingness to appear a *femme fatale* rather than a victim. The truth of that story is itself revealed to Roderick by Cousin Nettie, the wife of the recently deceased Francis Morris, an Anglo-Irish landowner who has unexpectedly left Roderick his Irish esate, Mount Morris. Nettie is confined to a home for the mentally ill, Wistaria Lodge, and it is plain when she tells Roderick the truth of his own family background—what he subsequently regards as 'quite a new story'—that she is not quite as out of her mind as she has given the impression of being. Her deception has been another story fabricated to enable her only conceivable exit from a marriage and an upper-class Anglo-Irish mode of existence which she had found intolerable: 'There should never have been any other story' in her relationship with Francis than that they were cousins, she tells Roderick, although she is tantalizingly inexplicit on the reasons for the failure of the marriage. *Hamlet* is alluded to when she she says this, as it is elsewhere in the novel too, and its hero's strategies of feigned insanity—if that's what they are, exactly ('O that subtle trick to pretend the acting only when we are very near *being* what we act', says Coleridge)—cast their dismal light across Nettie's dreadful necessitousness.[3]

After Roderick has taxed Stella with the truth of her marriage, she also thinks of her own life as a story, as she makes plain to Harrison. Acknowledging the fiction of 'the story that I had walked out on Victor', she says that 'Whoever's the story *had* been, I let it be mine . . . it came to be my story, and I stuck to it. Or rather, first I stuck to it, then it went on sticking to me: it took my shape and equally I took its' (224). Here the uncertain 'I' is shaped as derivative, imitative, and virtually random, an aggregate, a composite, a composition: the 'I' is only whatever story will stick to it for long enough. In this, Stella thinks herself typical of those who stay on in the wartime London in which, just after the fall of France in 1942, she and Robert first meet, 'people whom the climate of danger suited', for whom, she thinks, 'Life-stories were

---

[3] Terence Hawkes (ed.), *Coleridge on Shakespeare* (Harmondsworth: Penguin, 1969), 176. Barbara Bellow Watson sees *Hamlet*—in some far-fetched ways, in my view—as the novel's 'literary forebear' in what is nevertheless a valuable essay, 'Variations on an Enigma: Elizabeth Bowen's War Novel', repr. in Harold Bloom (ed.), *Modern Critical Views: Elizabeth Bowen* (New York: Chelsea House, 1987), 81–101.

shed as so much superfluous weight.' And she thinks of Harrison in a virtually Wildean paradox: 'By the rules of fiction, with which life to be credible must comply, he was as a character "impossible"—each time they met, for instance, he showed no shred or trace of having been continuous since they last met' (140).

There is a wry exposure of its own fictionality in the fiction that is *The Heat of the Day* here, and perhaps a rationale for what critics have often felt as a lack of solidity or adequate individualization in the novel's characterization; but life's being not 'credible' is the ethical and ontological chasm which yawns everywhere in the book. The virtually febrile self-consciousness about being narrated informs the entire narrative; and it also crosses with, just as individual stories leak into, the public narratives of wartime. The 'story' which Harrison tells Stella about Robert, and then the stories which this novel tells us about what both Stella and Harrison do with that story, have their direct public consequences since Robert's treachery is, presumably, even if only minutely, capable of altering the course of the war. But the sense of being narrated, of being part of a discourse you cannot control, is also congruent with the wartime narratives of propaganda; and *The Heat of the Day* has, as one of its sub-plots, a narrative profoundly to do with the perils of being narrated. The story of Louie Lewis and her friend Connie is a story of believing, and then choosing to disbelieve, the stories about yourself with which the state, through the machinery of the press, would wish to shape you, which the state would wish to stick to you. This plot is the place where story most exacerbatedly meets the authoritative voice of the public story which the country tells itself about itself during war; and in *The Heat of the Day* the propagandist narrative is deeply undermined.

W. J. McCormack has said that this is a novel in which we witness 'the absconding of action, or the abjuring of it by the author', which is certainly true in the sense that for a novel of war its action is remarkably muted.[4] However, in the crossing of public and private stories, its predominantly interior, temporary locations—rented flats, a house permanently on the market, an Irish Big House at a phase of acute historical crisis, a home for the mentally distressed, a sequence of unnamed restaurants and bars—are made to register or, as it were, to exude or sweat out or discharge the exacerbations of the public

---

[4] W. J. McCormack, *Dissolute Characters: Irish Literary History through Balzac, Sheridan Le Fanu, Yeats and Bowen* (Manchester: Manchester University Press, 1993), 219.

wartime world. *The Heat of the Day* is a kind of vortex which has sucked the outer wartime atmosphere into itself and vertiginously whirls it around, even in its syntactical structures, in a motion all the more unsettling for the confined space in which it occurs. It is an unillusioned treatment of the relationship between tiny human stories and the vast wreckage that is the public story between 1942 and 1944, the years between the fall of France and the victories of Montgomery in North Africa; and the novel, for all the interiority of its design and settings, does punctiliously remind us of the public events and the public dates.

II PARALLELS

Louie Lewis is topographically displaced in London, having been brought up in Seale (Bowen's version of Hythe in Kent, which also figures, as we have seen, in *The Death of the Heart*), where her parents have been killed by a bomb. She is also emotionally disoriented because her husband, Tom, is in the army overseas. Her friend Connie, an ARP warden, is an ardent, if sceptical, reader of the newspapers, to which she introduces Louie. In the pathos of Louie's disorientation, she is solaced by her belief in what they say: 'how inspiring was the variety of the true stories', she thinks, 'which made the war seem human, people like her important, and life altogether more like it was once'. In a passage which has a comically ironizing but uncondescending momentum, she measures herself against the definitions of the newspaper:

Louie, after a week or two on the diet [of newspapers], discovered that she *had* got a point of view, and not only a point of view but the right one. . . . Dark and rare were the days when she failed to find on the inside page of her paper an address to or else account of herself. Was she not a worker, a soldier's lonely wife, a war orphan, a pedestrian, a Londoner, a home- and animal-lover, a thinking democrat, a movie-goer, a woman of Britain, a letterwriter, a fuel-saver, and a housewife? She was only not a mother, a knitter, a gardener, a foot-sufferer, or a sweetheart—at least not rightly. Louie now felt bad only about any part of herself which in any way did not fit into the papers' picture; she could not have survived their disapproval. (152)

She becomes, indeed, a virtual worshipper of press opinion, and a fetishist of the newspaper as object, and of newsprint itself. As a result, she accepts the responsibility of making her own story coincide as closely as possible with the 'true stories' of the press; and these are prominently about how servicemen's wives should behave in the absence of their husbands. Which is why Louie conceives of herself as 'not rightly' a sweetheart: naturally flirtatious and highly sexed, she is wrongly a sweetheart when she picks men up, which is what we see her attempting with Harrison in the novel's opening scene. The 'true stories' of the newspaper are, therefore, stories which stick only very approximately to Louie.

The novel establishes an elaborate parallelism between Louie and Stella; and the almost geometrically accurate fit of this irritates some critics, including W. J. McCormack, who wants to dismiss it as a virtual *naiveté*: the parallelism, he says, 'is lightly laid down upon a far more fractured and fracturing treatment of character, and can be put aside without difficulty.'[5] I doubt this. Indeed, it may be read as part of that very fracture, since it is through her attitude to Stella that Louie is saved from the propagandistic version of herself; and it is therefore the parallelism between Louie and Stella which designs one of the novel's most striking ethical effects. At the most significant point of convergence between the main plot and this sub-plot Louie meets Stella in the grill-bar in the climactic scene with Harrison in Chapter 12. It is the moment when Stella, in front of Louie, codedly offers herself to Harrison in order to buy Robert's continued freedom, and Harrison decisively refuses the offer: his motives are never elaborated, here or anywhere else, merely hinted at, and that very darkly. Louie, who understands none of this, sees only a Harrison behaving extremely badly to Stella, in a way which transgresses, for her, all the established norms of wartime behaviour. After rebuking him, she forms an attachment to Stella which is socially admiring but also virtually sexual in its intensity: 'Lying in Chilcombe Street . . . Louie dwelled on Stella with mistrust and addiction, dread and desire . . . Louie felt herself entered by what was foreign' (247).

When, towards the end of the novel, Robert dies in a fall from Stella's roof, attempting to evade capture, Stella's evidence to the inquest is reported in the press as that of a *femme fatale*, a version of herself which she has already maintained for much of her life, and which she is only too ready to accept once more since it appears to supply a reason for Robert's otherwise suspicious death. Louie, still avidly reading the newspapers, is, as a consequence, undermined in her resolution to behave other than the way the newspapers tell her 'flighty

[5] *Dissolute Characters*, 230.

wives' behave since her new model, Stella, has now, it appears, been proven 'flighty' too. What the newspapers insinuate, wrongly, about Stella's sexual morality therefore induces in Louie a proper realization of her own. And this is stranger, more contingent, and altogether more subtle than the received opinion of the press: 'she felt nearer Tom with any man than she did with no man—true love is to be recognized by its aberrations; so shocking can these be, so inexplicable to any other person, that true love is seldom to be recognized at all' (145). And the consequence is Louie's pregnancy which, as we shall see, is crucial to the novel's climax.

Louie is an excellent study in self-lacerating inarticulacy and self-opacity, but there is no doubting the complexity of this alternative, unpropagandized knowledge. What may seem tendentious is, in fact, contrary, potentially chaotic, utterly unavailable to the ideologies of the public sphere; and it has been learned in loneliness and suffering, in a form of self-abjection, as Louie's truth.[6] We may also read such knowledge out of Elizabeth Bowen's treatment of love elsewhere too; and it is rendered all the more compelling by its being formed in Louie through an appreciation of a woman, not a man.[7] Patricia Coughlan is an excellent reader of Bowen but she mistakes Louie when she maintains that 'she seems to lack all capacity to be the author of her own life'.[8] Here, reading Stella wrongly—literally, reading her as she is reported in a newspaper—Louie becomes a newly enabled author of herself. And she does so in what is virtually an ironic *mise-en-abîme*: her own genuinely true story is discovered by her placing faith in the newspaper's 'true story'—that is, lie—about another. In the story of Louie *The Heat of the Day* intensively transforms the history of a cultural moment—what the novel epigrammatically calls 'that "time

---

[6] Gill Plain, in an excellent account of the novel, thinks that we are being offered here a view of 'male interchangeability'. Obviously, I think the ethical focus of the novel is very differently adjusted here. See *Women's Fiction of the Second World War: Gender, Power and Resistance* (Edinburgh: Edinburgh University Press, 1996), 187.

[7] There is certainly a lesbian sub-text here but, in general, I find such texts in Bowen's earlier novels much less insistent—and therefore altogether stranger and more compelling—than Renée C. Hoogland does in her book, *Elizabeth Bowen: A Reputation in Writing* (New York: New York University Press, 1994). Nevertheless, in this context Hoogland's alliance between the grill-bar and the hellish underground bar of Radclyffe Hall's *The Well of Loneliness* (1928) is arresting. The bar's 'intertextual value', Hoogland says, is as 'a sexually overdetermined subcultural space' (201).

[8] Patricia Coughlan, 'Women and Desire in the Work of Elizabeth Bowen', in Eibhear Walshe (ed.), *Sex, Nation and Dissent in Irish Writing* (Cork: Cork University Press, 1997), 121.

being" which war had made the very being of time' (100)—into the troubled, exacerbated, extreme story of characters caught between past and future, making their own more complicated stories in the face of the constrictingly singular narratives they are everywhere offered. Traversing the consciousnesses of their readers, the propagandist stories of the press may climax where they least intend.

As they do too in the 'story' of Robert, whose apologia to Stella is explicit about his resistance to the propagandist narrative, which, to him, is 'dead currency':

What is repulsing you is the idea of 'betrayal', I suppose, isn't it? In you the hangover from the word? Don't you understand that all that language is dead currency? How they keep on playing shop with it all the same: even you do. Words, words like that, yes—what a terrific dust they can still raise in a mind, yours even: I see that. Myself, even, I have needed to immunize myself against them; I tell you I have only at last done that by saying them to myself over and over again till it became absolutely certain they mean nothing. What they once meant is gone. (268)

If words are 'dead currency' Robert is nevertheless treacherous for no other currency: he is not paid for it, and to Harrison his only motivation is the no motivation of 'sheer kink'. But Robert is explaining here what it is that drives him: an opposition to the shop-soiled language of propaganda, in which language is what renders people into a reprehensible, even disgusting *schwärmerei*, precisely what Louie wants but misses in the grill-bar: 'The war-warmed impulse of people to be a people had been derisory; he had hated the bloodstream of the crowds, the curious animal psychic oneness, the human lava-flow' (275). Given this, it may seem peculiar that Robert should be attracted to fascism, which may well be thought to lie much further along that flow: but fascism is not, exactly, what attracts him. He is attracted, rather, to what Hitler will be a stage in, an anti-democratization of feeling or sentiment of the kind which produces the lies and evasions of British wartime propaganda. And for Robert, this focuses on Dunkirk, where he was badly wounded in the leg. Many accounts of *The Heat of the Day* locate Robert's fascism in his family background, which, in the shape of his mother and her house, Holme Dene, occupies central episodes of the book. Harrison interprets Stella's visit there as her attempt to discover 'the place where rot might start'; and, in the bullying antagonism of his mother, in what we learn of the spinelessness of his now dead father, and, crucially, in the house itself—one of the most heavily

moralized houses even in Elizabeth Bowen, with its rebarbatively alien-
ating spaces, its kitsch garden, its 'swastika-arms of passage leading to
nothing'—we are offered, and chillingly, a convincing genealogy for
the development of a fascist sensibility and psychology.

Nevertheless, in Robert's apologia Dunkirk is the issue, and the
source of his political reproof: rot may have 'started' at home, but it
found its permission there. 'It was enough to have been in action once
on the wrong side', he tells Stella, describing Dunkirk as an 'army of
freedom queueing up to be taken off by pleasure boats' (272). 'Can they
conceive', he asks, 'that's a thing you never do come back from?' And,
decisively rejecting the value of fighting for any such notion of 'freedom', he also asks, 'who could want to be free when he could be
strong?' (269). Propaganda about Dunkirk, the lies told in the interests
of protecting people against the reality of their own vulnerability and
defeat, is therefore the crucial impetus to Robert's treachery. And in
Robert's view this is a defeatism endemic to post-1918 English culture,
and incarnate in his father: so that his political realignment is more
than a politics, it is the refusal of a genetic heritage: 'I was born
wounded; my father's son. Dunkirk was waiting there in us' (272). And
if Dunkirk, then so also the extremity of this survivor's reaction to it:
'It bred my father out of me, gave me a new heredity' (273).

In Elizabeth Bowen's review of Angus Calder's *The Peoples' War* in
1969 she notes the appeal of its disaffection to a 'left-wing élite', and
tartly insists that 'Not only the People were people, so were others',
implying an element of sentimentally populist mythologizing in
Calder's own interested revisionism.[9] It is the more remarkable, then,
that she nevertheless has high praise for the book's, at the time, startling revelations of the 'other truths' untold by wartime propaganda
and post-war mythologizing: 'a drastic book', she says, 'but hon-
ourable'.[10] In particular, she opposes to received opinion her own
experience of 'disaffection, a raw black bitterness in the disarmed army
back from Dunkirk': this was, she says, 'on a scale not to be measured
then'.[11] It was not, of course, to be publicly measured then, but its measure was nevertheless being privately taken. *The Heat of the Day* is
dedicated to Bowen's wartime lover and subsequent long-term friend,
the Canadian diplomat Charles Ritchie. He published his diaries of the
period as *The Siren Years: Undiplomatic Diaries 1937–1945* after

---

[9] 'The People's War by Angus Calder', in *The Mulberry Tree*, 181–5, 182. The book
includes references to, and quotations from, *The Heat of the Day*, used as reportage.
[10] *The Mulberry Tree*, 184.   [11] Ibid., 183.

Bowen's death, in 1974. They form an admirably unillusioned, acerbic, sometimes mordant commentary on the time by a knowledgeable political insider; although his insider status was to some degree compromised, and his perceptiveness thereby arguably to some degree increased, by his Canadian nationality, since Canada, like Ireland, was a very new state during wartime. These diaries may be read, in places, as a kind of interstitial gloss on Bowen's novel. In an entry for 16 July 1940 Ritchie writes of having lunch with 'the wife of the British Minister to Sofia', who suggests that 'there was more than meets the eye in the British escape from Dunkirk—meaning that it was arranged for our special benefit by God. The latter idea is quite widely spread with the corollary that it was the response to our National Day of Prayer. It is not only old women who believe this but at least one contemporary of my own.'[12]

It is clearly not mere accident that he reports immediately after this on the fate of internees whom Britain has begged the Canadian government to take to Canada—'to save this country from their nefarious activities'—who turn out to be 'entirely inoffensive anti-Nazi refugees who have been shovelled out to Canada at a moment's notice where they may have a disagreeable time, as our authorities have no files about them and will not know whom or what to believe'. 'Part of the trouble', he adds, 'is due to the fact that the Home Office and the War Office seem barely to be on speaking terms.'[13] The reporting of religiose nonsense about Dunkirk, which is quite generally believed, is forced up against Ritchie's personal experience of the opportunistic cynicism of *realpolitik*. While *The Heat of the Day*, in the complex weave of its plotting and the exacerbations of its style, is very prominently a fiction, not a socio-history, it nevertheless manifestly inhabits the same psychic space as these diaristic notations: its exacerbation is, exactly, knowing 'whom or what to believe', and Charles Ritchie is its worthy dedicatee.

At crucial points *The Heat of the Day* knows as well as Calder's much later book that 'the people' do not always believe what they are told. When the church bells ring for the Allied landings in North Africa, 'they rang false', in one of Bowen's keenest sharpenings of the figurative against the literal: for a people who have experienced too much, this 'directive for feeling' asks for too cheap an emotion.

---

[12] Charles Ritchie, *The Siren Years: Undiplomatic Diaries 1937–1945* (London: Macmillan, 1974), 61.

[13] Ibid.

This also strongly proposes the collusiveness of the Church in the propagandist narrative, as Ritchie's diary entry does also. Similarly, newspaper photographs in 1943 of Berlin 'learning how it had been for London'—learning, that is, the reality of Blitz bombing—are reported by the novel as 'less to be relished than had been hoped': civilians who know this reality have no great desire to inflict it on others, however much those 'others' are to be regarded as 'the enemy'. In this detail—but it is a significant and ramifying detail—we may surely almost over-hear a conversation between Bowen and Ritchie since his diary asks, 'What is meant by the collapse of civilisation? It means that we are glad when we hear that Berlin is getting the same bombing we are.'[14] This is devastating, since it implies that the propagandist motive itself is the destruction of 'civilisation': but of course civilization is precisely what the propaganda insists you are fighting for.

As it draws to a close—but only then—the narrative of *The Heat of the Day* starts assuming the patriotic first person plural in its possessive adjectives and pronouns: 'we' and 'our' reverberate in the final pages. This is the imitation of a Churchillian rhetoric, the rhetoric of what the narrative calls the 'one voice' heard everywhere and always towards the end of the war; and it is the voice appropriate to the recounting of the stages of victory in Europe, almost a kind of 'Pathe News' voice-over. Nevertheless, against this single authoritative voice *The Heat of the Day* opposes its many other voices. It is a novel in which the uni-vocalism that is the discourse of propaganda is everywhere disrupted and distressed by the plurivocalism of individual stories, stories which refuse single authoritative interpretation. The novel itself is a sort of confession as to why many stories, now that Elizabeth Bowen comes to tell them, have no ending. Even so, propaganda, *The Heat of the Day* knows too, is endlessly recuperative: when Robert falls to his death, 'the country was spared a demoralizing story'. Propaganda, that is to say, inheres as much in the stories untold as in the stories told. The con-tortions of plot and style in *The Heat of the Day* derive in part from its knowledge, when it tells its own story, of all the other stories which are always there to be told too; and this is to subject all knowledge of wartime truth to a corrosive, even disintegrative, irony. Irony is so all-consuming in this prismatic novel—as it is in *Madame Bovary*, as it is in *Ulysses*—as to leave almost nothing standing, and certainly to leave us as readers entirely unsure where we stand.

[14] *The Siren Years*, 98–9.

III NAMES

Robert Kelway's crypto-fascism partly derives, then, from a war wound, from the physical and psychological damage done to him at Dunkirk. Stella, who has not known Robert prior to Dunkirk, is therefore attracted to a wounded man. Her husband, Victor—ironically named—had also been a wounded man. Invalided out of the First World War, he abandoned Stella and Roderick shortly after his marriage in order to live with the woman who had been his nurse. When Harrison leaves her flat in Chapter 7 Stella suddenly thinks of 'her vanished husband': 'Why of Victor now? One could only suppose that the apparently forgotten beginning of any story was unforgettable; perpetually one was subject to the sense of there having had to be a beginning *somewhere*' (133), in a way which suggests that our ends know our beginnings all too well, and that Stella is recognizing an affinity between Victor and Robert, and a continuity in the impulse behind her desire for both. The book nowhere emphasizes Stella's own woundedness, or even her vulnerability, and her name makes her a bright particular star: she is explicitly a highly independent woman, a cosmopolitan sophisticate and linguist, beautiful and capable, who has raised a child on her own, has an important wartime job, and is able to resist Harrison with the haughty threat that 'I am not a woman who does not know where to go' (40). Nevertheless, in the strangely quasi-mystical recognitions made by Louie immediately after she meets her, Stella is figured as a 'soul astray'; and the piercing phrase—already used, as we have seen, of Anna as a child in *The Death of the Heart*—is repeated as it comes to Louie once more, on the verge of sleep, in a way that makes her almost a medium to its other-worldly delivery:

Those three words reached Louie imperatively, as though spoken—memory up to now had been surface pictures knocked apart and together by the heavings of a submerged trouble. Now her lips seemed bidden. 'A soul astray,' they repeated with awe, aloud. (249)

And Louie's bedmate, Connie, brings the chapter (13) to a close with yet a further intensification of the expression as she reproves Louie for 'crying out like after a stray soul'.

There is a comparable, if less intense, moment in the novel during Cousin Francis's funeral when the Anglo-Irish Colonel Pole recognizes Stella's 'refugee glance' among Francis's disapproving relatives; and the word is not innocently used in this wartime novel, just as—we have already seen—it is not innocently used in *The Death of the Heart*. Stella is a woman profoundly aware of how even the wealthy may, in a moment, lose everything during a war, and of how numerous such people are, in fact, in the European moment she is living through, in the process of losing everything. Although we learn very little about Stella's background other than that she is the scion of landed gentry (we are not even told whether they are Irish or not), we do learn, insistently, that both of her brothers have been killed in the First World War, and that their absence from her life has partly enabled her acceptance of the 'story' told about her marriage, since it might dishonour her but it could not, now, dishonour them; and the story is also permitted, as we have seen, by Stella's terror of appearing the victim. In *The Heat of the Day* the vulnerable, the wounded, and the intensely lonely—who may superficially appear entirely otherwise—are attracted to one another by a network of recognitions. Robert has had an extremely difficult childhood with an unloving, authoritarian, mother and a pusillanimous father; Louie is a displaced person in London with an absent husband and dead parents; Harrison, who manifests, we are told, 'the defencelessness of the stricken person', has never been loved—he tells Stella this, twice—and, in a brief, uncharacteristic, revelation, again to Stella, he explains that he was abandoned by his mother in his own childhood. Cousin Nettie is someone almost certainly feigning insanity and confined to an asylum. Stella is a woman who has accepted a seriously disparaging story about her without demur, and she is recognized as a soul astray.

These shared vulnerabilities form part of the explanation for the novel's elaborate system of doublings and mirrorings which may be regarded as an intensification of the *doppelgänger* effect elsewhere in Bowen. Stella Rodney has a son called Roderick Rodney, a name which is, like Louie Lewis, a kind of nominal inversion, a doubling of, or return upon, itself. Stella's lover is Robert, the first two letters of whose name are repeated in both 'Roderick' and 'Rodney'. Harrison has made never adequately explained visits to Cousin Francis on his Irish estate, and when the servant Donovan confirms this for Stella, he mistakes the name for 'Robertson', where the initial two-letter configuration occurs once more, and where, of course, the full name 'Robert' is part of the configuration, in a way that may be regarded as amalgamating 'Robert' and 'Harrison'. Colonel Pole gets Roderick's name wrong when he is talking to Stella at Francis's funeral, and gets it wrong as 'Robert' ("Roderick," she impassively corrected.') And towards the very end of the novel, when he visits Stella in her new London flat during an air-raid two years after the main action of the plot, Harrison, for the first time, reveals his Christian name: it is (also) Robert.

These alphabetical, alliterative, and nominal coincidences—'algebraic variables', Maud Ellmann calls them—are accompanied by the sharing of physical distinctivenesses.[15] Robert has a peculiarly variable limp—the consequence of his wound; Harrison has what Donovan poetically calls 'a sort of a discord between his two eyes', a peculiarity noticed by other characters too; and Stella has one single patch of white hair standing back from her forehead. Further, characters manifest recognitions of affinity or even something approaching identity among themselves. Stella and Robert are said to share 'the complicity of brother and sister twins', and we hear of 'their doubled awareness'. Harrison tells Stella very early in the novel, without any entitlement whatever to say so, that 'there's something like nothing else between you and me'; and this is an act of presumption all the more notable for the manifest class differences between them, which are a major impulse, although always only implicitly, to his desire (when she picks up the telephone on their first encounter in her flat it is Harrison's 'first idea of poetry'). He is himself capable of a sometimes startling coarseness, even brutality, of speech, and is an upwardly mobile wartime opportunist (he has realized, he tells Stella, that 'This is where I come in'); and we may infer that, along with his sheer Ibsenic doggedness, or hangdoggedness, this is part of Stella's growing attraction to him, which has sometimes been seen as imperfectly explained.

Crucially, within this system of correspondences and recognitions, when Stella learns the truth of Robert's treachery, 'It seemed to her it was Robert who had been the Harrison' (275). Patricia Coughlan says, truly, that 'Bowen's verbal games with naming and with physical appearance as metaphor in this novel would not have disgraced a Freudian dream-text'; but this is extraordinary, even within the structure of identifications I have been delineating.[16] W. J. McCormack speculates that the name is here being used to mean 'spy' in something of the way in which the name 'Quisling' was contemporaneously being

---

[15] Maud Ellmann, *Elizabeth Bowen: The Shadow across the Page* (Edinburgh: Edinburgh University Press, 2003), 23.

[16] 'Women and Desire', 122.

used to mean 'collaborator'.[17] If Robert has been the Harrison, then
Harrison may be the Robert, of course; and the formulation certainly
invites us to speculate on whether, if Robert is the spy, Harrison may
be the traitor, and more corruptly so than Robert. He may certainly be
read as a cynical opportunist, infantile in his emotional development,
unconcerned for the fate of his country to the extent of bartering it for
Stella's sexual favours, whereas Robert has a principled, if repulsively
perverse, ideological commitment. When Harrison enters Stella's flat
for the first time, we remember, 'he looked about him like a German in
Paris' (44); and this just after the fall of France.

Such mirrorings, doublings, echoes, and inversions are in one sense
a manifestation of the mobilities of what the novel calls a wartime
'society of the garrison', in which people 'began, even, all to look a little alike' (94). Stella reminds Robert, after telling him what Harrison
has told her, that 'You have sometimes said that in one particular issue
which might be found, anybody is capable of anything' (190); and she
eventually says to Harrison himself that 'Below one level, everybody's
horribly alike. You succeed in making a spy of me' (138). Stella means
that she is herself, since Harrison has told her his 'story' about Robert,
forced to act as the close scrutineer of Robert's behaviour, motivation,
and background: but if Stella is a spy, then presumably that makes her
also 'the Harrison', with 'her dogging of the step of his thoughts, her
search for the interstices of his mind'. A vertiginously undermining
aspect of *The Heat of the Day*, and one that flies in the face of the
relentless positivity of wartime propaganda, is indeed the extent to
which, under certain circumstances, anyone is capable of anything,
including political and sexual betrayal. 'What is anyone?' asks Stella,
thinking specifically of Harrison: 'Mad, divided, undoing what they
do' (287). One gloss on this is supplied by the postscript to *The Demon
Lover and Other Stories*, where Bowen maintains that 'during the war
the overcharged subconsciousnesses of everybody overflowed and

---

[17] *Dissolute Characters*, 226. Robert Fisk, in his study of Irish wartime neutrality, *In
Time of War*, to which I shall refer below, tells us that one of the very few attempts to
explain neutrality in Britain was made in a book called *The Neutrality of Ireland: Why
it was Inevitable* (1940), written by 'a former supporter of Parnell who had won the
Military Cross while fighting as a British soldier in France in 1916'. His name was
Captain Henry Harrison. The name, and its alliteration, will, of course, strike any reader
of *The Heat of the Day*; and, as we shall see in a moment, Irish neutrality figures prominently in the novel and, in a major way, elsewhere in Bowen's wartime writing too. See
Robert Fisk, *In Time of War: Ireland, Ulster and the Price of Neutrality 1939–45* (1983;
Dublin: Gill and Macmillan, 1985), 291.

merged'. In war, she says, the 'feeling of slight differentiation was suspended: I felt one with, and just like, everyone else. Sometimes I hardly knew where I stopped and somebody else began.'[18]

But the word 'spy' alerts us to a further dimension in the almost feverishly reflex involutions of this novel. The word figures once in another book Elizabeth Bowen wrote during the war, her memoir of a Dublin childhood, *Seven Winters*, published by the Cuala Press in, the colophon says, 'the last week of August, nineteen hundred and forty two'.[19] Telling us that she was not allowed to read until she was 7, she represents herself as a frustratedly inquiring child, who, in the absence of text, took reality as her text, with the consequence that 'on my walks through familiar quarters of Dublin I looked at everything like a spy'.[20] Any student of the alphabetical repetitions, inversions, and ingenuities of *The Heat of the Day* will also be arrested by the information conveyed in the opening pages of *Seven Winters* that when she was conceived her parents had anticipated a son: 'the first male Bowen in each generation had been christened either Robert or Henry. My grandfather had been Robert, my father Henry—there was no doubt which name was waiting for me.'[21] This makes the process heavy with omen; and it seems clear that the name 'Robert', with its various alphabetical abbreviations and repetitions in *The Heat of the Day*, pervasively encodes an autobiographical inscription; and this indelibly marks the text with an Irish signature, impresses into it an Irish watermark. And a return to Ireland is central to the novel's complex figurings, motifs, and meanings, just as another text which Elizabeth Bowen wrote, partly in Ireland and exclusively about Ireland, during the war, may be perceived below the surface of the novel's text. In this sense the inscription of the name 'Robert' makes *The Heat of the Day* almost a kind of palimpsest; and if in one of its aspects the book is preoccupied with the official public narrative of wartime propaganda, in another it encodes the most private of all texts, the secret narrative of espionage.

---

[18] *The Mulberry Tree*, 95.
[19] Elizabeth Bowen, *Seven Winters* (Dublin: The Cuala Press [1942], repr. 1971 for the Irish University Press, Shannon), colophon.
[20] Ibid., 17.   [21] Ibid., 2–3.

IV SPIES

Just after Harrison has visited, or intruded on, Stella in her flat to tell her the story of Robert she is joined there by Roderick, on furlough from the army. Stella is still oppressed by the poisonous atmosphere of Harrison's earlier presence: 'Even the papers, letters, among which she had rested her elbow, listening to him, seemed to be contaminated; she shrank, even, from phrases in purple type on which, in the course of the listening, her eyes had from time to time lit' (57). In the Public Record Office in Kew it is possible to consult documents in purple type dated 1940 and 1942, marked 'SECRET', and entitled *Notes on Eire*, written by Mrs Elizabeth Cameron and delivered to the Ministry of Information. 'Mrs Elizabeth Cameron' was the married name of Elizabeth Bowen. The initial purpose of her reports—which she volunteered to write—was to test Irish opinion on the possibility of Britain's reclaiming the use of certain Irish ports: this was a matter of great concern in 1940, since it was generally thought that lack of access to these ports had cost numerous British lives in the North Atlantic, and the British press was clamouring for invasion. (Louis MacNeice's well-known poem 'Neutrality' expresses an Irishman's bitterness about the policy.) Shortly before Bowen's first report Churchill had made a belligerent speech on the matter in the House of Commons. She was not, therefore, performing a negligible function in Ireland, but a politically sensitive and significant one involving not only English attitudes to Irish neutrality but the development of English strategy in relation to a potential re-conquest of sovereign Irish territory: which is why her 1940 reports were passed on by Lord Cranborne, who received them in the Dominions Office, to Lord Halifax, the Secretary of State for Foreign Affairs, with the opinion that this is 'a shrewd appreciation of the position'.[22] In the novel Stella is employed 'in an organization better called Y.X.D., in secret, exacting, not unimportant work, to which the European position since 1940 gave ever-increasing point'

---

[22] Elizabeth Bowen, *'Notes on Eire': Espionage Reports to Winston Churchill, 1940–2; with a Review of Irish Neutrality in World War 2*, ed. by Jack Lane and Brendan Clifford (Millstreet: Aubane Historical Society, 1999), 10. Since this is the only form in which these documents have ever been published in full, I cite this text in my references to them. It is very badly edited, however, and its transcriptions are not always reliable. I have checked the references I make against photocopies of the original documents, which I have also read *in situ* at the Public Record Office. They are classified as FO 800/310 and DO 130/28.

(26)—where 'better called' suggests almost that the novel itself cannot reveal what it is actually called, and where the preposterous acronym is both a joke about the wartime habit of acronyms and a testimony to the pervasive necessity for guardedness.

In the context of English attitudes to Ireland in 1940, Mrs Cameron is bravely independent-minded and sensitively alert to the Irish mentality: 'I could wish some factions in England showed less anti-Irish feeling . . . The charge of "disloyalty" against the Irish has always, given the plain facts of history, irritated me . . . I could wish that the English kept history in mind more, that the Irish kept it in mind less.'[23] Bowen patiently explained, and justified, Irish neutrality in her reports, and did so again, publicly, in an article in the *New Statesman* in 1941. However, the reports are also the history of Bowen's change of mind on the issue, and she is markedly less sympathetic by 1942. The later reports are coolly hard-headed evocations of Irish mood, sentiment, and attitude, a succinct précis, and fascinating: she is very good at this. And these reports are now themselves part of 'history', since they are quoted in the histories of the period, extensively by Robert Fisk in his standard account of neutrality, *In Time of War*, which is of the opinion that 'the Irish Government could not escape the accusation—indeed should not have escaped the accusation—that dead British seamen were being washed up on Eire's shores because of her policy of neutrality . . . de Valera would not risk the lives of his people for the lives of British seamen. Truly, neutrality was a form of warfare.'[24]

However, in 1999 an organization based in North Cork called the Aubane Historical Society published Bowen's reports—and this is still the only way to read them in their entirety in published form—with the subtitle 'Espionage Reports to Winston Churchill, 1940–2', in a volume which includes an attack on Bowen as an 'English' spy in Ireland during the war, a lengthy defence of Irish neutrality along the de Valeran lines that the war was an imperial adventure, and an account of the controversy generated in the *Irish Times* and other Irish newspapers by an earlier attack on Bowen from this same source in 1997. The Aubane Historical Society's polemic is ignorant in some respects: it appears, for instance, unaware that some of Bowen's work is actually set in Ireland, and it nowhere refers to her *New Statesman* defence of neutrality. But

[23] Ibid., 13.
[24] *In Time of War*, 290. This view should, however, be measured against R. F. Foster's that 'the Irish approach amounted to pro-British neutrality.' See *Modern Ireland 1600–1972* (London: Allen Lane: The Penguin Press, 1988), 560.

it is not altogether unintelligent, and it is not unscrupulous; and it serves to show how great a strength of feeling there still is in certain circles in Ireland about the justification for neutrality itself and about the part played in Ireland during the war by people like Bowen (and John Betjeman) who were perceived, when their wartime work came to light, as espionage agents; a feeling all the more bitter in Bowen's case since she claimed to be Irish—or, in the formulation of Brendan Clifford, one of the Aubane editors, she 'polish[ed] up her Irish credentials' during the war as a deliberate 'cover for espionage'.[25]

When Elizabeth Bowen used the word 'spy' of her childhood self in the Dublin of the early years of the century in *Seven Winters*, therefore, she was well aware that she was at that very moment engaging in activities which others in Ireland, including those whose conversations she was reporting on, would certainly have defined as a contemporary act of espionage. Furthermore, although her motivation was, in part, like Robert Kelway's, ideological, it was also, it appears, unlike his, financial: her care to ensure that his has no taint of this lower motivation is, I believe, to be read as self-critical.[26] In Ireland during the war Bowen was so different from herself, so self-mobile, as to be readable by many as virtually a spy in neutral Ireland for the British government; and in my view her unease, insecurity, anxiety, and guilt about this, as well as her justification of it, are all inscribed in the wartime novel which, she said, she wanted to make 'enormously comprehensive'.[27] Coded into *The Heat of the Day*, in its deepest structures and stresses, is the nexus of espionage and putatively treacherous activities in which Bowen was involved in Ireland; and the coding may be deciphered not only in the novel's alphabetical play with the name 'Robert' but also in the way the word 'conversation' plays between the wartime reports and the novel.

She writes in the reports that she hopes to be able 'to continue conversations that had promised to be interesting'; she mentions her extensive 'conversation with Mr. Dillon'—James Dillon, a politician of the opposition—and then reports on 'a long conversation' with him

[25] 'Notes on Eire', 7.

[26] Heather Bryant Jordan, in *How Will the Heart Endure?: Elizabeth Bowen and the Landscape of War* (Ann Arbor: University of Michigan Press, 1992), 210 n. 106, tells us, citing the records of Bowen's literary agent, that in 1944–5 she was paid £115.10s. by the British government; not a negligible sum then. Also proof, of course, that Bowen went on writing these reports throughout the war, although the remainder—for whatever reason—are unavailable in the PRO.

[27] *The Mulberry Tree*, 95.

subsequently; she refers generally (and airily) to 'conversations that I have had'; and, presumably when she decides that there are things she doesn't wish to commit to paper, she says, 'I should prefer to expand these points in conversation.'[28] In the novel Roderick, when he finds what appears to be a note of some kind in Robert's dressing-gown, tells Stella that it may be a note on 'some conversation . . . conversations are the leading thing in this war . . . Everything you and I have to do is the result of something that's been said. How far do you think we'd get without conversations?' (63). Stella also imagines the relationship between outside and inside, what is said and what is acted or trans-acted in wartime: 'To her, tonight, "outside" meant the harmless world: the mischief was in her own and other rooms. The grind and scream of battles, mechanized advances excoriating flesh and country, tearing through nerves and tearing up trees, were indoor-plotted; this was a war of dry cerebration inside windowless walls' (142). For Roderick and Stella both personal and universal wartime action is compelled by conversation; and perhaps this is the crucial reason why action absconds in *The Heat of the Day*: as corrosively as its under-standing of the directives for feeling given by propaganda, it under-stands too how action is generated by the discourses of power. It has no use for anything approaching the conventional plot of a spy novel because it understands where the plots are ultimately generated. Both the narratives of her reports and of her wartime novel are also literally generated out of conversation: she told Virginia Woolf, of her activities in Ireland, that 'It will all mean endless talk, but sorting out talk into shape might be interesting.'[29] Which is exactly what the structure of her novel does too; and of no novel of hers is it truer that, as she claimed of the novel generally, and italicized the claim, 'Speech is what the characters *do to each other*.'[30]

As its own kind of spy novel, however, *The Heat of the Day* employs an extensive imagery of the theatrical. The cliché 'theatre of war' is used only once, in the closing chapter, where we are told that 'There were too many theatres of war'; but *The Heat of the Day* is one itself, opening in the open-air theatre in Regent's Park, where Harrison meets Louie, who thinks that he appears 'to *act* the thinker', while Louie her-self wants 'someone to imitate'. When Harrison first goes to Stella's flat he is said to 'make his entrance'. Roderick as a soldier considers that

[28] 'Notes on Eire', 14, 20, 23, 26.
[29] Letter to Virginia Woolf of 1 July 1940, in *The Mulberry Tree*, 214–16, 216.
[30] 'Notes on Writing a Novel', in *The Mulberry Tree*, 35–48, 41.

his 'ineptness to play any other part would have more distressed him had there been any other part to play' (49). When Stella and Harrison, in a moment of high sexual charge, stand together in the window embrasure of her flat, they are said to be 'depersonalized speakers in a drama' (140). And Stella in the climactic grill-bar chapter with Harrison is said to give a 'command performance' (227); and, again in this chapter, expecting Robert, she thinks that 'some major entrance' is 'overdue' (233), and, in fact, the entrance does occur but, joining the novel's main to its sub-plot, it is not Robert's—which would be the sheerest melodrama—but, as we have seen, Louie's.

In addition, if *Hamlet* is the play of Shakespeare's actually named in the text, we may well think that it is not *Hamlet* but *Measure for Measure* which runs its plot motif through Bowen's novel, that play in which a sister decisively refuses to part with her virginity to spare a brother's life: Stella, obversely but not perversely, decides to submit to Harrison's sexual blackmail in order to save a lover figured as a 'brother . . . twin' in a way quivering between suggestions of incest and asexuality. It is unsurprising, and particularly so given Shakespeare's presence elsewhere in Bowen's work too, as I have indicated, that Roderick figures his own callow ineptitude, in the last response we see him making to his mother, as an inability to say 'something that in a flash would give what Robert did and what happened enormous meaning like there is in a play of Shakespeare's' (300). Finally, what decisively undermines Stella's complacency about Robert's guilt is Harrison's suggestion that he might be a consummately good actor, and Stella is forced to consider the ultimate kind of personal—that is, sexual—deception: 'If actor, to her and for her so very good an actor, then why not actor also of love?' (173). Within this virtual technology of representations, subjectivity and interiority become extremely fragile, insecure, and almost, as it were, a matter of negotiation. So in this novel the 'I' which is always 'uncertain' in Elizabeth Bowen becomes destabilized even further as a consequence of the politics of wartime espionage. Against those critics who find a lack of adequate characterization in the novel, notably in Robert Kelway, it might be claimed, therefore, that its modes of theatricality undermine the very self-identity of character. *The Heat of the Day* is governed by an almost Berkeleyan metaphysics, in which you are what you are perceived to be.

Bowen's reports to Churchill are also much preoccupied with Irish attitudes to the fascist enemy, and, given the role of Kelway in the novel, these are of particular note. For instance, she finds Irish anti-

Semitism on the increase; she identifies James Dillon, whom she never-theless clearly admires in many ways, as a 'fascist' (peculiarly enough, since he is publicly anti-neutrality, and not pro-German); she discovers sympathy for Pétainist France; she finds particularly corrosive defeatism among the Anglo-Irish; and she speculates on the possibility of an Irish 'Catholic-Fascism'. W. J. McCormack says that Bowen's discoveries of fascist sympathies in Ireland make Kelway's fascism 'an Irish "trace"' in the novel.[31] This is understandable, but it may be to say too much, since Bowen would also have been aware that many thousands of Irish nationals were serving in the British armed forces too: an Irish address did not of itself at all signal hostility to the Allies. In any case, as such books as Richard Griffiths's *Fellow Travellers of the Right* make clear, you did not have to cross the Irish Sea to find sympathy for fascism.[32] Indeed, as late as February 1941, Charles Ritchie is telling his diary that

if this country is invaded successfully there is the possibility of a Pétain gov-ernment here whose names one can already guess plus, perhaps, an Anglo-German alliance. This is an ugly picture, but the other, the picture of Germany crushed, of England and America restoring democratic governments in Europe, seems to me incredibly remote. All this gloomy speculation goes on in the back of people's minds. They do not talk like this, they hardly allow themselves to think such things. Most are content to repeat that Britons never will be slaves and that Britain can take it. They do not think ahead of the next move, and this is doubtless very sensible. Also they are pretty well blanketed by propaganda.[33]

In that same month he also meditates on Hitler as 'the incarnation of our own sense of guilt':

When he attacks our civilisation we find him saying things that we have thought or said. In the 'burrows of the nightmare' such a figure is born, for as in a nightmare the thing that pursues us seems to have an uncanny and terrify-ing knowledge of our weakness. We spawned this horror; he is the byproduct of our civilisation; he is all the hatred, the envy, the guile which is in us—a sur-realist figure sprung out of the depths of our own subconscious.[34]

Kelway may well be read at least as well as what went on in the back of some English people's minds as what went on in some Irish minds; and Ritchie's diary entry alerts us to what the novel manages very well

---

[31] *Dissolute Characters*, 215.
[32] Richard Griffiths, *Fellow Travellers of the Right: British Enthusiasts for Nazi Germany, 1933–9* (London: Constable, 1980).
[33] *The Siren Years*, 90–1.   [34] Ibid., 92.

indeed too: a sense of the terrifying obligations and choices imposed on people under immediate physical threat, when one's own personal prognosis fails entirely to coincide with the official one, however much one wishes it could.

VI THE IRISH STORY

Wherever we source Kelway's fascism, however, the fact that all three major characters in the novel are, or are forced against their will to become, spies is most certainly an Irish trace. Adam Piette has arresting things to say about the Anglo-Irish crossings between Bowen's wartime reports and her wartime novel, offering a version of Anglo-Irish allegory:

> *The Heat of the Day* fictionalizes the England–Eire relationship by transposing the secret story of Bowen's spying on her country into Stella's spying on her lover. The 'hybrid' Anglo-Irish self is capable of a double allegiance, to country and to that country's 'enemy'. Eire is both the old home of that hybrid self and the Robert of fifth-column fantasy . . . In the end, Stella and Robert form a secret union, an Anglo-Irish union, a class in the middle of nothing, the Irish ghostly self obsessed by history, capable of betrayal in the name of revenge for historical indignities and loss of caste, the English self capable of spying on its loved ones, playing the propaganda game while secretively passing information to the loved one's enemy.[35]

This is penetrating and subtle in its mapping of self onto nation, that perhaps ultimate slippage between the literal and the figurative in Bowen, and does undoubtedly tune in to the correct frequency of the novel's Anglo-Irish signals; but it may be a little too schematic, not least because, as I have already observed, the novel never actually tells us, despite her Anglo-Irish marriage, that Stella is Anglo-Irish: indeed, the very brief reference made to her background suggests to me more the English squirearchical classes than Irish landlordism. *The Heat of the Day*, in my view, has more than this to say about Anglo-Irish relations, and it offers, at least up to a point, more an optimistic register of potential than the fixed and inevitably dangerous interlocking of attraction and antagonism which Piette's formulation suggests. In doing so, I propose, it aims to ally and reconcile divided traditions in a way which, if successful, would ensure that the kind of espionage

---

[35] *Imagination at War*, 172.

activity which Elizabeth Bowen engaged in during the war would have been unnecessary. The novel therefore encodes an apologia.

When Cousin Francis dies in Wistaria Lodge, he is visiting England to offer his services in the war, even though—as Colonel Pole, a childhood Anglo-Irish friend of his, tells Stella, in deeply baffled disappointment— he has been a defender of the post-Treaty Irish state to the extent of seeming to display a 'nearly nationalistic strain'. The fragile and fissured identity of the Anglo-Irish hybrid in neutral Ireland, the person who has one firm belief about Irish governance in his own country but must nevertheless act in a way quite contrary or hostile to it, is therefore perfectly caught in Francis; and this makes him too the representative of Bowen herself in the novel. His unexpected willing of his Irish estate, Mount Morris, to Roderick necessitates visits by Stella, first, and sub- sequently by Roderick himself to Ireland: so that Ireland as a topo- graphical presence enters the wartime space of *The Heat of the Day*; and, making a further fictional return to the country, Bowen now both makes the harshest critique in her entire work of Anglo-Irish history and also proposes, at a point of supreme crisis, an alternative to it.

Her return to Ireland is Stella's first since the failure of her marriage. Had the marriage not failed she would herself have lived, instead of the cosmopolitan life she has led, the generic life of the Anglo-Irish wife and mother. We already know that this is the life which has forced Cousin Nettie into feigned insanity and voluntary incarceration in a home for the mentally ill. Stella in Mount Morris contemplates an Anglo-Irish history of women as themselves victims incarcerated in such houses: as chattels, spoils, décor, signs of conspicuous consump- tion, whose leisured luxury is, in fact, a form of denial, an enforced maintaining of silence about perceived secrets, and, at the worst, a col- lapse into something like madness. Not even in *Bowen's Court*, which can be, as we have seen, harsh about the Anglo-Irish heritage—but per- haps sometimes a little too dutifully harsh—is there anything approaching the vapid desperation evoked when Stella feels alienated from 'the society of ghosts' which she senses in the history of the house's drawing-room:

After all, was it not chiefly here in this room . . . that Cousin Nettie Morris— and who now knew how many more before her?—had been pressed back, hour by hour, by the hours themselves, into cloudland? Ladies had gone not quite mad, not quite even that, from in vain listening for meaning in the loudening ticking of the clock . . . Therefore, her kind knew no choices, made no deci- sions—or, did they not? Everything spoke to them—the design in and out of which they drew their needles; the bird with its little claws drawn to its piteously smooth breast, dead; away in the woods the quickening strokes of the axes, then the fall of the tree; or the child upstairs crying out terrified in its sleep. No, knowledge was not to be kept from them; it sifted through to them, stole up behind them, reached them by intimations—they suspected what they refused to prove. That had been their decision . . . And though seated together, hems of their skirts touching, each one of the ladies had not ceased in herself to reflect alone; their however candid and clear looks in each others' [sic] eyes were interchanged warnings; their conversation was a twinkling surface over their deep silence. Virtually they were never to speak at all—unless to the little bird lying big with death on the path, the child being comforted out of the nightmare without waking, the leaf plucked still quivering from the felled tree. (174–5)

This passage on silence and extreme loneliness, on the reduction of women's insight and intelligence to inarticulate functions of nature, on apparent decisions in fact made under large cultural duress, is loud with implicit judgement. What the deep silence and the warnings comprehend is, in the end, the demise of the Anglo-Irish as a class, the exhaustion of a history. The passage's 'knowledge', like the 'discovery' made of a 'lack' in *The Last September*, is the knowledge of supersession. For Stella the further silence now existent in this suddenly historyless drawing-room is Irish wartime neutrality itself, since the war of independence in the 1920s was the consequence of this leisured existence, with its many victimizations, not only those of its own women— as *The Last September* makes plain. And the consequence of that was the creation of the political state which justified neutrality on the grounds which Bowen herself originally defended, as we have seen: that this was Eire's 'assertion of strength, [its] first major independent act', having 'a symbolic as well as moral significance . . . that identifies, for the people, Eire's neutrality with her integrity'.[36] The fact that Bowen always uses the appelation 'Eire', and that her wartime reports are punctiliously entitled 'Notes on Eire', indicates that she herself maintains the probity of accepting this integrity even while she is 'spying' on the state which asserts it, since 'Eire' was the new state's name for itself. The maintenance of silence about what is known but is not to be revealed to be known—which is, in this passage, portrayed as the inevitability of Anglo-Irish female history—is what Stella now decisively rejects. It is in Ireland that she decides to confront Robert with what Harrison has told her, and she does so as soon as she returns to

[36] 'Eire', reprinted in *The Mulberry Tree*, 30–5, 31.

London: so it is specifically her rejection of an Anglo-Irish history, made in Ireland itself, which impels her alternative behaviour in England.

She is also decisive in another way, however, which does not simply reject the burden of the history she identifies, or senses, in the Mount Morris drawing-room. Here the word 'story', which has been often enough in the novel the register of confinement and limitation, of an entrapment in the past, is oriented towards a future: 'That her own life could be a chapter missing from this book need not mean that the story was at an end', she thinks; 'at a pause it was, but perhaps a pause for the turning-point?' And it is Stella, who describes herself as a 'déclassée' outsider, who shows Roderick how his inheritance, if it is to work at all, must be managed: she recognizes that inheritance must now be more a matter of renovation and even rejection than the acceptance of any stable 'tradition': 'Required to mean what they had not, old things would be pushed into a new position; those which could not comply, which could not be made to pick up the theme of the new song, would go' (176).

Cousin Francis has willed Mount Morris to Roderick with an ambiguous clause: 'in the hope that he may care in his own way to carry on the old tradition' (72). Before Roderick will accept the inheritance he must resolve the ambiguity to his satisfaction: 'Does he mean, that I'm free to care in any way I like, so long as it's *the* tradition I carry on; or, that so long as I care in the same way he did, I'm free to mean by "tradition" anything I like?' (88). *The Heat of the Day* includes, in the relationship between Stella and Roderick, as none of Bowen's other novels do, for all their interest in the matter of mothers and children, a happy—if to some degree edgy—relationship between mother and mature, or maturing, son: and there is an unnervingly original irony in this relationship when it is Roderick, representative of the younger generation, rather than Stella, who is instinctively inclined to be simply appreciative of the old order. It is for Stella to correct his readiness 'to entertain a high, if abstract idea of society'; it is for her to modify his 'idealization of pattern'; it is she who knows that tradition is an invention. Critical of Roderick's primness, she locates its origin self-recriminatingly, in one of the most delicate, and surprising, mother-and-child passages in all Bowen:

when he had been a baby she had amused him by opening and shutting a painted fan, and of that *beau monde* of figures, grouped and placed and linked by gestures or garlands, he never had, she suspected, lost interior sight. The fan on its fragile ivory spokes now remained closed: she felt him most happy when they could recreate its illusion in their talk.   (61)

It is as though Roderick, the male inheritor of Mount Morris, is, as it were, instinctively Anglo-Irish, inescapably drawn to a *beau monde* of, here, Watteau-like proportions; and indeed when he first visits his estate he transforms this into a quasi-Wordsworthian mysticism of attachment: 'Forms, having made themselves known through no particular sense, forms whose existence he was not to doubt again, loomed and dwelled within him' (311). Whereas it is Stella, the mother and self-impelled outsider, who understands how such an 'old tradition' is now mere 'illusion', outmoded and impossible, and she acts as the corrective agent for her son's deluded and dangerous romanticism. In these perceptions of necessity, justice, and corrective continuity, we should see Elizabeth Bowen inscribing herself in yet another way in *The Heat of the Day*, since they are a fictionalized version of the recommendations she also makes in her essay 'The Big House', published in 1940 in the first issue of Sean O'Faolain's journal *The Bell*, which I touched on in my opening chapter. It is an essay which offers an Anglo-Irish apology rather than an apologia and which hopes (but very much against hope), and recommends to the younger generation, that 'the European idea' sustained by the social tradition of the big house at its best may be made newly available to those hitherto not welcomed behind its walls: that is, although they are nowhere actually specified, the now politically powerful Catholic middle classes. This itself opposes that pragmatic and opportunistic strain in many more of the Anglo-Irish of the post-revolutionary period, represented in the novel by the otherwise entirely benign Colonel Pole, for whom the big house is 'a thing of the past', simply to be sold off.

In the retrospect of Irish history, it is clear that Colonel Pole has the better of the argument; and *A World of Love*, published seven years after *The Heat of the Day*, is, as we have seen, the textual location of an Anglo-Irish near-posthumousness. In *The Heat of the Day*, however, Stella imagines a corrective re-orientation of the 'tradition', in which Roderick will, 'in his own way', learn to farm his estate in a manner profitable to, rather than exploitative of, the local community, and in which he may even—it is hinted she may feel—make a marital alliance with the once exploited class. Fantasizing a wife for Roderick, Stella imagines someone 'unspent and fearless'; and at the moment

when Donovan at Mount Morris announces Montgomery's Alamein
victory Stella's eyes rest on Donovan's beautiful 16-year-old daughter,
Hannah. The writing in parts of this Irish chapter (Chapter 10) has an
almost Lawrentian vitalism never attempted by Elizabeth Bowen anywhere else—occasionally of a rather over-egged kind, it has to be
said—in a way which suggests the extent of the investment of authorial interest and self-interest; and the large concepts are certainly
reached for as, at the chapter's close, Stella gazes at Hannah standing
in front of the house, and Hannah gazes back:

Childish for sixteen years, she wore the gravity of her race; something was
added to her beauty by her apartness from what was going on; her mountain-
blue eyes had inherited the colour of trouble but not the story. Having not a
thought that was not her own, she had not any thought; she was a young girl
already upon her unmenaced way to Heaven . . . Stella, also making for the
house, became embalmed in the orbit of Hannah's gaze. She smiled at the girl,
but there was nothing—most of all at this moment nothing—to be said.
Whenever in the future that Mount Morris mirage of utter victory came back
to her, she was to see Hannah standing there in the sunshine, indifferent as a
wand. (179)

'Embalmed in the orbit of Hannah's gaze' is a rivetingly intricate
metaphor, and one with a marked erotic element. It may be thought to
revise in the direction of reconciliation and harmony the anxiety and
dread in the exactly comparable metaphor of mummification which I
have already discussed in relation to Anna and Portia in *The Death of
the Heart*. Here in *The Heat of the Day* the effect is, precisely, to still
anxiety into the spellbound; and the word 'story' is used now with a
high political charge, since the failure of the Irish Catholic serving-class
daughter to inherit the 'story of trouble' would bring to completion,
and move towards some new possibility, the long story of Irish and
Anglo-Irish 'trouble', the long history—of which Irish neutrality is the
ultimate heritage—of 'the Troubles'. It is that history which Stella also
recognizes among the other ghosts of the Mount Morris drawing-
room, with its paintings of 'horsemen grouped apprehensively at midnight' and of the sinking *Titanic*, prominently dated 1912; which was
the year the ship, built in the exclusively Protestant shipyard of
Harland and Wolff in Belfast, sank, but also the year of the Solemn
League and Covenant signed in Ulster as a pledge of resistance to Home
Rule for Ireland. It is unsurprising that, for the politically corrective
Stella, this is 'one picture to banish'.

'Indifferent as a wand' figures Hannah in a suddenly almost Yeatsian transformation, since the word 'indifferent' appears emphatically in Yeats, sometimes with a certain approbatory Anglo-Irish *hauteur*—in love poems such as 'A Woman Homer Sung' and 'The Living Beauty', for instance—and the hazel wand is a pastoral property of his early poetry. What could be more 'unspent and fearless' than this? Nothing explicit is said, and nothing explicit need be said: but the novel is, I think, brushed here by the possibility of a marriage—by, indeed, the spellbound Stella's nascent desire for a marriage—between the new master of the house and the young Catholic servant. The prospect of an alliance between Roderick and Hannah, if that is what is being almost subliminally raised here, is surprising, even for the politically corrective Stella, since not much political correctiveness would have gone so far either in 1942 or even on the novel's publication in 1948, when such an alliance might have been regarded—and not only by the Anglo-Irish— as a form of miscegenation. But wartime Ireland in *The Heat of the Day* is moved on, in the end, from the nullness of neutrality and the ter- giversation of espionage and treachery into the figuration of a potential alternative, in which Catholic nationalist Ireland will be doubled with England, married to it, rather than separated from it by the now alto- gether uncertain hyphen between 'Anglo' and 'Irish'.[37]

VII FUTURES

Stella projects a future for Roderick, and we could say that she also makes a future for Louie when Louie responds to her in the way I sug- gested earlier in this chapter. Louie's sense of a new future prompts her into a 'gaze'—comparable to Stella's exchanged gaze with Hannah—

---

[37] In an interview in *The Bell* in 1942 Bowen speculated very interestingly on the pos- sibility of an Irish *Comédie humaine*. In a way that strikingly complements what I am claiming here about a 'marriage' of traditions, she says, 'I don't think it will be written until we produce a writer who thoroughly understands both the Catholic and the Protestant points of view . . . When that Really Great Irish Novel comes to be written, I fancy you'll find that it has been written by a Protestant who understands Catholicism and who, very probably, has made a mixed marriage.' See 'Meet Elizabeth Bowen', *The Bell*, 4: 6 (September 1942), 420–6, 425. It is notable that she clearly does not consider *Ulysses* the 'Really Great Irish Novel', although she is several times highly commenda- tory of it in her critical prose. The criteria she offers here would, of course, disqualify Joyce as its author; which makes it more than usually significant that she makes these her criteria.

when she looks at Tom's photograph (which she has previously been unable to bear, associating it with a deathly absence): 'she felt herself beckoned into that gaze of absention and futurity—was she not in her own way drawing ahead of what was to be?' (325). These gazes are the reconciliatory and benevolent transformation of the largely negative and malevolent imagery of scrutiny elsewhere in the novel. 'In her own way' here is code for Louie's pregnancy by another man: news of Tom's death is, in fact, delivered before he can be told about this. But the phrase echoes, or rhymes with, the phrase in Francis's will to Roderick; and there are further rhymes, or secret, or even occult correspondences, between the book's English conclusion, when Louie returns to Seale with her baby, and its Irish element. Louie calls the baby 'Thomas Victor' which is to name him after her husband and—although, of course, she has never known his name—after Stella's husband and Roderick's father. And *The Heat of the Day* climaxes in Seale when Louie holds Tom out of his pram to see, 'and perhaps remember', three swans 'flying a straight flight': 'They passed overhead, disappearing in the direction of the west' (330). The direction of the west is the direction of Ireland; and three Yeatsian symbolic swans have already appeared in the novel when they are seen by Stella at Mount Morris: 'In the morning, dressing at her window, she watched three swans come down the river to pause in midstream looking up at the house with her in it' (148). The projected English future and the projected Irish future, both figured as pacific in the repeated figure of the three swans, are here dreamed by the novel itself into a new harmony of post-war interrelationship, even if the figure is, in its first Irish appearance, ambivalently associated too with what is not so much peace as the absence of war, the nullity of neutrality, since the 'assurance of being utterly out of reach added annulingness to [Stella's] deep sleep that night'.

In such moments *The Heat of the Day*, a novel of great emotional and political bruise and damage, seems obliged to unsettle or distress its own potential affirmations; and there are other unsettlements too as it reaches conclusion. Louie's baby may grow up the victim of an enabling or self-justifying fiction: because to Louie he is starting 'to look like Tom'—who might have been her husband, but was certainly not the child's father. It is one thing to have an individually evolved and emotionally credible sexual morality, in which unfaithfulness becomes— perversely but not disingenuously—a kind of higher faithfulness; but it is quite another to encourage in a child a belief in an unreal paternity. Louie's prospective 'story' is, therefore, ambivalently positioned between affirmation and something more discouragingly or even, potentially, more disintegratingly, self-justifying, a newly opportunistic attunement to the old morality, and a false start for a child. Similarly, Roderick's story, for all that Stella plots it, and for all that he desires to manage his inheritance 'in his own way', has a potentially undermining element too. When Stella imagines, or fantasizes, a wife for Roderick—and she realizes that a wife is a necessary element of the inheritance—she cannot conceive, at least before her exchanged gaze with Hannah, of anything other than a version of herself. Marriage is 'so far so inconceivable in the case of Roderick that she had not bestirred herself to envisage her daughter-in-law' (175): but what she does conceive is as bizarre as anything in Bowen: 'since Stella having no daughter could not conjure up youthfulness other than her own, the daughter-in-law curled forming like ectoplasm out of Stella's flank' (175). Stella becomes here a kind of spiritualistic medium out of whose quasi-Adamic, and therefore cross-gendered, body a spooky bride forms; and all that can be imagined for Roderick in the way of a bride is an emanation of his mother, a version of herself when young. It is an odd conception, in several senses, combining the maternal, the erotic, and the spiritualistic; and it suddenly recalls some of the odd conceptions of conception in *The House in Paris*. It hardly suggests that a flesh-and-blood bride is very immediately in prospect for this son.

Roderick, it is true, tells Nettie that he will call his son after Francis; but when, in Ireland for the first time, he vaguely thinks about a wife, as if out of mere dutifulness, he immediately falls asleep:

Roderick reflected that, as things were, there would be nobody but his mother to be *his* heir, either: he felt this with chagrin both for himself and her— between them, they should have come to something further than this. He began to mutiny—which took the form of striking match after match till he had succeeded in relighting the little lamp. That done, he was once more inside four walls: drawing down in the bed he immediately fell asleep.   (313)

And that is exactly as long as Roderick dwells on the subject. Given what we have previously seen of Stella's very interested fantasy, this cannot but seem strikingly abrupt. Roderick certainly does not himself notice, as Stella, of course, does, the beauty of Hannah Donovan; and we see him not noticing. While he is in the kitchen, 'The face of either Hannah or Mary appeared from time to time in the darkness of the doorway, but then always footsteps were to be heard padding lightly away again down the stone passage' (314). 'Hannah or Mary', one or the other, indistinguishably: it is all one to Roderick.

Nowhere in *The Heat of the Day* do we witness Roderick having any dealings with, or even thinking about, women: indeed, his only intimate relationship, apart from Stella, as he acknowledges to her, is with his fellow-soldier Fred, who almost ubiquitously accompanies him, and on whom he appears almost hero-worshippingly dependent, but who is, on his every appearance in the novel, on the enigmatic verge of a disappearance. Stella also thinks of Roderick as 'unattachable' in nature, 'passive in his relations with people'.[38] Bowen is, of course, as we have seen, a novelist in whom the homosexual theme assumes growing prominence over the course of the *œuvre*. It figures as a doubt at the back of the reader's mind in the failure of Nettie's marriage to Francis, since this appears to involve, if obliquely, a catastrophic sexual failure: she says to Roderick, 'You see I could not help seeing what was the matter—what he had wanted me to be was his wife; I tried this, that, and the other, till the result was that I fell into such a terrible melancholy that I only had to think of anything for it to go wrong too . . . so I took to going nowhere but up and down stairs, till I met my own ghost' (217). Although many of the novel's critics assume that Nettie's condition is the consequence of her inability to provide Francis with an heir, I think that this leaves it open whose the cause of the failure is: Nettie's trying 'this, that, and the other' sounds far more as though she is valiantly attempting to persuade Francis with variety than as though she is attempting to motivate herself. While Nettie could be a version of the sexually terrified wife in Charlotte Mew's great poem 'The Farmer's Bride'—although one who finds her own, extreme, way of organizing a necessarily separate life—the possibility that the failure of the marriage is, for whatever reason, Francis's fault undoubtedly inheres in Nettie's 'story'. If homosexuality is coded into this 'story' and also into Roderick's story, then the true Anglo-Irish heritage has become the impossibility of consummating sexual relationships between men and women. And, as the 'tradition' conceives of itself, this is its extinction, whatever anyone manages 'in his own way'. It is as though Elizabeth Bowen can manage many ways of rethinking a tradition for a radically reconstituted present but she cannot, in the end, imagine how or where a woman would fit in.

[38] The *OED* ascribes the first use of 'passive' in relation to homosexuals to 1916.

If the futures evoked for both Roderick and Louie at the end of *The Heat of the Day* are, then, such dubiously ambiguous ones, the novel's main plot harmonizes with them to the extent of actually itself using, self-referentially, the word 'open' of its own closure. Having been silent and absent for the intervening period, Harrison visits Stella in her new London flat two years after Robert's death, during yet another air raid. Stella tells him that she is engaged to be married; and Harrison feels 'relief'. Nevertheless—with genuine desire, or possibly tauntingly, since she accuses him of killing Robert—Stella invites him to stay the night: 'Prospects,' she says, 'have alternatives . . . I always have left things open' (322). As the raid comes to an end Harrison looks at his watch but asks, 'Or would you rather I stayed till the All Clear?' It is one of the most provokingly, fascinatingly, and frustratingly 'open' culminations of a relationship even in modern fiction. The screenplay which Harold Pinter made from the novel for a television film by Christopher Morahan is very inward with its ambiguities, as we might anticipate from a writer himself so preoccupied with personal and political treacheries; its 'spider's web of dubious loyalties and betrayals' he says he 'found compelling'.[39] It is also knowingly allusive when it offers the following concluding stage direction:

> They sit in silence.
> After a time the All Clear sounds.
> They do not move.[40]

'They do not move' is also the unforgettable final stage direction of both acts of Samuel Beckett's *Waiting for Godot* (1956) after a meaninglessly hollow 'Yes, let's go' has, on both occasions, been uttered by Estragon. Beckett, another Irish Protestant writer, encodes in his postwar novel, *Watt* (1953), a view of de Valera and neutrality ('in our windowlessness, in our bloodheat, in our hush'); and *Waiting for Godot*, also written in the aftermath of the Second World War, in which its author was heavily involved too, is, like *The Heat of the Day*, a text in which a ' "time being" ' has become 'the very being of time'. But if prospects have alternatives—like the prospect and the alternative of Pinter discovering Beckett in Bowen—then in the political as well as in the erotic realm, *The Heat of the Day* goes on leaving things open. Or, as the novel itself says, in a phrasing nervously strung, with characteristic ambivalence, between affirmation and inertia, 'Questions to

[39] Harold Pinter, *Collected Screenplays* 3 (London: Faber & Faber, 2000), p. vii.
[40] Ibid., 242.

which we find no answer find their own' (327–8). Which reads to me like a dejected and disabused recasting of Jane Austen's great observation on Emma's contentment with Highbury (which we perhaps only partly believe): that 'A mind lively and at ease, can do with seeing nothing, and can see nothing that does not answer.' In *The Heat of the Day* a writer's extremely lively but deeply uneasy mind, attempting to cope with the trauma of modern history, can see nothing that does.

Works Cited

BY ELIZABETH BOWEN

Fiction

The Hotel (1927; London: Penguin Books, 1987).

The Last September (1929; with an introduction by Victoria Glendinning, London: Vintage, 1998).

Friends and Relations (1931; London: Penguin, 1943).

To The North (1932; with an introduction by Hugh Haughton, London: Vintage, 1999).

The House in Paris (1935; with an introduction by A. S. Byatt, London: Vintage, 1998).

The Death of the Heart (1938; with an introduction by Patricia Craig, London: Vintage, 1998).

The Demon Lover and Other Stories (London: Jonathan Cape, 1945).

The Heat of the Day (1948; with an introduction by Roy Foster, London: Vintage, 1998).

A World of Love (1955; with an introduction by Selina Hastings, London: Vintage, 1999).

The Little Girls (1964; with an introduction by Penelope Lively, London: Vintage, 1999).

A Day in the Dark and Other Stories (London: Jonathan Cape, 1965).

Eva Trout (1969; with an introduction by Eibhear Walshe, London: Vintage, 1999).

The Collected Stories of Elizabeth Bowen, with an introduction by Angus Wilson (1980; London: Penguin, 1983).

Elizabeth Bowen's Irish Stories, with an introduction by Victoria Glendinning (Swords: Poolbeg Press, 1978).

Non-fiction

Bowen's Court (1942); in Bowen's Court and Seven Winters: Memories of a Dublin Childhood, with a new introduction by Hermione Lee (London: Virago Press, 1984).

Seven Winters (Dublin: The Cuala Press, 1942; repr. 1971 by photo-lithography in the Republic of Ireland for the Irish University Press, Shannon).

English Novelists (London: William Collins, 1942).

Collected Impressions (London: Longmans Green & Co., 1950).

A Time in Rome (1960; New York: Alfred A. Knopf, 1965).

Afterthought: Pieces about Writing (London: Longmans, Green & Co., 1962).

Pictures and Conversations, with a foreword by Spencer Curtis Brown (London: Allen Lane, 1975).

The Mulberry Tree: Writings of Elizabeth Bowen, selected and introduced by Hermione Lee (London: Virago Press, 1986).

'Notes on Eire': Espionage Reports to Winston Churchill, 1940–2; with a Review of Irish Neutrality in World War 2, ed. by Jack Lane and Brendan Clifford (Millstreet: Aubane Historical Society, 1999).

Uncollected:

'Meet Elizabeth Bowen', *The Bell*, 4: 6 (September 1942), 420–6.

'Ireland Agonistes' [review of J. G. Farrell's *Troubles*], *Europa*, 1 (1971), 58–9.

'In Praise of Shem the Penman', *Irish Times*, 12 January 1991, 9, reprinted from *The Bell*, March 1941.

OTHERS

Ackroyd, Peter. *Dickens* (London: Sinclair-Stevenson, 1990).

Ashworth, Ann. '"But Why Was She Called Portia?": Judgment and Feeling in *The Death of the Heart*'. *Critique: Studies in Modern Fiction*, 28 (Spring 1987), 159–66.

Barthes, Roland. *Camera Lucida*, trans. by Richard Howard (London: Jonathan Cape, 1982).

Bennett, Andrew, and Royle, Nicholas. *Elizabeth Bowen and the Dissolution of the Novel: Still Lives* (London: Macmillan, 1995).

Borhan, Pierre. *André Kertész: His Life and Work* (New York: Bullfinch, 1994).

Brown, Terence. *Ireland: A Social and Cultural History 1922–1985* (London: Fontana, 1985).

Coates, John. 'The Misfortunes of Eva Trout', *Essays in Criticism*, 48: 1 (1998), 59–79.

Coughlan, Patricia. 'Women and Desire in the Work of Elizabeth Bowen', in Eibhear Walshe (ed.), *Sex, Nation and Dissent in Irish Writing* (Cork: Cork University Press, 1997).

Coveney, Peter. *The Image of Childhood* (Harmondsworth: Penguin, 1967).

Cunningham, Valentine. *British Writers of the Thirties* (Oxford: Oxford University Press, 1988).

Dylan, Bob. *Lyrics 1962–1985* (London: Paladin, 1988).

Eagleton, Terry. *Heathcliff and the Great Hunger: Studies in Irish Culture* (London: Verso, 1995).

Eliot, T. S. *The Use of Poetry and the Use of Criticism* (1933; London: Faber & Faber, 1964).

Ellmann, Maud. *Elizabeth Bowen: The Shadow across the Page* (Edinburgh: Edinburgh University Press, 2003).

Fisk, Robert. *In Time of War: Ireland, Ulster and the Price of Neutrality 1939–45* (1983; Dublin: Gill and Macmillan, 1985).

Flaubert, Gustave. *Selected Letters*, ed. Geoffrey Wall (London: Penguin, 1997).

Ford, Ford Madox. *The Good Soldier: A Tale of Passion* (1915; Harmondsworth: Penguin, 1972).

Foster, R. F. *Modern Ireland 1600–1972* (London: Allen Lane: The Penguin Press, 1988).

—— *Paddy and Mr Punch: Connections in Irish and English History* (1993; London: Penguin, 1995).

—— *The Irish Story: Telling Tales and Making it up in Ireland* (London: Allen Lane: The Penguin Press, 2001).

Freud, Sigmund. 'The "Uncanny"', in *The Penguin Freud Library*, 14: Art and Literature, ed. by Albert Dickson (London: Penguin, 1985).

—— *The Interpretation of Dreams*, trans. by Joyce Crick with an introduction and notes by Ritchie Robertson (Oxford: Oxford University Press, 1999).

Gilbert, Sandra, and Gubar, Susan. *No Man's Land, volume 2: Sexchanges* (New Haven: Yale University Press, 1989).

Glendinning, Victoria. *Elizabeth Bowen: Portrait of a Writer* (1977; London: Phoenix, 1993).

Golding, William. *Pincher Martin* (London: Faber & Faber, 1966).

Griffiths, Richard. *Fellow Travellers of the Right: British Enthusiasts for Nazi Germany, 1933–9* (London: Constable, 1980).

Harrison, Tom. *Living through the Blitz* (1976; Harmondsworth: Penguin, 1978).

Hart, Peter. *The I.R.A. and its Enemies: Violence and Community in Cork, 1916–1923* (Oxford: Clarendon Press, 1998).

Hartley, L. P. *The Go-Between*, ed. by Douglas Brooks-Davies (London: Penguin Books, 1997).

Hawkes, Terence (ed.). *Coleridge on Shakespeare* (Harmondsworth: Penguin, 1969).

Heath, William. *Elizabeth Bowen: An Introduction to Her Novels* (Madison: University of Wisconsin Press, 1961).

Hildebidle, John. *Five Irish Writers: The Errand of Keeping Alive* (Harvard: Harvard University Press, 1989).

Hoogland, Renée C. *Elizabeth Bowen: A Reputation in Writing* (New York: New York University Press, 1994).

Innes, C. L. *Women and Nation in Irish Literature and Society 1880–1935* (Hemel Hempstead: Harvester Wheatsheaf, 1993).

James, Henry. *What Maisie Knew* (1897; London: Penguin, ed. with an introduction and notes by Paul Theroux with additional notes by Patricia Crick, 1985).

Jordan, Heather Bryant. *How Will the Heart Endure?: Elizabeth Bowen and the Landscape of War* (Ann Arbor: University of Michigan Press, 1992).

Kershner, R. B. Jr. 'Bowen's Oneiric House in Paris', *Texas Studies in Literature and Language* (Winter, 1986), 407–23.

Kiberd, Declan. *Inventing Ireland: The Literature of the Modern Nation* (London: Jonathan Cape, 1995).

Kincaid, James. *Child-Loving: The Erotic Child and Victorian Culture* (London: Routledge, 1992).

Kinsley, James (ed.). *The Oxford Book of Ballads* (1969; Oxford: Oxford University Press, 1989).

Lassner, Phyllis. *Elizabeth Bowen* (London: Macmillan, 1990).

Leavis, F. R. *The Great Tradition* (London: Chatto & Windus, 1948).

Lee, Hermione. *Elizabeth Bowen* (1981; rev. edn., London: Vintage, 1999).

McCormack, W. J. *From Burke to Beckett: Ascendancy, Tradition and Betrayal in Irish Literary History* (1985; rev. and enlarged edn., Cork: Cork University Press, 1994).

—— *Dissolute Characters: Irish Literary History through Balzac, Sheridan Le Fanu, Yeats and Bowen* (Manchester: Manchester University Press, 1993).

Miller, Jane. 'Re-reading Elizabeth Bowen', *Raritan*, 20: 1 (2000), 17–31.

Milosz, Czeslaw. *To Begin Where I Am: Selected Essays*, ed. and with an introduction by Bogdana Carpenter and Madeline G. Levine (New York: Farrar, Straus and Giroux, 2001).

Moynahan, Julian. *Anglo-Irish: The Literary Imagination in a Hyphenated Culture* (Princeton: Princeton University Press, 1995).

Muldoon, Paul. *To Ireland, I* (Oxford: Oxford University Press, 2000).

O'Faolain, Sean. *The Irish* (Harmondsworth: Penguin, 1947).

—— *The Vanishing Hero: Studies in Novelists of the Twenties* (London: Eyre and Spottiswoode, 1956).

Parsons, Deborah. 'Souls Astray: Elizabeth Bowen's Landscape of War', *Women: A Cultural Review*, 8: 1 (Spring 1997), 24–32.

Piette, Adam. *Imagination at War: British Fiction and Poetry 1939–1945* (London: Papermac, 1995).

—— *Remembering and the Sound of Words: Mallarmé, Proust, Joyce, Beckett* (Oxford: Clarendon Press, 1996).

Pinter, Harold. *Collected Screenplays 3* (London: Faber & Faber, 2000).

Plain, Gill. *Women's Fiction of the Second World War: Gender, Power and Resistance* (Edinburgh: Edinburgh University Press, 1996).

Proust, Marcel. *Remembrance of Things Past*, Vol. III, trans. by C. K. Scott Moncrieff and Terence Kilmartin; and by Andreas Mayor (London: Chatto & Windus, 1981).

Radford, Jean. 'Late Modernism and the Politics of History', in Maroula Joannou (ed.), *Women Writers of the 1930s: Gender, Politics and History* (Edinburgh: Edinburgh University Press, 1999).

Ricks, Christopher. *Tennyson* (London: Macmillan, 1972).

Ritchie, Charles. *The Siren Years: Undiplomatic Diaries 1937–1945* (London: Macmillan, 1974).

Segal, Naomi. *The Adulteress's Child: Authorship and Desire in the Nineteenth-Century Novel* (Cambridge: Polity Press, 1992).

Smith, Patricia Juliana. *Lesbian Panic: Homoeroticism in Modern British Women's Fiction* (New York: Columbia University Press, 1997).

Sontag, Susan. *On Photography* (1977; London: Penguin Books, 1987).

Stevens, Wallace. *Opus Posthumous*, ed. by Samuel French Morse (1957; New York: Alfred A. Knopf, 1977).

Tanner, Tony. *Adultery in the Novel: Contract and Transgression* (Baltimore: Johns Hopkins University Press, 1979).

Tillinghast, Richard. 'Elizabeth Bowen: The House, the Hotel and the Child', *New Criterion*, 13: 4 (1994), 24–33.

Watson, Barbara Bellow. 'Variations on an Enigma: Elizabeth Bowen's War Novel', repr. in Harold Bloom (ed.), *Modern Critical Views: Elizabeth Bowen* (New York: Chelsea House, 1987).

Index

adultery, novel of 2, 5, 89–90
anamorphisms 130, 133–5, 141, 143
Ann Lee's and Other Stories 30–5
anti-Semitism 96–7
'Art of Bergotte, The' 5
Ashworth, Ann 124 n. 14
Aubane Historical Society 185–6

'Back Drawing Room, The' 30–5
Barthes, Roland 68
Baxter's World of Spirits, see *The Certainty of the World of Spirits*
Beckett, Samuel 63, 200
Bell, The 24, 37, 76, 194, 196 n.
'Bend Back, The' 11
Bennett, Andrew, and Nicholas Royle 128 n. 2
  on *The House in Paris* 83 n., 87
  on *The Last September* 41 n. 3, 49–50
  on *A World of Love* 63 n. 2, 66, 73
betrayal:
  The Death of the Heart 112, 113, 122
  The Heat of the Day 175–6, 182
'Big House, The' 37, 194
Bowen, Elizabeth
  on childhood reading 8–9, 10–11
  Irish, reports on 184–7, 188–9
  mannerism 3–4
  on *Troubles* 2, 61
  on writing 3–4, 5
Bowen, Henry (father) 23
Bowen, Henry I 26–7, 28
Bowen, Henry III 29
Bowen, Henry IV 29
Bowen's Court (family home) 22, 24, 25 n. 9, 30, 60
Bowen's Court 21–30, 34–5, 36–8
  'affair of the Apparition' 26–7, 30
  dispossession 36–7
Brown, Terence 60

Calder, Angus 176
Cameron, Mrs Elizabeth, *see* Bowen, Elizabeth

Cape, Jonathan 25
Certainty of the World of Spirits, The 27
'Cheery Soul, The' 148, 154
childhood 5, 109–10, 142
  reading in 8–9, 10–11
childlessness:
  Eva Trout 134, 141, 144
  The House in Paris 85–6
Christian imagery 70–1, 136–8, 140, 142
Clifford, Brendan 186
Coates, John 132 n. 7
Coleridge, Samuel Taylor 170
comedy 42, 45
  comédie noire 131
  social 45, 61–2, 69
conception 86
Conrad, Joseph 104
Coughlan, Patricia 51 n., 126 n., 128 n. 3, 174, 181
critical essays 29
Cunningham, Valentine 98
Cushin, Elizabeth 28

death and the dead 19–21, 71–2, 131; *see also* 'The Demon Lover'
Death of the Heart, The 6, 102–25
  betrayal 112, 113, 122
  diaries 3, 103, 115, 122–4
  doubles 114–18
  dreams and dreamworld 121–2
  Portia: significance of name 124–5
  reading 121–3
  refugees 102–10
  servants 103, 118–21
  sexuality 107–10, 111–12, 115, 117
  and Shakespeare 124
  survivors 110–14
  What Maisie Knew, relationship with 106, 109–10
  writers and writing 121–4
'Demon Lover, The' 4, 120, 153, 154, 158–65
  ghosts 2, 58, 148
  letters 2, 158–9, 160–2
  returning, theme of 148, 149–50, 158–63

Demon Lover and Other Stories, The
  5, 147–67, 182–3
  'The Cheery Soul' 148, 154
  'The Demon Lover' 2, 4, 58, 120, 148,
    149–50, 153, 154, 158–65
  dreams and dreamworld 148, 150,
    166–7
  ghosts 2, 58, 148, 155
  'Green Holly' 148
  'Happy Autumn Fields, The' 2, 22 n.,
    148–9, 150, 153–4, 156, 165–6
  'In the Square' 147, 154
  'The Inherited Clock' 148, 155
  'Ivy Gripped the Steps' 148, 151–3,
    155–6, 157, 165
  letters 2, 158–9, 160–2
  literary allusions 149–54, 160, 163, 166
  'Mysterious Kôr' 147, 150–1, 152, 156,
    166–7
  'Pink May' 148
  possession and self-possession 163–4
  returning, theme of 147–50, 152–3,
    154–6, 158–63
  sexuality 150–1, 153, 156–8
  and Shakespeare 151, 153
  'Songs My Father Sang Me' 148, 155,
    156–7
  'Sunday Afternoon' 147, 151, 152, 154,
    165
Derrida, Jacques 28–9
diaries 3, 103, 115, 122–4
Dickens, Charles 122
  and *Eva Trout* 5, 140, 141–3
dislocation 12–13, 28, 29, 149
'Disloyalties' 6
dispossession 28–30, 32–5, 36–7
dissolution 41, 72
doppelgänger (doubles) 9, 27, 28, 31,
  58–9, 67
  The Death of the Heart 114–18
  The Heat of the Day 180
dreams and dreamworld 41–2, 92, 166
  The Death of the Heart 121–2
  The Demon Lover and Other Stories
    148, 150, 166–7

Eagleton, Terry 29, 36, 53
Eliot, George 21
Eliot, T. S. 9, 160
  Four Quartets 70, 71, 72
Ellmann, Maud 41 n. 5, 181
  on *The Death of the Heart* 124 n. 14
  on *Eva Trout* 128 n. 2, 130 n.

  on *The House in Paris* 88
  on *A World of Love* 69 n., 72 n.
Encounters 8
eroticism 122
  Eva Trout 127–8
  The Last September 51
  A World of Love 65, 67, 69 n., 77
Eva Trout 2, 4, 5, 7, 12, 78, 126–44
  anamorphisms 130, 133–5, 141,
    143
  childlessness 134, 141, 144
  Christian imagery 136–8, 140,
    142
  and Dickens 5, 140, 141–3
  eroticism 127–8
  film imagery 139
  identity issues 129, 139–40
  letters 2, 141
  motherlessness 129–30
  parentlessness 132–3
  and Shakespeare 126
  writers and writing 140–2

Farrell, J. G. 2, 41, 61
First World War memories 56–7, 58, 68,
  156, 157–8
Fisk, Robert 182 n., 185
Flaubert, Gustave 37
Foster, R. F. 23, 35–6, 38, 39 n., 71,
  76
Freud, Sigmund 9, 164
Friends and Relations 93–4
  lesbianism 128
  letters 2
Frost, Robert 37

Gardner, Alexander 68
gender issues 23–4
ghosts and ghostliness:
  Bowen's Court 26–7, 30
  The Demon Lover and Other Stories
    2, 58, 148, 155
  The Last September 50, 54, 58, 59
  living ghosts 28, 29–34, 64
  A World of Love 75
Glendinning, Victoria 28, 31, 46, 88 n. 5,
  136 n.
Gollancz, Victor 88 n. 5
gothic 5, 29–30, 52–3, 153
  The House in Paris 92–3
gothic supernatural 69–71
Green, Henry 5, 119, 121
'Green Holly' 148

Haggard, H. Rider 5, 150, 153
'Happy Autumn Fields, The' 22 n.,
   148–9, 150, 153–4, 156,
   165–6
  letters 2
Hart, Peter 46, 52
Hartley, L. P. 156
Hawthorne, Nathaniel 153
Heaney, Seamus 116
Heat of the Day, The 37, 38, 67, 97–8,
   116, 168–201
  betrayal 175–6, 182
  futures 196–201
  identity issues 168
  the Irish story 190–6
  lesbianism 128
  names, significance of 179–83
  newspapers 3
  parallelism 172–8
  and Shakespeare 170, 188
  spies 181–90
  stories 168–72, 180, 190–6, 197–8,
   199
  theatrical imagery 187–8
Heath, William 76 n. 14, 124 n. 14
'Her Table Spread' 132
Hildebidle, John 41 n. 3, 76 n. 14
homosexuality 69 n., 128–9, 199
Hoogland, Renée C. 174 n. 7
Hotel, The 1, 4
  letters 2
hotels 103–5, 106, 111
House in Paris, The 1, 3, 5, 12–13, 67,
   81–101, 136 n.
  anti-Semitism 96–7
  childlessness 85–6
  gothic 92–3
  letters 1–2, 88
  parentlessness 81–3
  returning, theme of 86
  sexuality 87–8, 93, 100–1
  treachery 90–1

identity issues 3, 9, 68
  Eva Trout 129, 139–40
  The Heat of the Day 168
  Last September, The 50
'In the Square' 147, 154
'Inherited Clock, The' 148, 155
IRA 25 n. 9
Ishiguro, Kazuo 121
'Ivy Gripped the Steps' 148, 151–3,
   155–6, 157, 165

James, Henry 5, 6, 124 n. 14, 142
  'The Jolly Corner' 31, 34
  What Maisie Knew 92, 106, 109–10,
   114
Jordan, Heather Bryant 186 n. 26
Joyce, James:
  Finnegans Wake 5
  Ulysses 56, 120
'Jungle, The' 122

Keats, John 19–20, 21
Kershner, R. B. Jr 92
Kiberd, Declan 35, 36, 49
Kincaid, James 109

Lang, Andrew 150–1, 166
Lassner, Phyllis 124 n. 13
Last September, The 1, 19, 22, 30, 37,
   39–60, 136 n.
  Daventry's role 55–60
  ellipses 39–47, 52, 53, 58
  eroticism 51
  ghosts 50, 54, 58, 59
  identity 50
  lesbianism 128
  letters 2, 41, 69
  Lois and Laurence 47–51
  mill episode 51–5
  sexuality 40–1, 51–3, 57
  and Shakespeare 43–4
  social comedy 61–2
  A World of Love, relationship with
   62–3, 66–9, 74, 77
  writers and writing 41–2
Le Fanu, Sheridan 7, 29, 55, 132, 149
Leavis, F. R. 21
Lee, Hermione 66, 96, 120
lesbianism 128–9, 174 n. 7
letters:
  'The Demon Lover' 2, 158–9, 160–2
  Eva Trout 2, 141
  Friends and Relations 2
  'The Happy autumn Fields' 2
  The Hotel 2
  The House in Paris 1–2, 88
  The Last September 2, 41, 69
  To the North 2–3
  A World of Love 1, 64–5, 68, 69, 73
Little Girls, The 7–8, 28, 78, 136 n.

mannerism 3–4
McCormack, W. J. 48–9
  on *The Demon Lover* 4, 158 n.

McCormack, W. J. (*cont.*):
  on *The Heat of the Day* 171, 173,
    181–2, 189
  on *A World of Love* 64 n.
Mansfield, Katherine 112
mental instability, hereditary 27–8, 29,
    30
Miller, Jane 96
Milosz, Czeslaw 111 n.
Modernism 4–5
motherlessness 116
  Eva Trout 129–30
  The House in Paris 81–3
mourning 72
Moynahan, Julian 53, 54
Muldoon, Paul 50, 63, 158 n., 162
'Mysterious Kôr' 147, 150–1, 152, 156,
    166–7

Nabokov, Vladimir 126 n.
  Lolita 109–10
neutrality, Irish 24, 184–7, 188–9, 192
newspapers 3, 172–4

O'Faolain, Sean:
  The Bell 24, 37, 76, 194, 196 n.
  The Irish, 24
  The Vanishing Hero 19
  'Out of a Book' 8–9, 10
Owen, Wilfred 83

parentlessness:
  Eva Trout 132–3
  The House in Paris 81–3
Parsons, Deborah 166 n. 20
photography 68, 70, 99, 130–1
Piette, Adam 4, 169, 190
'Pink May' 148
Pinter, Harold 121, 200
Plain, Gill 174 n. 6
Poe, Edgar Allan 52
possession and self-possession 66, 163–4
Proust, Marcel 5, 45–6, 151–2

Radford, Jean 97
reading 3, 4, 6, 9–10, 121–3
  in childhood 8–9, 10–11
refugees 98, 102–10
returning, theme of 8, 9, 147–9, 156,
    158–63
  The Demon Lover and Other Stories
    147–56, 158–63
  The House in Paris 86

Richardson, Samuel 2
Ricks, Christopher 150
Ritchie, Charles 118 n., 176–8, 189
'Roving Eye, The' 10–11, 14
Royle, Nicholas, and Andrew Bennett
    128 n. 2
  on *The House in Paris* 83 n., 87
  on *The Last September* 41 n. 3, 49–50
  on *A World of Love* 63 n. 2, 66, 73

Segal, Naomi 89
self-possession 163–4
servants:
  The Death of the Heart 103, 118–21
  To the North 118
Seven Winters 27, 81, 144, 183, 186
sexuality:
  The Death of the Heart 107–10,
    111–12, 115, 117
  The Demon Lover and Other Stories
    150–1, 153, 156–8
  The House in Paris 87–8, 93, 100–1
  The Last September 40–1, 51–3, 57
  A World of Love 65
Shakespeare, William 5–6
  and *The Death of the Heart* 124
  and *The Demon Lover and Other
    Stories* 151, 153
  and *Eva Trout* 126
  and *The Heat of the Day* 170, 188
  and *The Last September* 43–4
  and 'Sunday Afternoon' 151, 153
  and *A World of Love* 67, 73, 77
Smith, Patricia Juliana 128–9
social comedy:
  The Last September 45, 61–2
  A World of Love 69
'Songs My Father Sang Me' 148, 155,
    156–7
Sontag, Susan 68
spies 126 n., 134, 181–90
Stevens, Wallace 12
'Sunday Afternoon' 147, 151, 152, 153,
    154, 165

Tanner, Tony 89
Tennyson, Alfred, Lord 5, 150, 153
Tillinghast, Richard 119
Time in Rome, A 13, 19–21, 41 n. 5
To the North 9, 75, 98, 102 n.
  lesbianism 128
  letters 2–3
  servants 118

Traherne, Thomas 70–1
treachery 90–1; *see also* betrayal

Wade, Eliza 24
Woolf, Virginia 5, 134–5
 Mrs Dalloway 56, 73–4
 To the Lighthouse 64
World of Love, A 1, 7, 30, 60, 61–78,
  194
 eroticism 65, 67, 69 n., 77
 ghosts 75
 Last September, The relationship with
  62–3, 66–9, 74, 77

letters 1, 64–5, 68, 69, 73
sexuality 65
and Shakespeare 67, 73, 77
social comedy 69
writers and writing 3–4, 5, 6–7,
  8 n. 14, 10–11, 14
 Death of the Heart, The
  121–4
 Eva Trout 140–2
 Last September, The 41–2
writing and reading 3, 9–10

Yeats, W. B. 36